**Inviting Women's Rebellion**

# ANNE N. COSTAIN

# Inviting Women's Rebellion

A Political Process Interpretation
of the Women's Movement

**THE JOHNS HOPKINS UNIVERSITY PRESS**

BALTIMORE & LONDON

© 1992 The Johns Hopkins University Press
All rights reserved
Printed in the United States of America on acid-free paper

The Johns Hopkins University Press
701 West 40th Street
Baltimore, Maryland 21211-2190
The Johns Hopkins Press Ltd., London

Library of Congress Cataloging-in-Publication Data

Costain, Anne N., 1948–
  Inviting women's rebellion : a political process interpretation of the women's
movement / Anne N. Costain.
      p.    cm.
Includes bibliographical references and index.
ISBN 0-8018-4333-2
1. Women—Government policy—United States.   2. Feminism—Political aspects—
United States.   3. Women in politics—United States.   4. Women's rights—United
States.   I. Title.
HQ1236.5.U6C67   1992
305.42—dc20       91-39293

*To my parents*
Frances A. Nicholas
*and*
James E. Nicholas

# Contents

Acknowledgments   ix

Introduction   xi

1   Interpreting the Contemporary Women's Movement   1

2   The Opening of Political Opportunity for Women   26

3   A New Women's Movement Emerges   44

4   The High Point of the Women's Movement   79

5   Fighting Decline   100

6   If Government Gives, Can It Also Take Away?   122

7   For a Continuing Movement   136

Appendix A: Coding Women's Events Data   143

Appendix B: Assessing the Relative Influence of
Government, Public Opinion, and the Women's Movement   150

Notes   157

Index   181

# Acknowledgments

As with all projects that have endured so long, I have incurred many debts along the way. I am grateful to Ruth Mandel, Marilyn Johnson, and Ida Schmerz at the Center for the American Woman and Politics at Rutgers for launching me on this decades-long project through my first funded research. I thank Gilbert Steiner and James Sundquist of the Brookings Institution, who saw that I had a place to work while I was in Washington. Also, Gil helped to disabuse me of some of my more naive ideas about how Congress works. Carol Bray, then a graduate student at the Johns Hopkins University School of Advanced International Studies (SAIS), and Valerie Gilpeer, then a graduate student at George Washington University, provided crucial assistance in helping me with congressional interviews as my time in Washington was running out. The lobbyists, members of Congress, and staff whom we interviewed were surprisingly generous with their time in view of their overloaded schedules.

The Bunting Institute at Radcliffe provided both time and stimulation for considering the larger implications of the study. I am particularly grateful to Naomi Chazan, Diane Margolis, and Jane Martin, who were always willing to discuss issues ranging from writing books, to gender difference, to women's political place. Ed Greenberg, as chair of the Political Science department at Colorado, found money in the budget to support a research assistant to help me code first the congressional bill introductions and laws and, afterwards, the *New York Times* events data. The University of Colorado provided essential support at the end of the project. The IMPART (Implementation of Multicultural Perspectives and Approaches in Research and Teaching) program contributed partial support over one summer, a Faculty Teaching Fellowship from the Council on Teaching gave me a semester of released time, and a Dean's Summer Fellowship allowed me to finish writing the manuscript. Finally, a National Science Foundation grant (SES-8908063) assisted me in exploring the relationship between American public opinion, congressional action, and the women's movement during these years. The results of this work, undertaken with Steven Majstorovic, are reported in chapter 6 and Appendix B. Michelle Marcu, Cory Sher, Tiffany Moehring, and Kathy Westphal helped validate footnotes and undertook many of the last minute tasks needed to turn a manuscript into a book. John McIver's help with printing the figures is also gratefully acknowledged.

I owe a number of personal debts. Doug Costain joined me in coding thousands of bills introduced and laws passed. He has also read and offered advice on countless versions of this manuscript. Jo Freeman, Milton C. Cummings, Jr., and Andy McFarland have provided valued insights and encouragement about this project over the many years. Craig Jenkins, Carol Mueller, Paul Burstein, and Doug McAdam, as sociologists and experts on social movements, have shared insights and warned me about pitfalls in social movement research. Sidney Tarrow organized, to our collective benefit, a conference at Cornell that brought together political scientists and sociologists interested in social movements. Evonne Okonski, Oneida Mascarenas, Will Moore, and Steven Majstorovic, while graduate students at the University of Colorado, were involved in collecting, coding, or critiquing the data gathered and my interpretation of it. I am grateful to them. Last, but by no means least, Henry Tom, at the Johns Hopkins University Press, believed that a book would emerge from all this even at times when I myself was not sure this was true. His encouragement and wise suggestions at many points during this project kept it on track and helped shape the final product. The results of these many efforts are certainly less than the sum of their separate parts. My hope is that this book will raise questions about the relationship between the women's movement and the U.S. government that may help our children make choices when, in the next century, they embark on a third women's movement.

# Introduction

In summer 1974, with support from a small research grant awarded by the Center for the American Woman and Politics at Rutgers University, I was in Washington, D.C., interviewing and observing lobbyists for women's groups and selected members of Congress and their staff aides. I was trying to compare the goals and lobbying methods used by women's groups with the perceptions of those members in Congress who had recently worked on important pieces of women's rights legislation. At the time, I thought I was engaged in a simple study of interest group tactics. Because Congress had already passed a number of major laws dealing with women's issues,[1] I fully expected to discover a dynamic group of women's lobbyists who were reasonably well funded and working cooperatively to prod the legislature to take action on policies of concern to women.

What I found instead were severely underfunded lobbyists who were frequently divided over issues and split by rivalries among their respective groups. This "women's lobby,"[2] on the one hand, seemed relatively ineffective, according to standard methods of measuring lobbying success, yet, on the other hand, it was achieving an undeniable political impact. The newer women's groups, such as the National Organization for Women (NOW), Women's Lobby, Women's Equity Action League (WEAL), and the National Women's Political Caucus (NWPC), all products of the women's movement, acted as catalysts and organizers for most of the campaigns to pass legislation on women's issues. But, despite the leading role these groups played, only NOW and Women's Lobby had full-time lobbyists. The NWPC and WEAL had part-time lobbyists who were most often unavailable during the critical periods leading up to elections, when campaign work drew them away from Washington. Even the groups that did lobby continuously expressed frustration at the volume and press of work in their offices. A legislative director for one movement organization reported telling congressional offices to hire their own feminists rather than calling on her group's overburdened staff for information.[3] The head of one legislative office offered me a job during the interview. Some of these early women's movement lobbyists ran their offices out of private homes (Women's Lobby) or places of business (WEAL); others, such as the NWPC, were moving around Washington seeking affordable rent.

The effective lobbying that they did was often aided by both traditional women's groups, such as the National Federation of Business and Professional Women, the American Association of University Women, and the National Council of Jewish Women, and liberal organizations, including the National Education Association and the American Civil Liberties Union. This assistance was crucial because it allowed women's movement groups to gain access to Congress more rapidly than would otherwise have been possible and to work together buffered by the presence of groups that were not competing with them for the same members. But it also meant that much of the Washington agenda of the women's movement depended on the support of other groups, many of which were uncomfortable with a feminist label.[4]

Not only did I find the "women's lobby" in the mid-1970s poor in resources and new to the art of lobbying, but when I began to interview members of Congress and their staff, I discovered that most were hardly aware of its existence.[5] Congressional opinions of groups such as NOW and WEAL varied from "No one from that group has ever visited the office" to "I think I remember someone from that group testifying at the hearings." The few Capitol Hill offices that had worked closely on legislation with these lobbyists expressed opinions ranging from praise for their information and professionalism to accusations of political naivete and undiplomatic behavior. A key congressional office reported frustration at two instances in which its representative was sharply criticized by women's groups despite his hard work in pushing a bill they favored toward passage. His legislative assistant noted that "Congressman —— got yelled at as a sell out, and he had taken a lot of flack from enemies on the issue, so he wasn't very happy to get criticism from people he was trying to support."[6] She attributed these misunderstandings to the inexperience of the women's groups.

Despite this evidence of scanty resources and sometimes amateurish lobbying, the fact remained that Congress was engaged in passing new legislative initiatives on women's issues to an extent that was unprecedented in U.S. history (see Fig. P-1). There seemed to be an unknown factor X that was causing this outburst of political activity without the expected intermediation of lobbying groups or any noteworthy new influx of resources into Washington lobbying efforts. A discussion with Jo Freeman during a meeting at the Eagleton Institute at Rutgers University in spring 1975, persuaded me that the women's movement was a prime candidate to be factor X. After talking with Freeman, I went back through my Washington interviews with women's lobbyists, members of Congress, and congressional staff. It became clear that all, to varying degrees, were responding to the size, intensity, and political

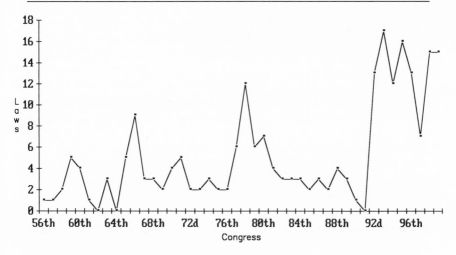

Fig. P-1. Women's laws passed by Congress.

power of the women's movement. From a spokeswoman at the League of Women Voters who marvelled at how psychologically empowering it was for League members to work on the Equal Rights Amendment (ERA), to movement lobbyists who insisted that all their access and influence on Capitol Hill depended on the mobilizing, organizing, and letter writing carried on by movement activists at the grass-roots level, to the leader of one women's group who felt her organization could now get a hearing because of the "wild-eyed, extreme" women's groups that made her appear moderate, it was evident that the movement created the wedge that allowed Washington groups to gain access to decision makers.

Although members of Congress and their staffs were anxious to deny the existence of any bloc of votes in their districts that was responsive to women's issues, they, in the same breath, affirmed that, of course, they supported policies helping women anyway. Reasons for denying the existence of a "women's" vote in the early 1970s varied. Several male members of Congress, who were interviewed after committees they served on had successfully reported out women's rights bills, asserted that only their sisters-in-law ever raised women's issues to them.[7] Other male members expressed concern that the emergence of a bloc of women's votes might lead women candidates to challenge them for their seats in Congress, a prospect they found unsettling. Finally, other representatives talked about women's rights as an issue of morality, something that needed to be done regardless of the amount of pressure mobilized behind it. At this point, I was not at all sure why groups and members of Congress were responding to the movement as they were, or, indeed, how they saw the women's movement and its supporters.

In 1980-81, I spent a year as a fellow at the Bunting Institute of Radcliffe College in Cambridge, Massachusetts, studying social movements. I read much of the scholarly literature on social movements in sociology, primarily, but also in history and political science. I participated in two faculty study groups—one on social movements, organized by Carol Mueller of Harvard, and the other on studying women, begun at the Bunting Institute, organized by fellows Naomi Chazan, Diane Margolis, Jane Martin, and me. The social movement study group allowed me to understand better how sociologists view the political actions of movements. The group on women sharpened my awareness that it was possible to view women, in certain circumstances, as legitimately different from men, without foregoing the notion of equality or implying inferiority. During this period, I also read the documents in the NOW and WEAL archives which are housed in the Arthur and Elizabeth Schlesinger Library at Radcliffe College.

Although I felt I understood the politics of the women's movement better, I was still dissatisfied with the dominant theory explaining movement development, a theory called resource mobilization.[8] Resource mobilization is based on the idea that successful movements acquire resources and create advantageous exchange relationships with other groups as they achieve success in fulfilling their goals. My earlier work in Washington convinced me that the major impact of the women's movement had been largely independent of political resources, strong allies, or very effective political tactics.

I believed that the women's movement, with its passion and anger as well as organization, was the stimulus causing members of Congress to work for, vote for and brag in their campaigns about their support for women's issues. Thus I was particularly uneasy about assumptions surfacing in much of the scholarly literature on the women's movement that women's legislative success had resulted from their moderate demands and tactics.[9] Many analysts were starting to write that women had focused their attention early on achieving equal rights with men. By asking for equality, women were thought to be both linking their cause to the congressional majority that supported civil rights legislation in the sixties and, at the same time, minimizing their challenge to the status quo. Women's issues were subsumed in the incremental politics of adding "and sex" to new and existing civil rights guarantees. Yet, this incremental and "clever" politics bore little relationship to the messianic, ideological, and often angry politics I had observed in Washington.

Lobbyists for most of the women's movement groups described their activity as a kind of crusade to change the world. There were many variants on the theme "If I die tomorrow, my life will have had meaning because I will know that I played a significant role in getting Congress to pass ERA." Much of the undiplomatic behavior by lobbyists, such as chastising male members of Congress for pushing congresswomen out of the way when it was time to claim credit for legislation that was about to pass, stemmed from a kind of feminist consciousness that women were no longer willing unquestioningly to stand aside for men. Women had organized through social movements in the early 1900s and the 1960s, at least in part, to achieve legislative impact. If they genuinely had the option of couching their concerns in language that asked for small changes rather than major restructuring of women's social and political roles, it was difficult for me to imagine that the major effort and commitment necessary to form movements would have been undertaken.

When I read Doug McAdam's and Sidney Tarrow's research on how the structure of political opportunity affects new social movements, the separate pieces of my research began to fall into place.[10] The idea that much of the policy success of social movements is dependent on the receptivity of the *political process* during the time that potential supporters of a new movement are psychologically and organizationally ready to challenge the status quo corresponded to my observations of the women's movement. According to political process theory, when government is strong and committed to repressing a social movement, the movement will usually fail. By contrast, when government is weakened and, as a result, the relative balance of power between movement and government is more nearly equal, the movement will acquire leverage within the political system and be successful.

It is the nature of politics that, for a time at least, political success breeds further success as people rush to join a winning cause. As the crumbling of the New Deal coalition ushered in a period of political uncertainty in the late sixties and early seventies and the potential electoral impact of a women's bloc of votes began to attract attention, strategically placed politicians saw the value of making a serious effort to attract women's support. This allowed the women's movement to gain early legislative victories without possessing many resources or tactical skills. Presidential and then congressional facilitation first of the women's movement's formation and then of that part of the movement's agenda that focused on legal equality helped to establish both the timing and emphasis on issues within the movement. Because of the long legislative history of the ERA and its logical link to civil rights bills of the previous decade, Congress was ready to move on this issue and complementary civil rights statutes that extended equal treatment to women. It was not as ready to move on issues that singled women out for special consideration. So, as laws mandating equality prospered, that part of the women's agenda addressing child care, abortion, and women's de facto segregation within the workplace floundered.

By looking at the women's movement as a social movement that posed a greater challenge to government than seemed warranted by the material resources that it controlled, it is easier to understand why government responded to the movement as early as it did. It is also possible to evaluate the range of strategic options that were available to the movement, without tying this assessment to the necessity for incremental political change. Nonincremental change is a possibility if the government's relative weakness leaves it open to pressure from the movement rather than if the movement is successful in framing its agenda in a nonthreatening way.

To analyze the women's movement this way means incorporating political process theory from sociology into political science. Although other scholars have made use of process theory (sometimes labeled political opportunity theory), it is still not well known in the political science discipline as a whole.[11] In many respects, resource mobilization theory, with its emphasis on money, membership, and external allies, fits more smoothly than process theory into the political science literature on groups. Yet, process theory has a capacity, which resource mobilization theory does not, to show how rapid, nonincremental changes in public policy can take place when a number of external factors are conducive to groups that are presenting a challenge to government. It also does a better job of explaining why multiple movements arise during the same historic periods.

Using a mixture of research techniques ranging from interviews and archival research to content analysis of news reports and official documents, I attempted to relate the mobilization of the women's movement and the strategies employed by groups within the movement to government responses, focusing on presidential statements and congressional introduction and passage of legislation. My emphasis throughout is on the *political impact* of the women's movement. I have no doubt that the movement has also produced significant changes in language, childrearing, education, the arts, individual psychology, and a myriad of other areas affecting our life and culture. And yet, the women's movement from its inception has attempted to change *laws* that perpetuate gender difference, seeking to free both sexes from rigid regulations that assumed women were not willing to sit on juries, men alone were fit for military combat, married women had no resources to get financial credit in their own names, boys did not need to take home economics in school, or girls woodworking classes, and men should have the sole responsibility after divorce for alimony and child support.

A large part of the movement's thrust, as well as its successes and failures, have been political. I have tried to take account of the contributions of radical groups within the women's movement as well as the more conventional groups, but with the national political focus of this analysis, many radical activities are left out.[12] One of the founders of a Washington-based women's group whom I interviewed in 1974 noted that sustained radical activity was very difficult in the nation's capital. She laughingly observed that if members of her group wanted to picket or sit-in at the offices of a corporation engaged in sexist employment practices, the D.C. corporate offices would probably contain just two or three employees. In her view, echoed by many other Washington representatives, politics (and, by and large that meant conventional politics) was the only game in their town.

## Methodology

Many sources of data are used in this political process analysis of the women's movement. To understand the emergence and subsequent political activity of the women's movement, I spoke with lobbyists for the major feminist groups represented in Washington, including NOW, WEAL, and the NWPC, in four waves of interviews (1974–75, 1977, 1981, and 1984). These interviews were initially intended to show the development of an effective lobby representing women's interests and to help explain why Congress was passing an unprecedented number of bills responsive to women. Especially in the early years, the interviews instead suggested how effective a disorganized, poorly funded lobby could be *when* it was linked to a large social movement. Second, I examined the papers of NOW and WEAL housed at the Arthur and Elizabeth Schlesinger Library in Cambridge, Massachusetts. These documents revealed much about the goals, strategies, and organizational priorities of these two important movement groups. Third, I analyzed and coded the abstracts of news stories about U.S. women using the *New York Times Annual Index* for the period 1950 to 1986, concentrating on events that reflected agitation on behalf of women's rights. I followed a procedure similar to McAdam's coding of black insurgent events from 1940 to 1970 reported in his well-known study of the civil rights movement[13] (see Appendix A). This provided a means of assessing variations in social activism on behalf of women's rights as well as public awareness of women's concerns. Fourth, I have drawn heavily on what is by now a rich secondary literature in political science, history, and sociology that analyzes the contemporary women's movement.

To examine the role of government in changing public policy toward women, the *Congressional Record* is especially useful in coding bill introductions, and *U.S. Statutes at Large* contains the information on the passage of laws that make gender their focus. There are fewer precedents for using *U.S. Statutes at Large* and the *Congressional Record* to measure congressional action than for using the *New York Times Annual Index* to study movements. Benjamin Ginsberg's article, "Elections and Public Policy,"[14] is one of the few pieces of research that uses *U.S. Statutes at Large* as a source for assessing the impact of events (in his case, elections) on policy.[15] Ginsberg justifies a count of laws passed as the most systematic way to measure the results of congressional policy. Although a numeric categorization of laws ignores important qualitative differences by weighting each piece of legislation equally, it is hard to conceive of an alternate procedure capable of coding new laws qualitatively over time.

In reading through a large number of statutes, it soon becomes clear how much laws build upon each other. When Title IX was added to the Educational Amendments Act of 1972, its significance in expanding women's opportunities to engage in competitive sports was barely recognized. The real political battle over funding and women's access to athletics came three years later, when efforts to weaken enforcement of the legislation were beaten back in Congress. A numeric count of legislative activity does more to highlight the importance of policies developed in a given area than it may first appear, for there are very few major "one-shot" laws.

The one difficulty that does arise in constructing a yearly measure of congressional activity is the congressional pattern of passing a whole wave of laws during the second session of Congress, just before adjournment. This sessional fluctuation was handled by emphasizing the percentage of women's laws for each year rather than the absolute number. Percentages give a better representation of the share of the agenda occupied by these issues, since yearly legislative output fluctuated widely during the period studied, from a low of 145 new laws passed in 1981 to a high of 505 laws passed in 1970.

Before ratification of the so-called "lame duck" amendment (the twentieth) to the U.S. Constitution in 1932, Congresses frequently spanned three years, with a short session running from January to the beginning of March of the year following the election of a new Congress.[16] The Twentieth Amendment changed this, moving the beginning date for the new Congress back to January to coincide with the start of the presidential administration and creating the now familiar two-year length of Congresses.

In coding bill introductions, a problem arose that was not a factor with laws passed. During this period, Congress has varied its rules regarding the number of cosponsors allowed on a single piece of legislation. This has led researchers such as Paul Burstein to count the number of legislative sponsors of legislation rather than the number of bills.[17] Because of the diversity of the laws tracked in this study, I treated this problem like the yearly fluctuation in laws passed. That is, the number of bills introduced dealing with women's issues is represented as a percentage of all bills introduced during that year. After looking at yearly changes in the number of bill sponsors on a wide range of issues, I concluded that there are not significant differences in patterns of sponsorship among issue areas. There is no reason to believe that there are either fewer or more cosponsors of women's bills than of any other type of bill in the same year, and so it seems just as reasonable to represent the proportion of women's bills before Congress as to represent the number of sponsors. Coding the percentages of women's bills introduced and passed by year, provides a picture of the timing, pace, and subject matter of "women's" issues handled by Congress.

I conducted the one and a "half" waves of interviews in 1974–75 and 1977 with members of Congress and their staff who were involved in considering several pieces of women's rights legislation in subcommittee. These interviews suggested that members of Congress were sensitive to women's issues without quite realizing where pressure for these bills was coming from. Finally, I examined the public papers of the presidents holding office from 1952 to 1988 for references to women and women's issues. I also used concordances of State of the Union messages, as well as nomination and inaugural addresses, to compare presidential statements about women and women's issues.[18]

This mixture of events analysis, interviews, archival records, and content analysis of presidential rhetoric is designed to show both the public and some of the private faces of the women's movement. It also provides a picture of governmental involvement with women's issues in this period.

This book is organized so that the first chapter examines the development of the current women's movement and tests competing theories of social movement behavior. The second chapter focuses closely on the conditions that led up to the appearance of a new women's movement in the 1960s and attempts to explain why this social movement emerged at this time. The third chapter concentrates on the formative period of the women's movement and analyzes choices that were made within the movement and in government, which set the direction for the movement's future development. Chapters four and five trace the movement through its peak years and into its current decline and show the tactics, issues, and alliances that characterized the movement in these periods. Chapter six focuses on government's role in determining the political outcomes of the contemporary movement and explores the initiatives that brought about its current political gains. Chapter seven examines the degree to which the women's movement has succeeded in institutionalizing itself within the American political system and summarizes the lessons to be learned from the political struggles of this movement and their relevance for contemporary American politics.

**Inviting Women's Rebellion**

# 1

# Interpreting the Contemporary Women's Movement

There are many difficulties in trying to study the women's movement. Its longevity, with all the transformations needed to survive into its fourth decade, is one. Its size is another. There are so many different facets of a women's movement to study. The guerrilla theater acted out by young feminists of the 1960s, disrupting congressional committee hearings to demand consideration of the ERA, is one type of movement.[1] The feminist political action committees of the 1980s, distributing money to candidates for office, is another. The angry, weeping, shouting women of Mills College in 1990, demanding that their college's trustees reverse a decision to admit male undergraduates, is still a third. Diane Feinstein's capture of the 1990 Democratic gubernatorial primary in California is a fourth. Yet, the political strength of the women's movement owes a great deal to its persistence, diversity, and scope. To understand the women's movement, it is necessary to determine what gives it energy, holds it together, and sustains its many forms.

Like most social movements of the 1960s in America, the women's movement seemed to burst onto the political scene with little warning. Many observers at the time felt that it would disappear just as quickly. They viewed the women's movement as a transitory phenomenon, imitating the black civil rights movement, but without that movement's capacity to endure. They felt that women would soon realize how well off they were relative to other groups in society and return to their homes, abandoning protest.[2]

Yet, the women's movement, far from fading, proved more enduring and adaptable to changing political conditions than most other movements of the same period. Each decade since its emergence has witnessed a somewhat different thrust to the women's movement. In the sixties, the movement used flamboyant and sometimes disruptive tactics to win adherents and publicize its issues. A typical action was the 1969 protest by a group of women from NOW, who interrupted the New York governor's committee on abortion-law reform by chanting, "No more male legislators" and "Every woman resents having her body controlled by men."[3] The women's movement in this period was commonly referred to as the "women's liberation movement." Movement activists intended for the name to evoke women's desire to be treated as individuals, and to avoid media characterizations of the "woman problem" in the way that the "black problem" had gained currency in the popular press.[4] However, the term "liberation," like sixties-style protest, quickly became dated, fading in the 1970s, as the movement picked up increasing public support.

In the seventies, more conventional organizing tactics predominated. Most women's groups referred to the movement as simply "the women's movement." This terminology evoked the presuffrage appellation of the "woman movement," with its connotations of the unity and homogeneity of women's interests.[5] Along with a modified name, the movement's public presence shifted from confrontation to organization. In the early 1970s, most of the major groups that had arisen from this new social movement opened Washington offices to increase pressure on government to respond to women's new political interests.[6] Mass marches began to replace small-scale disruptive actions. Ten thousand people paraded down Fifth Avenue in New York in 1970, marking the fiftieth anniversary of women's suffrage and "a new crusade for equality."[7]

In the 1980s, there was a further shift, as women activists began to forsake organizing for actually exercising political power. A gender gap in voting estimated from 6 to 8 percent, between men's and women's candidate preference which first became evident in the 1980 elections, gave movement members a vehicle for attracting politicians' attention.[8] Women were not only starting to vote differently from men, but they were turning out to vote in larger numbers as well.[9] A tilt by women voters toward the Democratic party helped make Geraldine Ferraro that party's vice presidential nominee in 1984. Ever increasing numbers of women were running for electoral office.[10] The women's movement, through these three decades, shifted its political tactics from protest, to organizing, to exercising electoral clout, making it different from most other social movements of this period.

The other major social movements of the sixties and seventies adapted to changing political circumstances more slowly and might have suffered for it. The black civil rights movement pioneered the tactics of civil disobedience and defiance of authority that became the protest politics of the sixties.[11] Civil rights leaders varied the intensity of their challenges to authority from the relatively passive tactic of sit-ins to the raised fists of black power, but they always confronted established power. When these methods became less effective, the movement largely faded from the public eye. The consumer movement, with its Ralph Nader-inspired style of engaged citizens doing research to test corporate claims, used these tactics throughout the decades. Consumerism began to lose a large national audience when some of its amateurism and questionable research techniques damaged its credibility with the public.[12]

Finally, the environmental movement has always been more diverse tactically than either the civil rights or consumer movements.[13] Unlike the women's movement, which is similarly diverse, it has used a wide variety of political approaches *simultaneously*. Politically conservative environmentalists write letters protesting misuse of public lands, while groups such as Greenpeace and Earth First! commit civil disobedience to halt whale hunting and tree harvesting. Emphasizing the traditional stance that corporate greed and unthinking destruction of the ecological balance threaten the land, air, and water, environmentalism has successfully incorporated new issues ranging from acid rain and the clubbing of baby seals to nuclear safety and the destruction of Brazilian rain forests. Movement activists range from hunters to preservationists. Yet, the environmental movement has paid a price for its inclusiveness. The militancy of some groups led important officials within the Reagan administration to express open disdain for environmentalists, branding them "bird-nesters," "druids," and "tree huggers," launching an effective political attack on environmental issues throughout the 1980s.[14] The actions of extreme groups made it easier to attack the moderates.

The size of the women's movement also sets it apart from most contemporary movements. From its earliest days, it seemed to spring from a multitude of sources. Freeman has chronicled the emergence of the "older" and "younger" branches of the movement.[15] The former was started by professional women, many of whom were brought together either by John F. Kennedy's Presidential Commission on the Status of Women or by separate state commissions on the status of women, which formed as offshoots of the presidential commission. The younger branch, by contrast, often started on college campuses, attracting activists from the civil rights, antiwar, and new left movements. From the beginning, the movement also had international ties; Simone de Beauvoir's *The Second Sex*, first published in 1949, had lit the fires of feminism in Europe.[16] Clearly, there is no *single* unified women's movement, but there are a multitude of groups, organizations, and individuals that although diverse, identify with the goal of improving the status of women around the world.

# The Dominant Perspectives
# on the Women's Movement

Scholars do not agree about how to define social movements, let alone how movements emerge and develop.[17] Movements are difficult to categorize because they assume a much broader range of public postures than do institutionalized political actors and have the potential to alter their stances more quickly in response to changing conditions. For example, the women's movement was able to shift from nonpartisanship to a fairly close alliance with the Democratic party in less than ten years. Environmentalists have embraced both bipartisanship and partisan events such as the "bush-whacking" of presidential candidate George Bush before the 1988 election. By contrast, it took the Democratic party more than sixty years after the Civil War to replace the Republicans as the party perceived by the public as more supportive of black civil rights.[18] The Republican party similarly took almost sixty years to reverse its historic stands in support of an equal rights amendment and women's rights.[19] There is little agreement among those studying social movements about a "typical" pattern of movement development.

The argument over why specific movements behave as they do divides into three competing schools of thought—mass society, resource mobilization, and political process. Each perspective singles out a specific set of factors with the greatest influence on the timing and direction of social movements.

## Mass Society

Traditional mass society theories, such as those developed by William Kornhauser, Philip Selznick, and Hannah Arendt, grew out of observation of the increasing incidence of political movements in European industrial societies in the early decades of the twentieth century.[20] Theorists who adhered to the mass society model concluded that circumstances surrounding the creation of industrial mass societies, including alienation of the individual from his or her work, the breakdown of families, and the abandonment of traditional values, gave rise to new political movements. They hypothesized that rootless, alienated, and socially marginal workers are most likely to join movements of protest and discontent.

This theory was applied to American politics after McCarthyism in the early 1950s, isolationism in the 1930s, and a score of other right-wing movements in the United States led American intellectuals such as Seymour Martin Lipset, Daniel Bell, and Richard Hofstadter to conclude that conditions similar to those observed in Europe before the rise of Naziism in Germany now existed in the United States. The growth of urban America, as young people deserted rural communities to look for work in the cities, created conditions producing lonely, cut-off, rootless individuals who, according to mass society theory, would be prime recruits for mass movements that offered them social contacts and a purpose in life.[21] More recently, some neoconservative scholars have used the justifications inherent in a mass society model to group together the liberal social movements of the 1970s (including the environmental, antinuclear, women's, and consumer movements) into one "new class" movement, bent on subverting the public interest in favor of elite groups.[22] Although there are a variety of formulations of this critique, in general, neoconservatives conclude that a new class movement has grown as "an outgrowth of conditions in post-industrial society which made a mass phenomenon of the educated class, the producers of knowledge and culture and their followers in the upper rungs of the tertiary sector of the economy, those involved in communications, in the application of scientific technology, in welfare related activities."[23] These individuals in modern society are believed to be ideal movement adherents, according to mass society theory, because of their alleged alienation from the means of production and their "adversary orientation to traditional American values and institutional practices."[24] Mass society theorists see political movements as unpatterned and frequently irrational collective efforts to bring about or resist change using unorthodox means.[25] According to this perspective, one would expect movements to form and flourish when a group's grievances are increasing, its social ties are weakening, and traditional values are being questioned by a substantial portion of the public.

A more complex variant of this view of social movements is presented in Gurr's *Why Men Rebel*,[26] which stresses the absolute level not of dissatisfaction in society but of relative dissatisfaction. This variant of the mass society theory is known as relative deprivation. According to Gurr, movements form when individuals begin to perceive a great difference between their value expectations (what they believe that they should be able to achieve) and their value capabilities (what they actually can achieve in society). They then become frustrated and angry. When this discontent is politicized and so widespread that the power of the opposition nearly equals the government, social movements and even rebellion may occur. Both the psychological state of actual and potential movement adherents and the relative power of the movement in relation to the government play a crucial role in molding the movement.

Jo Freeman, using relative deprivation, did one of the earliest analyses of the women's movement.[27] Freeman marshalled evidence supporting her view that relative deprivation among women college graduates in the 1960s contributed to the rise of the women's movement in this decade.[28] She argued that when women compared their job and social prospects with men of the same age and educational background (including their spouses), they felt unjustly treated. While males were put in management-trainee positions, women with college degrees in the 1960s were routinely channeled into secretarial or clerical jobs or expected to become full-time wives and mothers. Men advanced quickly in their careers and income, while women lagged behind, breeding a sense of injustice and smoldering frustration.

Freeman's work also introduced an aspect of resource mobilization theory by noting that communication networks among college women were already in place through the student and new left movements. These networks were coopted and used to organize and spread information about the women's movement, helping it to grow rapidly. Freeman's analysis combines Gurr's work on relative deprivation with early emphasis on the acquisition of a vital resource by women. Freeman's book is the only well-known application of any part of mass society theory to the women's movement.

Most analyses, including all of Freeman's later work, have instead put primary emphasis on the ability of the women's movement to attract external resources and create new organizations, including a national network linking the movement together.[29] Women's grievances and isolation in the home are generally seen as less significant than their access to new resources.

## Resource Mobilization

This brings us to resource mobilization theory, which was formulated by sociologists in the 1970s to challenge mass society theory and its relative deprivation variant. Most recent studies of movements use resource mobilization theory to evaluate politically active social movements.[30] This theory has much in common with the traditional study of interest-group politics. Resource mobilization theorists define social movements as "a set of opinions and beliefs in a population which represents preferences for changing some elements of the social structure and/or reward distribution of a society."[31] This definition fits public interest groups like Common Cause and Public Citizen as well as those social movements that come more quickly to mind, such as the women's and environmental movements.[32] Resource mobilization theory suggests that the principal problems most movements, like most conventional groups, face are organizational. Among these, the hardest is the task of starting up. A close second is adding new followers while retaining existing members.

Resource mobilization theory examines these obstacles, incorporating many of Robert Salisbury's ideas about exchange in identifying ways that movements succeed.[33] According to resource mobilization theory, entrepreneurial organizers are likely to play a leading role in forming movements. These individuals often invest capital, which may include material resources, raise funds, or even make use of something as intangible as charisma in recruiting members. The entrepreneur or other leaders of the movement will first offer material benefits, such as a newsletter, a glossy magazine, or even travel discounts. The benefits of friendship and comradery, which create solidarity, will then be used to draw and hold followers. Finally, purposive incentives, such as the feeling of contributing to a worthwhile cause, will win additional adherents. Within this context, resource mobilization theorists view movements as realistic alternatives to conventional politics for excluded groups that desire access to the political system.[34]

In addition to obtaining resources from entrepreneurs, movements can gain resources at the outset through the patronage of established groups. If movements are able to attract allies, develop communications networks, gather material resources, and utilize entrepreneurial leadership, they are likely to achieve political impact; if not, they will probably fail.[35] The success of a movement seems most likely in periods of relative economic prosperity, when the discretionary resources of elite and mass publics increase. People have extra money and time to invest in movements. Individual movements will use self-advertisement and cite their success in accomplishing goals to command their share of available resources, competing with other potential movements. The availability, quantity, and type of resources that a movement has access to, in this view, will shape the movement's development.

Most research to date on the women's movement has adopted this perspective, treating these factors as crucial in allowing the movement to form originally and succeed in the medium term. Still, it was necessary to recast resource mobilization theory considerably to accommodate the case of the women's movement. In influential books, Gelb and Palley and Mansbridge stress the importance to the movement of framing women's issues in terms of role equity—attempting to gain equal treatment for women—rather than role change—trying to open new opportunities to women (e.g., the right to have an abortion) or changing women's accepted role in a fundamental way (e.g., drafting them into the military).[36] In their view, this new emphasis among women activists, which limited the extent to which the movement directly challenged the status quo, created the tactical environment that the movement used to coax change from government with existing resources.

Gelb and Palley argue further that entrepreneurs and a large number of new resources were not directly required in the women's movement because the movement had found a way, through its tactics, to make existing resources sufficient. This variant of resource mobilization theory may be called issue-based. Mansbridge's work on the ERA, by contrast, laments that many activists within the women's movement did not sufficiently moderate their demands to attract the political support needed to pass the ERA. According to this view, in the end the ERA was caught in a difficult situation. While it had become more of a symbolic than a real effort to achieve change in women's traditional roles, a number of Americans still perceived it as too threatening to pass. At the same time, it meant too little to many movement supporters to sustain the extraordinary effort necessary to add an amendment to the U.S. Constitution.

Conover and Gray's analysis of the women's movement is also premised on resource mobilization.[37] The thrust of their analysis is that self-interest, broadly defined, motivates individual participants in social movements. That self-interest may include preexisting loyalties to groups that aid the movement and a desire to act upon principles. The issues that a movement advocates have an important effect on whether mobilization will occur. Issues help individuals determine the nature of the good the movement seeks, the utility of the good, and the urgency of mobilizing. Finally, entrepreneurial leaders and external actors, including the government, the mass media, and other interest groups in society, play a role in helping or hindering the process of mobilizing a new movement. So rational self-interest, buttressed by loyalty to groups that became supportive of the women's movement, external sponsorship, and definition of issues, led to the emergence and success of the women's movement.

McGlen and O'Connor[38] also use an analysis driven by resource mobilization theory. They conclude that the movement arose when outside resources, a communication network linking the potential leaders of the movement, and a sense of collective outrage among women were sparked into activity by the publication of Betty Friedan's *The Feminine Mystique* in 1963.[39] Their perspective emphasizes the combination of new resources and psychological readiness that gave rise to the women's movement.

The major implications of resource mobilization theory as applied to the women's movement, then, are that the movement emphasized

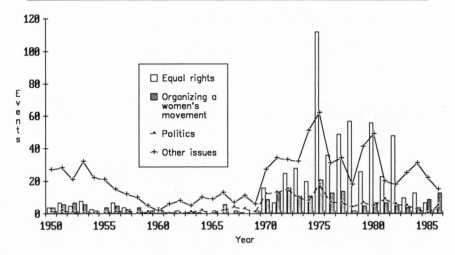

Fig. 1-1. Women's events raised in the *New York Times.*

its nonthreatening characteristics, appearing politically innocuous, and that an early accumulation of resources followed from this focus. The movement, by urging the incremental extension of equal treatment to women, used legislative gains of the civil rights movement to add protection for women. Consequently, moderate groups from the civil rights and women's communities joined forces with the new women's movement, providing resources to sustain it. Coding separate stories using the *New York Times Annual Index* reveals the number and nature of separate events or incidents related to women's rights in this period. (See Appendix A for more complete information.) These events provide a picture of the frequency of movement-related activity over time. From roughly the mid-seventies through the early eighties, equality is clearly the focus of most of the women's events reported in the *New York Times* (Fig. 1-1). Yet, a resource mobilization perspective suggests that issues of equality in fact paved the way for new alliances and women's movement growth in its earliest years. This is not borne out in *New York Times* reports, which show only a scattering of equality-related events from the early 1960s to the mid-1970s.

Similarly, such a cautious strategy on the part of the women's movement neither accords with the public face of the movement in the late sixties, when protest and radical rhetoric most often got into newspaper headlines, nor fits in with the actions of the early lobbyists for women's rights in the late sixties and early seventies. These individuals were acutely aware that winning legislative change on the basis of adding "and sex" to existing laws banning racial discrimination would not be enough to change the status of women. Their insistence upon passage of the ERA, day-care legislation, and the Equal Credit Opportunity Act reflected their view that women could not simply piggyback black civil rights issues. Women must come up with their own program for change, one that would explicitly suit women's needs. Later on, as organized opposition to the movement grew, lobbyists for the movement became more contented with "small" victories, eked out on the political margins, but the early years were quite different.

A cautious strategy also leaves unanswered the larger question of why women bothered to organize as a social movement. If it was possible for them to use a careful, incremental approach to achieve genuine change, why create a large movement for that purpose? Figure 1-2, showing the volume of congressional legislation on women's issues back to 1899, seems to suggest that, historically, social movements, world wars, or occasionally both were needed for women to be heard and responded to politically. The first major upsurge in the number of bills introduced occurred in the 65th Congress (1917 to 1919) during the height of the women's suffrage movement. Bill passage in these early years hit its highest point in the 66th Congress (1919 to 1921), the Congress that was in session as women first got the right to vote in federal elections. The next peak in the number of women's rights laws passed came in the 78th Congress (1943 to 1944) as legislation that mobilized women into the war effort went into effect. In more recent times, the number of women's bills introduced began to rise in the early 1960s (87th Congress), followed by the largest number of new laws addressing women's concerns ever passed by a Congress, the 93rd (1973 to 1974). The effect of the two women's movements of the century and World War II are all too apparent in this graph. If framing women's issues in terms of role equity was crucial to the movement, one would expect to see more continuity in congressional treatment of women's issues. Standard interest-group politics should have been enough to win changes from Congress. Instead, the pattern of activity is one of peaks and valleys, suggesting intense periods of change and long periods of neglect.

In addition, the women's movement's explicit rejection of hierarchical leadership as a replication of the sex-role dominance that existed within society, which they were fighting against, eliminates the most obvious tactic the movement could have used to accumulate resources. There was little room for entrepreneurial leaders to raise the outside resources necessary for the movement to attract adherents and achieve political leverage, given the movement's principled rejection of leaders. In the early days, there were neither groups nor individuals touting cheaper life insurance or group health policies to entice members

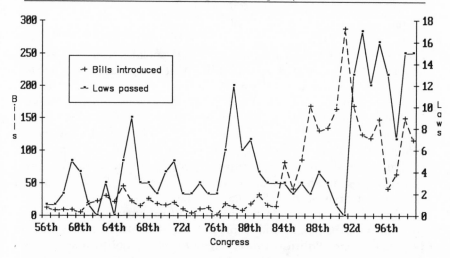

Fig. 1-2. Number of women's bills introduced and laws passed, 1899-1986.

into women's groups and win support for the movement. By the mid-seventies, organizations such as the League of Women Voters raised more than a million dollars by selling ERA bracelets, but the movement did not emerge from this kind of entrepreneurial spirit. The rejection of leadership was very costly to the new movement, as scholars were, even then, quick to note.[40] But this rejection of hierarchy was accepted almost from the beginning as an integral part of the movement's values.

Finally, there were few obvious patrons of the women's movement in its early years. Established women's groups, including the League of Women Voters and the American Association of University Women, helped train lobbyists for the new movement and eased their access to congressional offices. Aside from women's groups, most traditional liberal and labor groups steered clear of close involvement with this interest. There is little evidence that they supplied significant material resources to the movement in the sixties. Resource mobilization raises more questions than it answers in evaluating the experience of the women's movement.

## Using a Political Process Approach

### Political Process Theory

Another theory appears to coincide more closely with the development of the women's movement. The political process approach grew out of resource mobilization, but instead of concentrating exclusively on resources, it places more emphasis on the political system, indigenous accumulation of resources, and psychological aspects of movement identification.[41] Process theory defines social movements as the actions of "excluded groups to mobilize sufficient political leverage to advance collective interests through non-institutionalized means."[42] The definition itself suggests the problems these groups confront. Lacking political access and employing noninstitutionalized methods, movements are viewed suspiciously by the public. Nascent movement groups are political outsiders, representing interests that not only challenge the status quo but frequently seek to upset traditional political processes. They are dedicated to pursuit of *collective* interests rather than divisible benefits that can be used to attract members. Finally, they work outside dominant political institutions, making them at once mavericks and unpredictable elements in a very stable political system. Political process theory sees the political system as the crucial determinant of the movement's timing and success within a forbidding environment.[43]

Like Gurr's theory of relative deprivation,[44] those with this perspective recognize that movements are most likely to form when political elites are vulnerable and the difference in power between challengers and the government is lessened. Process theorists also acknowledge the importance of organizational readiness for the movement's success. Unlike some resource mobilization theorists, they retain a psychological dimension to the study of movements. McAdam labels this aspect "cognitive liberation."[45] According to the political process perspective, for a movement to emerge, its followers must believe that problems have political roots and that they can do something to change existing conditions. They need to have organizations in place to direct action. Most important of all, the government must at least be willing to tolerate the movement's appearance. While resource mobilization theory is closely related to theories of organizational formation (e.g., it asks if sufficient resources exist to sustain the new entity), process theory emphasizes the structure of political opportunity for a particular group within American society.

Several studies of the women's movement have adopted a political process approach. In *Gender Politics*, Ethel Klein deemphasizes organizational factors and focuses on the favorable structure of political opportunity that allowed the women's movement to form when it did. Klein notes that the mid-sixties was the first time since the suffrage movement in the teens and nineteen twenties when sociodemographic trends were arrayed so that fertility among women was declining, job participation was rising, and the number of unmarried women was going up. This coincidence, in her view, made conditions ideal for a

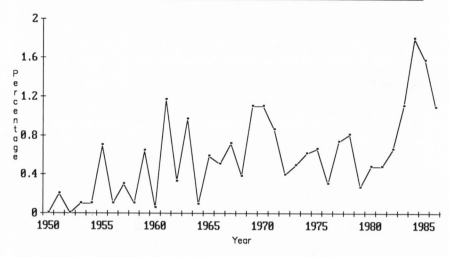

Fig. 1-3. Women's bills introduced as a percentage of all bills introduced.

new movement to emerge.[46] Klein and Carol Mueller argue that a new consciousness was developing among women at this time, which helped sustain the political force of the movement.[47] Women were starting to abandon the view that their lack of status was their own fault as they identified themselves as victims of a social and economic system that denied them opportunities because of their sex.[48] At the same time, politics seemed to provide a feasible and legitimate vehicle to bring about change.

Katzenstein and Mueller's book, with contributions by various authors who compared European and American women's movements, is also structured by political process theory.[49] The volume emphasizes the creation of feminist consciousness, the relationship between movements and political parties, and the interactions among organized labor, women's movements, and the state. It concludes with the somewhat puzzling finding that women's movements seem to be most successful in political systems with either very strong or very weak left-wing forces. The moderate, socially progressive governments favored by many political scientists turn out to be the least likely to pass policies urged by women's movements, although it is not completely clear why this is so.

Many aspects of the women's movement on their face seem to make more sense in the context of process theory than resource mobilization theory. First, the timing is better. Figure 1-3 shows the pace of congressional activity on women's issues. By 1961, for the first time since the end of World War II, women's issues comprised more than 1 percent of all bills introduced in Congress. This may not seem like a big impact for a group comprising 52 percent of the population, but it represents 150 bills, a large increase from earlier years. Most of these legislative introductions were versions of the ERA, which quite early became Congress's premier women's issue.

In 1961, President Kennedy followed the advice of his party and organized labor and appointed the first Presidential Commission on the Status of Women. Democratic party leaders and labor union officials still opposed the ERA in the early sixties, but they were afraid that without executive initiative, Congress might pass it anyway.[50] The commission was established, at least in part, to thwart the ERA. However, under the guidance of Esther Peterson, who was director of the Women's Bureau of the Department of Labor in the Kennedy administration, it unearthed sufficient evidence of discontent among women about the social, legal, and economic discrimination against them to play a major role in creating the early agenda of the women's movement.[51]

These events suggest that before the onset of the women's movement in 1966, initiated by the formation of NOW, Congress and the executive branch were already engaging in a low-key competition to position themselves out in front of this incipient movement. The most obvious reason for this competition was the perceived instability of political alignments in the 1960s and 1970s.[52] Since neither political party had a firm governing majority, both parties and politicians were openly searching for pivotal blocs of votes to stabilize a winning coalition. Government seemed to play an active role in encouraging the formation of a women's movement in the sixties. By contrast, there were few signs of other resources, leaders, or potential allies that might have directly facilitated the movement's emergence in this period.

The differing implications of resource mobilization and political process theory for understanding the development of a women's movement are clear. A resource mobilization perspective, especially one that is based on selecting issues that are relatively "cheaply" won in the political marketplace, argues that the women's movement arose when a requisite level of resources was brought together to push for change. The movement reached this point by couching its demands in nonthreatening, incremental terms, which reduced the political costs both for potential allies and for government in accepting these demands. The movement's ability to remain active was related to its skill in continuing to command new resources.

By contrast, a political process model stresses the balance of power between a weakened government and a newly empowered group of likely movement supporters. The openness of the government to new interests, the stability or instability of political alignments, the availability of allies and supporters willing to help form the new movement, and the psychological readiness of members of the excluded group together determine the political opportunities available for a women's movement to form and achieve its political goals. The movement demonstrates new organizational strength while government either lessens repression of the group or actually takes steps to facilitate its actions.

## An Empirical Test of the Two Approaches

To test the relative explanatory power of these two dominant theories of social movement development as applied to the women's movement, all activities dealing with women's rights that occurred between 1950 and 1986 were coded using the *New York Times Index*. (See Appendix A for coding information.) This period encompasses the earliest stirrings of the contemporary movement, its peak in the mid-1970s, and its subsequent decline. Events were coded to indicate (1) who initiated each; (2) the type of activity involved; (3) the target of the event; and (4) the issues at stake. This information makes it possible to compare the broad outlines of the women's movement's initial appearance and subsequent development with patterns predicted by resource mobilization and political process theories to see which of these theories best explains the growth and decline of the movement.[53]

Although a number of problems leading to possible inconsistencies in coding results have been identified,[54] efforts to show systematic bias in the *New York Times* coverage of social movement activity have generally failed. McAdam reports that the *New York Times* covered 83 percent of all dated events between 1955 and 1962 on the black civil rights movement that were mentioned in nine books written about the movement.[55] Jenkins and Perrow compared the *New York Times* coverage of events in the farm workers' movement with the *Los Angeles Times* and the *Chicago Tribune* coverage.[56] There was no evidence that the *New York Times* emphasized stories different from those in the other papers, but the *New York Times* did pick up more stories than either of the other sources. The one bias that has been demonstrated in *New York Times* reporting is the higher probability that "hard news," including demonstrations, riots, and national meetings, will be covered, as compared with "soft news," such as speeches and internal movement debates over tactics.[57] Most scholars who employ

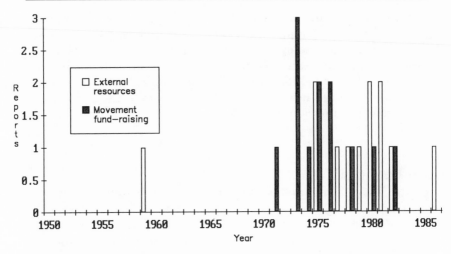

Fig. 1-4. Reports of new resources entering the women's movement.

events data exclude from events totals all editorials or other *New York Times*-generated stories, such as retrospectives on the movement or Sunday magazine articles. That practice was also followed here to cut down on the extent that the *New York Times'* editorial judgments might skew the results.

In analyzing the development of the women's movement, resource mobilization theory suggests that a successful movement will quickly attract allies, funds, and volunteer labor. This ability to gain external support itself provides the basis for future movement growth. Figure 1-4 shows the number of events coded in the *New York Times* that involved either outside resources coming into the women's movement or the accumulation of resources through fund-raising by women's groups. The flow of internal and external resources into the movement does not pick up significantly until the 1970s, after the formation of the movement and a number of its early successes.

Based on this data, it is difficult to argue that the timing of the movement depended on a new-found ability to attract outside resources. There is somewhat more evidence that allies helped the movement to emerge. A variety of interest groups generated positive news about women and their aspirations in the mid-sixties. As Figure 1-5 shows, civil rights and liberties groups, along with traditional women's, labor, and business groups, were all involved to a degree in promoting news events favorable to women and women's rights. There is again the curiosity that there were far more supportive events by these groups, with the single exception of those backing civil rights and liberties, in the 1950s, yet no women's movement emerged.

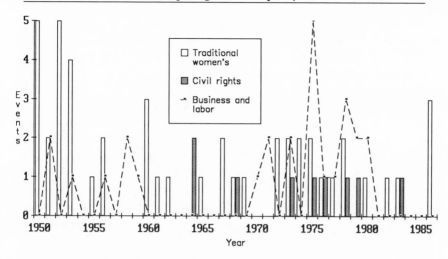

Fig. 1-5. Supportive events initiated by allied groups.

Most work that applies resource mobilization theory to the women's movement stresses the way that movement adherents moderated their political demands to compensate for lack of resources to bring about change. Data from the *New York Times* cannot give us a true picture of the degree of moderation or intensity of women's demands. Figure 1-6 shows which issues women raised and how the issues fluctuated over time. In the 1960s, women, like the other actors who raised women's concerns, were unlikely to focus on specific complaints. This early generality of issues changes among women, as among all actors, in the 1970s, as the focus on legal equality becomes increasingly predominant.

Although demands for legal equality and particularly the addition of an equal rights amendment to the Constitution were historically the uncompromising stands of the extreme feminists, Jane Mansbridge makes a strong case in her book, *Why We Lost the ERA*, that movement adherents in the seventies and eighties were, to a great degree, successful in making the ERA more a symbolic recognition of the new social reality of equality between the sexes than an extreme position. Yet, it remains hard to view the movement's interest in a new amendment to the U.S. Constitution as evidence of moderation. The extreme nature of the remedy clearly raised red flags for its opponents.

The decline of the movement in the 1980s, according to resource mobilization theory, should also be accompanied by a falling away of allies and a reduction of resources beyond a minimum necessary to support the movement. Both supportive actions by movement allies and new resources entering the movement do fall off in the 1980s (Figs.

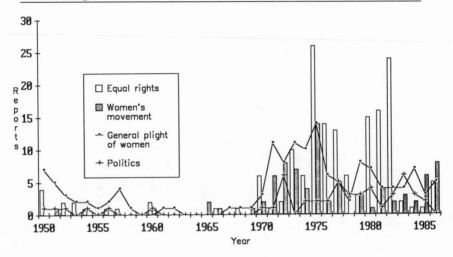

Fig. 1-6. Issues raised by women, as reported in the *New York Times.*

1-4, 1-5). It is difficult to determine if this is a cause or a result of the movement's overall drop in activity. Examining the actions of feminist groups during this period shows continuing initiation of new events (Fig. 1-7). Protest activities actually jump in frequency (Fig. 1-8). While events as a whole decline, some activities (e.g., protest by feminists) increase. In summary, there is some evidence that the availability of outside resources had an impact on the level of activity carried out by the women's movement. There is not enough data to conclude that resources were the decisive factor in movement development.

Political process theory shifts attention from resource accumulation toward government support as the key factor for the success of the movement. Government's behavior toward women would be expected to change noticeably before the mobilization of a new movement. Change may involve a significant cut-back in efforts to harass or oppress the group, or it may be a shift from government neutrality to positive facilitation of the group's political aspirations. Figure 1-9 shows the number of favorable, unfavorable, and neutral events dealing with women's issues reported by the *New York Times* that were carried out by all levels of government. The chart demonstrates a possible link between the rise in supportive government actions toward women between 1962 and 1966 and the emergence of a women's movement. The absence of negative, government-sponsored acts in this same period is also noteworthy.

Once again, there is the confounding appearance of even more supportive government acts relating to women in 1951 and 1953 when no

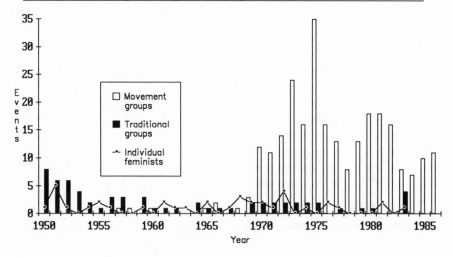

Fig. 1-7. Events initiated by groups and individual women.

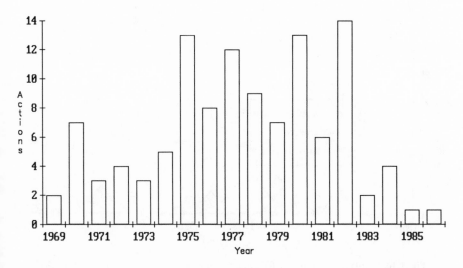

Fig. 1-8. Total reported protest actions.

movement organized than in the early sixties when it did. But during the fifties, the government sponsored more negative and ambiguous activities related to women than in the sixties. Separating the actions of the *federal* government from state and local governments clarifies the picture (Fig. 1-10). There was a relatively close balance between

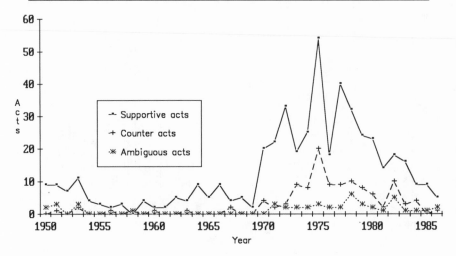

Fig. 1-9. Events initiated by all levels of government, as reported in the *New York Times.*

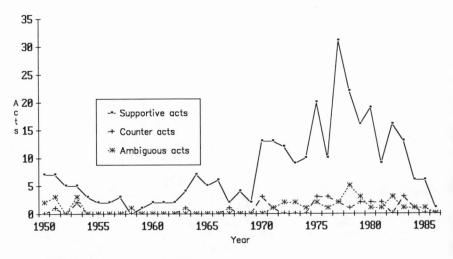

Fig. 1-10. Events initiated by the federal government.

positive and negative or ambiguous events for the federal government in the fifties. This shifted by the early sixties, as the actions of the national government became almost uniformly supportive of women's rights. The shift from a friendly but somewhat ambiguous relationship between government and women in the fifties to unalloyed support at the federal level in the sixties seems promising as an explana-

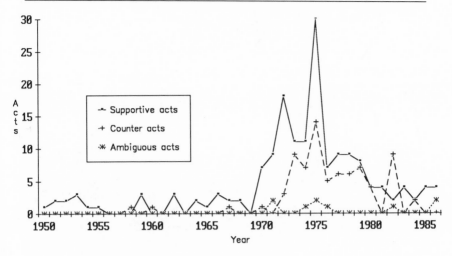

Fig. 1-11. Events initiated by state and local governments.

tion for the timing of the women's movement. Strong signals that government would help facilitate a movement's growth could have spurred the movement's formation. By contrast, state and local governments moved from positions of nearly unalloyed support to more negative postures from the mid-1970s to the early 1980s (Fig. 1-11). The majority of negative acts coming out of state governments were unfavorable votes in state legislatures on ERA ratification.

At the same time, according to political process theory, the group should become better able to organize itself. There is a perceptible psychological shift, as group members begin to see that their difficulties are amenable to political solutions. In the case of women, one should observe an increase in mutual cooperation, as diverse women's groups start to coordinate their efforts, creating enough resources to apply pressure more effectively on the government. Figure 1-12 shows some evidence of women working in concert during the sixties, yet the early fifties was actually a more active time. Figure 1-13, however, provides a somewhat different view of women's activities. In the early sixties, individual feminists and groups of women got together at conferences; in the late sixties and early seventies, they started to organize the underpinnings of a new women's movement by forming new groups.

The explanation for the small number of reported events publicizing women's growing consensus is probably linked to the history of intense struggles in the past between factions representing women's interests. Recent efforts to reconcile differences between women's

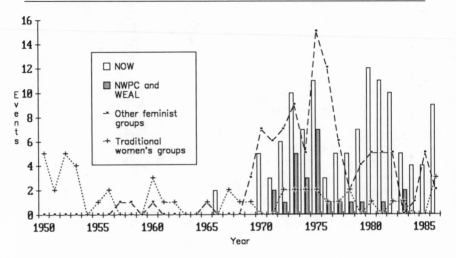

Fig. 1-12. Positive events initiated by women's groups.

groups remained particularly problematic in this context and were done as quietly as possible (see chap. 2). The empowering of individual women necessary to allow a new movement to form cannot be evaluated on the basis of news events. Yet, of the two theories, the aggregate data suggest that political process theory, with its emphasis on the relationship between government and a new movement along with the mobilization of indigenous resources, goes furthest in exposing what appear to be key factors underlying the timing and development of the women's movement.

## Clarifying Process Theory

An important aspect of process theory—the role of government as a facilitator of movement activity—requires additional clarification before it can be used to analyze the women's movement. As both the aggregate events data in this chapter and the historical analysis in chapter 2 indicate, the government played a far more supportive role toward the women's movement than toward most other movements that have been looked at using a process approach. The government tolerated or repressed the black civil rights and most poor peoples' movements rather than playing a facilitating role. When repression lessened, a movement became possible.[58] Charles Tilly is one of the few process theorists who even discusses the possibility that governments may facilitate movements. He defines facilitation as

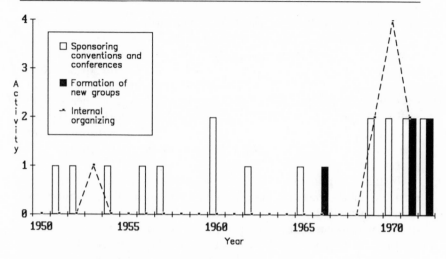

Fig. 1-13. Organization and resource accumulation by women.

promobilization activities such as giving a group publicity, legalizing membership in it, and simply paying it off; activities directly reducing the group's costs of collective action, such as lending information or strategic expertise, keeping the group's enemies out of the action, or simply sending forces to help the action along.[59]

In the case of the women's movement, the government clearly "reduc[ed] the group's costs of collective action," by establishing the Presidential Commission on the Status of Women to bring women together to decide on a common agenda, passed information from inside government to women activists, and used the media glare of the presidency and Congress to help women educate the public about bias toward women.

Yet Tilly's recommended method of determining whether government will facilitate or repress particular movements does not fit the women's case very well. His two critical factors for deciding whether facilitation is likely are the scale of movement activity and the power of movement actors. The smaller the scale of activity, the greater the prospect that government will tolerate it. The greater the movement's power, the more likely that government will facilitate it. The ultimate case in which facilitation may be predicted, according to Tilly, is when a group closely tied to the government initiates a small-scale action. Although some women activists were closely tied to the government and, for the first few years, engaged in small-scale activities, this is not the case for the vast number of women who eventually identified with the movement. It also obscures the extent to which most women had little to say about governmental policy decisions.[60]

It is preferable to consider different factors to understand why the government played such a supportive role in the case of the women's movement. The first, as was mentioned earlier, is the instability of political alignments in the 1970s. Piven and Cloward made a strong case that government is far less likely to repress movements of the politically powerless when elites are engaged in battles for electoral predominance.[61] Tarrow tied this notion of stable or unstable alignments to determination of the "political opportunity structure" in process theory.[62]

Unstable alignments indicate governmental weakness, which in turn lessens the costs for new movements to form. While alignments remain unstable, politicians and political parties are actively involved in seeking out bases of political support. A group of newly organized people will be viewed as potential supporters by political entrepreneurs. In the case of women, although a gender gap did not become a media phenomenon until the 1980 election firmly linked it to party preference, there is ample evidence that issue-based gender differences go back much further in time. As has been argued in relation to blacks, neither party could afford to forfeit competition for women's votes, even though their immediate impact as a bloc may not be very great.[63]

The second explanation rests on the idea of independent state action. Competition within political elites may result in government action because subgroups within government routinely act independently under certain conditions. James Q. Wilson's chapter in his book *The Politics of Regulation* ascribes this independence to "power triads" in American politics.[64] These power triads, which in Wilson's view help determine outcomes within specific areas of policy, consist of economic producer groups that are organized to lobby government, countervailing groups that counter-organize to provide a balance to the producer groups (often falling into the public interest category), and government agencies that possess a degree of autonomy, due in large measure to the conflict between producers and public interest groups. Andrew S. McFarland extends Wilson's model by pointing out that agencies have a clear interest in fostering countervailing pressure to increase their own autonomy. McFarland identifies social movements as important sources of countervailing pressure.[65] Left-wing movements often lobby against the interests of economic producer groups, while right-wing movements are more likely to lobby against agency autonomy.[66]

Application to the women's movement seems clear historically. A variety of subgroups within government or individuals in those subgroups found it useful to encourage pressure from women as a counterweight to competing interests and as a vehicle to increase agency autonomy. For example, Richard Graham, a commissioner on the Equal Employment Opportunity Commission (EEOC), encouraged the formation of NOW, at least partly in reaction to the overwhelming influence of black civil rights groups over the commission, which made it very difficult to give serious attention to sex-discrimination complaints.[67] By encouraging competing constituencies, the EEOC—the agency responsible for implementing the employment provisions of the 1964 Civil Rights Act—could gain greater freedom to set policy.[68]

The combination of electoral instability and the recognition of independent governmental power in particular areas of policy set the stage for interpreting government's willingness to assist the movement. This formulation bypasses the pitfalls in political process theory of either attributing too much latent power to women or making hasty assumptions about a unified government interest in women's policy.

## Conclusions

Process theory, with its emphasis on the centrality of political factors in determining the timing and chances for success of new movements, seems to be the most promising theory for understanding the development and political impact of the contemporary women's movement. The movement's success seemed to depend more on the heightened consciousness of its followers and the structure of political opportunity it confronted in the sixties and seventies than on either the availability of new resources or its skill in exploiting the political situation. Because the government played an unusually early, active, and supportive role in relation to this movement, it is necessary to expand process theory slightly to explain why government was so centrally involved in facilitating the women's movement. The instability of political alignments and the independence of some actors within government seem to offer the best explanations of government's involvement. The three components of political process theory used to analyze the development and impact of the contemporary women's movement are, then, (1) mobilization of indigenous resources, (2) empowerment of potential supporters through consciousness raising, and (3) government facilitation of the movement.

# 2 The Opening of Political Opportunity for Women

By the early 1960s, the women's movement displayed all three factors singled out by process theory as crucial for the formation of a new social movement.[1] New organizational strength was obvious as women's groups resolved many of the long-standing grievances that separated them, and they began to work together on a common agenda to improve women's status. Political opportunities for women also brightened considerably as both Presidents Dwight Eisenhower, toward the end of his term, and John Kennedy turned new attention toward women as a significant political constituency. Finally, there is scattered but persuasive evidence that women were starting to see their problems as collective and amenable to political solutions, which government seemed willing to provide.

## Organizational Capability: An End to Factional Strife

For many years, scholars have concluded that women's groups became less organized and less politically active during the period from the end of the suffrage movement in 1920—the year the Nineteenth Amendment was ratified—to the start of the contemporary women's movement in the 1960s. This seemed to explain their shrinking political influence. However, new historical research has convincingly shown that women's organizations neither shrank in size nor lapsed into inactivity in this period but instead became more diverse and disunited.[2] This new interpretation, which stresses the increasing variety of women's groups, argues that women's groups began to mirror the complexity of American society and the growing opportunity for women to enter spheres of life that were previously denied them.[3] New organizations, composed primarily of women, proliferated in the late teens and early nineteen twenties. While the principal suffrage organizations, the National Woman's Party and the more moderate National American Woman Suffrage Association—which renamed itself the National League of Women Voters in 1920—lost membership, women joined other groups in large numbers. In 1919 alone, the National Federation of Business and Professional Women was organized along with the Voluntary Parenthood League and the Women's International League of Peace and Freedom.[4] These groups, by their very existence, showed that women's concerns had broadened, as more women entered the work force, and women inside the home expanded their world view to encompass issues ranging from reproduction to peace.

The disunity among women's groups, by contrast, was a product of the monumental unresolved issue of the suffrage movement— whether women would fare better in society if they had the same legal rights and responsibilities as men or whether their biological and social differences from males required laws tailored to meet their special needs. This philosophical disagreement split women's groups into two often warring camps around the issue of an equal rights amendment to the U.S. Constitution.[5] Pro-amendment forces led by the National Woman's Party, whose leaders first drafted the amendment in 1921, and had it introduced in Congress by suffragist Susan B. Anthony's nephew in 1923, felt that if women were equal under the U.S. Constitution, they would have the greatest opportunity for individual achievement and full participation in all aspects of American life. An equal rights amendment would eliminate laws that assigned individuals to separate categories simply on the basis of gender. Women could no longer be barred from such occupations as bartending and police work nor forced to resign from jobs if they married or became pregnant. A males-only military draft would probably become unconstitutional under an equal rights amendment, as would social security benefits that paid more to men than women. Among the National Woman's Party's allies in this quest for an equal rights amendment over the next forty years were the National Federation of Business and Professional Women's Clubs, the General Federation of Women's Clubs, the National Association of Colored Women, the National Association of Women Lawyers, the American Bar Association, the National Education Association, and prominent women such as Senator Margaret Chase Smith (R, Me.), actresses Katharine Hepburn and Helen Hayes, and anthropologist Margaret Mead.[6]

Anti-amendment groups historically were closely tied to labor and reform organizations. They accused amendment supporters of a lack of realism about the conditions experienced by most women. They argued that women desperately needed the protective laws that were already on the books. If a woman's right to be supported by her husband were taken away, or if maximum hours, lifting limitations, and other labor laws that safeguarded the health and safety of working women became unconstitutional, they held that women would be worse off. Groups opposing the amendment in the late 1950s were part of what historians have labeled the "Women's Bureau (of the Department of Labor) coalition" and included, along with the Women's Bureau, the League of Women Voters, the National Consumers League, the National Women's Trade Union League, the Young Women's Christian Association (YWCA), the National Councils of Jewish, Catholic and Negro Women, and the American Association of University Women.[7]

After four decades, from the 1920s to the 1960s, in which fighting over the desirability of an amendment as a way to improve the status of women blocked the possibility of any legislative gains for women at the federal level, women's organizations were presented with a new opportunity to change national policy toward women. Kennedy's Presidential Commission on the Status of Women became a forum to put forth a legislative program supported by a majority of organized women's groups. Esther Peterson had persuaded Kennedy to establish a presidential commission as a way to thwart pressure for the ERA (pleasing organized labor) at the same time as he was building his support among women's groups, which would support a commission.[8] She hoped that the commission could formulate women's problems in such a way that it would put an end to the animosity that had split women's groups. The effort succeeded to an extent that few could have anticipated.

In a series of steps, the commission narrowed the differences between pro- and anti-ERA backers and demonstrated the opportunity for women to make legislative gains when their ranks were not divided. This process began with commission member Pauli Murray's proposal that the commission urge the U.S. Supreme Court to begin to interpret the Fifth and Fourteenth Amendments to the Constitution, which guaranteed all citizens "equal protection" under the law (the Fifth implicitly requiring this of the federal government, the Fourteenth explicitly demanding this of state governments), as granting women constitutional equality. Murray persuasively argued that such an interpretation would eliminate many of the legal disabilities that women suffered, including exclusion from juries and restrictions on controlling property and making binding contracts, while retaining protective laws.[9] This was not precisely what pro-ERA groups wanted, but this approach acknowledged the desirability of equal legal treatment of women in a way that anti-ERA groups had been reluctant to do before. The closing language of the commission's final report, entitled *American Women*, followed Murray's lead and read as follows: "Early and definitive court pronouncement, particularly by the United States Supreme Court, is urgently needed with regard to the validity under the Fifth and Fourteenth Amendments of laws and official practices discriminating against women, to the end that the principle of equality become firmly established in constitutional doctrine."[10] Although it was almost ten years until the Supreme Court, in the case of *Reed v. Reed* (1971),[11] took the first step toward making this interpretation official doctrine, holding that the state of Idaho could not have laws automatically preferring men over women as executors of estates, this formulation of the equality/difference debate did much to heal old divisions among women's groups.

Esther Peterson, head of the Women's Bureau, lobbied successfully to pass the Equal Pay Act of 1963, further lessening the conflict between pro- and anti-ERA women's groups by demonstrating that when most women agreed on legislation and cooperated, they could get action from Congress. This piece of legislation was the first major law furthering the legal rights of women enacted by Congress since the early 1930s, when it revised the Cable Act of 1922 to make a wife's citizenship fully independent of her husband's. Peterson's success reminded women's groups of what could be achieved when they cooperated.

The Women's Bureau's further willingness, under Peterson, to tolerate the addition of sex to other categories covered under the Civil Rights Act of 1964, in which Congress prohibited employment discrimination, despite the opposition of organized labor, contributed to the elimination of the long-standing dispute over the relative value of equality as contrasted with protective labor laws. The courts quickly interpreted the Civil Rights Act of 1964, with its absolute bar on employment discrimination that was based on sex, as making it impossible to uphold most protective laws that treated men and women differently. Protective laws for women were no longer legally viable with or without an ERA.[12] The passage of the act was a great legislative victory for the National Woman's Party without being a defeat for the Women's Bureau, which had little choice but to support the Civil Rights Act after the category of gender was added to it. Despite its mixed feelings the bureau could not have risked defeat of the entire legislative package by fighting inclusion of this single provision.[13]

As the final step in the process of reconciliation, on November 1, 1963, Kennedy signed into law an executive order which created two ongoing bodies to monitor implementation of the recommendations of the presidential commission—the Interdepartmental Committee on the Status of Women and the Citizens' Advisory Council on the Status of Women. These groups would continue the process of building a unified body of support for women's issues and a network that would help give rise to a new women's movement in America.

Since the suffrage movement, women had enough organized groups possessing the membership, leadership, and financial resources needed to push for change. However, until their collective experience with the presidential commission, they lacked both a consensus on the type of change they wanted to bring about and the ability to work together. Many of the resources they expended to influence government went to neutralize the political influence of other women's groups, either those favoring or opposing an equal rights amendment to the constitution.[14]

By 1963, these groups had found a way to work together on the national level, through the presidential commission and its executive branch successors, the Citizens' Advisory Council and the Interdepartmental Committee. They had also established a preliminary political agenda, embodied in the recommendations of the commission's report, *American Women*, that all could accept. Near the end of 1962, this cooperation was extended to the state level, as the National Federation of Business and Professional Women's Clubs met with Kennedy and received his approval to launch a campaign to persuade each state governor to appoint a state commission on the status of women, modeled after the president's commission. By 1967, all states had established commissions.[15]

At the same time that the older groups had begun to work together, the simmering discontent of young women in the civil rights and new left movements of the early sixties created a new group of potential movement recruits with skills in protest activities lacking in most members of older women's groups.[16] Women in the civil rights movement often found themselves pushed into menial tasks, "kitchen work, mimeographing [and] typing."[17] Insult was added to injury with the Student Nonviolent Coordinating Committee (SNCC) leader Stokely Carmichael's widely reported remark that "the only position for women in SNCC is prone."[18]

Women in the new left, a social movement that advocated the spread of participatory democracy in American life, fared no better. As one new left activist wrote:

> This kind of desperate attempt by men to defend their power by refusing to participate in open public discussion with women would be amusing if it were not so effective. And one sees the beginnings of it even now, while still students, in SDS [Students for a Democratic Society] meetings. You are allowed to participate and to speak, only the men stop listening when you do. How many times have you seen a woman enter the discussion only to have it resume at the exact point from which she made her departure, as though she had never said anything at all?[19]

Efforts to discuss women's issues at a 1965 SDS convention were shouted down with calls of "She just needs a good screw."[20]

Many women made the passage from other social movements of the 1960s into the women's movement by the end of the decade. Typically, they first joined, or formed, local "women's liberation" groups. The actions of these groups, including the picketing of the Miss America pageant, drew the attention and frequently the scorn of the mainstream press. When members of women's groups picketed the Miss America contest in Atlantic City, New Jersey, carrying signs that read "I am a Woman—not a Toy, a Pet, or a Mascot" and setting up a "freedom trash can" into which they hurled copies of *Playboy* and women's magazines, girdles, padded bras, and false eyelashes, this famous "bra-burning" incident became a widely known national symbol of the movement.[21] This was the case even though no fire was ever set and no bras were burned.

Those within women's liberation groups had an anger and passion that was typically lacking in more traditional groups. Several verses of a song (to the tune of "There Was an Old Woman Who Swallowed a Fly"), distributed by the Boston-based group Bread and Roses, give a sense of the concerns of these young women's liberationists:

> There was a young woman who swallowed a lie,
> We all know why she swallowed that lie,
> Perhaps she'll die.

> There was a young woman who swallowed a rule,
> "Live to serve others," she learned it in school;
> She swallowed the rule to hold up the lie,
> We all know why she swallowed that lie,
> Perhaps she'll die.

> . . .

> There was a young woman who swallowed a line,
> "I like 'em dumb, baby, you suit me fine;"
> She swallowed the line to tie up the fluff,
> Lipstick and candy and powder and puff;
> She swallowed the fluff to sweeten the rule
> "Live to serve others," she learned it in school, . . .
> (repeat)[22]

Many of these women slowly moved into nationally organized groups, such as NOW and the NWPC. Their entry, while sometimes producing conflict over group priorities and values, also energized and brought new organizational skills to the existing groups (see chap. 3).

In addition, the transition of these radical women out of liberation groups and into more moderate political organizations in the seventies helped create a more staid image for the women's movement as a whole.

The problem of organizing well enough to mount a challenge to established authorities was serious in the sixties. Yet on balance, it created fewer difficulties for movement formation than did the absence of a favorable structure of political opportunity or the need to raise women's consciousness. Because the disagreement between pro- and anti-ERA groups had prevented women from putting together the resources needed to press for change, a widespread public perception that favorable action by government on women's issues was imminent would have generated enormous pressure on the two sides to resolve their differences. As it was, most of the legislative initiatives put forth by either the pro- or anti-ERA factions, from the "Status Bill" supported by the National Committee to Defeat the UnEqual Rights Amendment to the ERA itself, never made it out of Congress.[23] As Jo Freeman documented, both major political parties were in the process of purging the ERA from their party platforms in the sixties after several decades of support.[24] There was little reason for any but the most relentlessly optimistic to believe that lack of organization and resources was the only problem holding back formation of a women's movement in America.

## The Structure of Political Opportunity

There were signs that political institutions were becoming more vulnerable to challenges from women in the 1950s and the 1960s. The most broad-gauged evidence comes from the weakening of the New Deal electoral coalition in this period. There is a great deal of evidence that both parties were working to solidify an electoral majority during these years; it would have been hard for them to ignore as large a bloc of voters as women. More has been written about efforts to capture the black vote than women's votes, but there are obvious parallels between the two concerns. Piven and Cloward observed that Clark Clifford, President Harry Truman's chief campaign strategist, was concerned about the president's support among blacks.[25] Clifford told Truman, who was a Democrat, that the Republicans were taking extraordinary steps to win back the black vote after the New Deal. He warned Truman that the Republicans might promise legislation to get rid of poll taxes, to end lynchings, and to establish a fair employment practices commission.

Historian Steven Lawson argued that the Republican party competed actively at the presidential level for a share of the black electorate throughout the fifties. After President Eisenhower's major heart attack in the fall of 1955, Republican strategists, chief among them Attorney General Herbert Brownell, began to devise a plan to improve Republican voting support among Northern blacks. With the prospect that the popular general might not be a candidate, they recognized that the black vote might swing the election. A half million blacks had migrated from the South in the previous thirty years, settling disproportionately in seven states that had cast 197 electoral votes for the president.[26] This Northern black vote was important to Republican strategic calculations. The Civil Rights Act of 1957, drafted and pushed by the Eisenhower administration, was a highly publicized legislative success aimed at attracting this vote.

Women were similarly objects of interparty competition, although less has been written about it. Eisenhower was elected to two successive terms in the White House with the benefit of a gender gap. Fifty-eight percent of women, as contrasted with 53 percent of men, preferred Eisenhower to Adlai Stevenson in 1952.[27] In 1956, the percentage widened slightly as 61 percent of women favored Eisenhower over Stevenson, as compared with 55 percent of men. Although women's issues were not a pressing concern of Eisenhower's (neither was civil rights), he clearly made concessions to the interests of organized women's groups during campaigning and his presidency.

A number of Eisenhower's public addresses made significant appeals to women. In his State of the Union message in January 1956, Eisenhower held, "Legislation to apply the principle of equal pay for equal work without discrimination because of sex is a matter of simple justice. I earnestly urge Congress to move swiftly to implement these needed labor measures."[28] In his 1956 speech accepting the Republican nomination, he again raised the issue of equal pay for women.[29] At the end of October, before the 1956 election, Eisenhower held a radio and television broadcast called "The Women Ask the President." In his opening remarks, he observed that women had cast a majority of the ballots in the last election and that in the future they would play a big role in managing government as well as their homes.[30]

In Madison Square Garden in New York City, Eisenhower elated ERA supporters by announcing, twelve days before the 1956 election, that his administration would fulfill the pledge in the Republican platform and seek equal rights for women in America.[31] In 1957, after his reelection, Eisenhower confessed to having a special interest in women voters while speaking to the National Conference of Republican Women. "Now of course I always have a peculiar satisfaction in addressing women. This is not only because there are more women than men and therefore more voters, but. . . . "[32] In his budget message to Congress that same year, he endorsed the ERA again, urging Congress to pass it.[33]

In addition to his rhetoric, Eisenhower had a better record of appointing women to high public positions than did his predecessor. With members of commissions included, Eisenhower appointed over four hundred women to government posts. Comparing the records of the Eisenhower and Truman administrations, Eisenhower named twenty-eight women to posts confirmed by the Senate, as compared with twenty by Truman. Each president had a woman in the cabinet. Eisenhower appointed ten women to posts that a woman had never before held, as compared with nine first appointments by Truman.[34] Eisenhower drew attention to his accomplishments in this area when addressing Republican women in 1957. He declared that the administration had worked to bring ever greater numbers of women into government.[35]

Presidential appointments of women were the main fruits of the Eisenhower administration in the area of women's rights. But Eisenhower's speeches, particularly before the 1956 election, clearly indicate that his administration, to a degree unmatched in the Truman administration, was appealing to women as an electoral constituency. The strong women's vote in favor of Eisenhower helps confirm that this strategy had the desired effect.

When John Kennedy was elected president in 1961, after winning by the narrowest of margins, he quickly consulted with advisers about how to gain support from women and women's groups.[36] He took most of his advice from Esther Peterson. In an important strategic shift from earlier presidents, he decided to deemphasize federal appointments for women and instead to pursue a strategy that combined the passage of legislation and the appointment of the Presidential Commission on the Status of Women.

It is clear, in hindsight, that the three years of the Kennedy administration were crucial both in constructing a unified agenda for the contemporary women's movement through the commission and in providing a necessary opening for a new women's movement to form. There is too much evidence, including the extent to which Kennedy's actions were presaged by those of the Eisenhower administration, to conclude that these were unanticipated results of Peterson's access to the president. Women were entering the labor force and voting in record numbers in the early sixties. These two factors could have important consequences for both political parties. Kennedy was no more of a feminist than Eisenhower, but both were astute politicians who wanted to fall on the right side of any electoral gender gap that opened up.

Kennedy had an unusual degree of personal involvement in publicizing the work of the commission. An examination of the news stories in the *New York Times* in the three years of the Kennedy administration, when there was little public pressure or attention to women's issues, shows that Kennedy, his commission, and Peterson dominated the discussion that did exist. Of a total of just twenty-five news events that featured women's issues from 1961 to 1963, the Kennedy administration initiated seven. In 1961, Kennedy's remarks on women's issues made the news twice, first seeming to pledge his support for the ERA in response to a question asked at a news conference, although this was clearly not the stance of his administration, and second announcing the establishment of the presidential commission.[37] In 1962, Kennedy was featured on the front page of the *New York Times* when he attended the first meeting of the commission.[38] In 1963, the administration generated four of the seven stories that year about women. The first was a speech given to the International Women's Council by Esther Peterson, whom Kennedy had appointed assistant secretary of Labor, in which she compared women's and blacks' fights for equality.[39] The second and third featured the twenty-four recommendations of the presidential commission to curb bias based on sex.[40] Kennedy's announcement of the cabinet-level commission to aid in the effort to raise women's status was the final story.[41]

By contrast, during the eight years of the Eisenhower presidency, of the 197 news events covered by the *New York Times* that dealt with women's issues, only 4 were initiated by the president or the Women's Bureau of the Department of Labor. Eisenhower's 3 stories were his endorsement of the ERA; his response to a press-conference question in which he stated that women were qualified to be president of the United States, but he doubted that any wanted to be; and finally his appointment of Clare Booth Luce as the first woman U.S. ambassador to a major nation—Italy.[42]

Kennedy also went further than his predecessors in talking about women in his State of the Union messages. While Eisenhower referred to women seven times in his eight State of the Union addresses, Kennedy acknowledged women nine times in just three addresses. It is part of the ambiguity surrounding Kennedy's role, however, that whereas at least one of Eisenhower's mentions of women was tied to their unequal treatment and his proposal for an equal pay act, Kennedy's mentions were all symbolic. Roughly half of Kennedy's references acknowledged women as workers along with men. The others urged both young men and women to join the Peace Corps.

In his 1963 address, he mentioned his first recurring theme, his expression of pleasure that "well over a million more men and women are working today than were working 2 years ago."[43] His second theme is also clear in his 1961 speech introducing the Peace Corps. "An even more valuable national asset is our reservoir of dedicated men and women—not only on our college campuses but in every age group— who have indicated their desire to contribute their skills, their efforts, and a part of their lives to the fight for world order. We can mobilize this talent through the formation of a National Peace Corps."[44] Kennedy seemed to see women as an integral part of the American labor force, and young women as part of a new generation entering public service.

One of Kennedy's most revealing discussions of his understanding of women's problems came during a television interview in 1962 conducted by Eleanor Roosevelt. In response to a question from Mrs. Roosevelt about the contribution of educated women to American society, Kennedy reflected that

> well, I think when you look at Radcliffe College, that the curve of academic excellence at Radcliffe is higher than it is at Harvard. And therefore you assume that this is really the most highly developed student body. What happens to those girls 2 or 3 years later? They get married, many of them become housewives, and all that talent is used in this family life but is not used outside. . . . But I wonder whether they have the full opportunity to develop their talents. As the Greeks said, the definition of happiness is full use of your powers along lines of excellence, and I wonder whether they have that opportunity.[45]

In 1963, Kennedy remarked at the mid-October ceremony where he accepted the report of his presidential commission that civilization could be judged on its opportunities for women. His executive order establishing two ongoing bodies to carry out its work proclaimed: "Enhancement of the quality of American life, as envisioned by the Commission's report, can be accomplished only through concerted action . . . within the Federal Government, and through action by States, communities, educational institutions, voluntary organizations, employers, unions, and individual citizens."[46] This language might almost be a prelude to the next twenty years of agitation and progress on women's rights in the United States.

Kennedy's efforts to reach out to women as a constituency are surprising, given that the lack of coordinated pressure on behalf of women's rights was matched by almost stagnant public opinion on women's changing roles. Burstein compiled two sets of public opinion data covering this period: the first on women working and the second on voting for a woman for president.[47] He found that public opinion toward women working and women as presidential candidates rapidly became more favorable until the late 1940s at an estimated rate of 2.2 percent per year on labor-force participation and 3.8 percent on the presidency. Then the rate of change slowed for both sets of attitudes (changing only 0.7% per year on women in the labor force and 0.3% on women as president) until the late 1960s, when the pace of change again quickened.[48] Kennedy appears to have led public opinion through his recognition that women were assuming new political and economic roles in American society.

Kennedy was not alone in this realization. Another sign that political opportunities were widening was the emergence of a new voting majority in Congress willing to pass legislation that equalized the treatment of women and men. In 1962, for the first time since its introduction in 1945, an equal pay bill won positive votes in both houses of Congress. The bill died that year, after it failed to achieve the unanimous consent necessary to proceed to a joint conference committee. In 1963, the Kennedy administration-backed proposal again passed by voice vote and was subsequently signed into law. This was the first substantive proposal extending rights to women to become law in twenty years.

The following year, by a narrower margin (168 to 133), an amendment to Title VII of the Civil Rights Act of 1964 added sex to the other categories of race, creed, color, and national origin in which Congress prohibited employment discrimination. Although the unrecorded teller vote in the House to add sex was widely described as a coalition of female House members, who genuinely supported it, and Southern white male members, who hoped to defeat the entire legislative package through inclusion of this amendment, passage of the bill with this addition encouraged women's rights advocates to believe that Congress would now pass other legislation equalizing the treatment of men and women.[49] The votes for final passage (290 to 130 in the House of Representatives and 73 to 27 in the Senate) gave shape to women's hopes that a supportive coalition might now act favorably on women's concerns.

In addition to these new laws, starting in 1961, members of the Eighty-seventh Congress began to introduce more bills dealing with women's concerns (Fig. 1-2). By far the greatest increase came in ERA introductions, with 140 members of the House of Representatives introducing joint resolutions to amend the constitution and guarantee equal rights under the law (Fig. 2-1). Other legislation that was offered included bills to equalize men's and women's pay; to protect the health benefits of married women federal employees; and to stop wage dis-

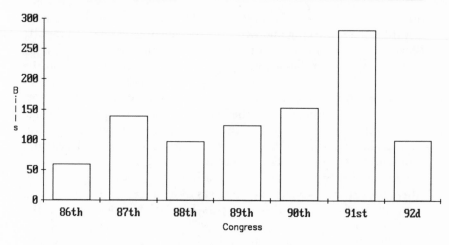

Fig. 2-1. Number of ERA bills introduced in the House of Representatives.

crimination based on sex. The near doubling of bills introduced, from 85 in the Eighty-sixth Congress to 168 in the Eighty-seventh, suggest that members of Congress along with the president sensed that politically women's hour was approaching. Clearly, this mounting pressure within Congress for an equal rights amendment was influential in pushing Peterson and Kennedy to form the Presidential Commission on the Status of Women and to propose an equal pay act as a possible alternative to it. Congress, in turn, was pushed to greater legislative activism by the recommendations put forth by the Presidential Commission.

Evidence of a split among political elites over new legislation granting women rights is easy to find in the early sixties and crosses party lines. Peterson fought Secretary of Labor Willard Wirtz's opposition to adding sex to other federal affirmative action categories, convincing President Lyndon Johnson to include sex.[50] Representative Howard Smith's (D, Va.) amendment to the Civil Rights Act of 1964, which prohibited employment discrimination based on sex, brought almost every woman in the House, regardless of party, to the floor to comment. The levity with which the amendment was initially greeted by liberal male members added urgency to the women's public remarks. Representative Martha Griffiths (D, Mich.) chastised House members, observing that "if there had been any necessity to have pointed out that women were a second-class sex, the laughter [on the House floor] would have proved it."[51] Griffiths urged support for the amendment, reminding House members that both women of color and white women worked side-by-side to win suffrage.[52] Veteran legislator Katharine St. George (R, N.Y.) argued defensively in response to the mocking tone of the House debate,

> Protective legislation . . . prevents women from going into the higher salary brackets. Yes, it certainly does.
>
> Women are protected—they cannot run an elevator late at night and that is when the pay is higher. . . . But what about the offices, gentlemen, that are cleaned every morning about 2 or 3 o'clock in the city of New York and the offices that are cleaned quite early here in Washington, D.C.? Does anybody worry about those women?[53]

Even Representative Edith Green (D, Oreg.), the one woman to take the floor opposing the amendment, held,

> Any woman who wants to have a career, who wants to go into the professions, who wants to work, I feel cannot possibly reach maturity without being very keenly and very painfully made aware of all the discrimination placed against her because of her sex.[54]

Within the EEOC—the agency charged with enforcing the employment-discrimination provisions of the Civil Rights Act of 1964—there was sharp disagreement. Commissioners Richard Graham and Aileen Hernandez wanted to proceed with enforcement of the anti-sex bias provisions in the law. The rest of the commissioners did not, speaking facetiously of every man's right to have a woman secretary.[55] Both Graham and Hernandez quietly counseled women to follow the example of blacks and form a kind of National Association for the Advancement of Colored People (NAACP) for women to apply pressure on the agency and the government. Graham and Hernandez left the EEOC in 1966. Lyndon Johnson, who became president in 1963, did not reappoint Graham as EEOC commissioner. Hernandez resigned later that year in protest over Johnson's failure to make new appointments to the commission in a timely fashion. Both subsequently became national officers of NOW— Hernandez, eventually, NOW's president.

In addition to these public instances of disagreement within the government over the appropriate course of action to take on women's concerns, the government was populated by what Freeman aptly labeled "woodwork feminists."[56] As Freeman noted, in many instances these women and men had been interested in women's rights for years. With the emergence of a popular women's movement, they could now claim a public demand for solutions to these problems. In interviews I conducted in Washington in 1974 and 1975 with congressional staff members, women's rights activists, and some agency personnel, the most common off-the-record comments told of giving and receiving clerical assistance and inside information from government workers to women's movement groups. These types of under-the-table assistance frequently allowed organized women's groups to achieve a political impact much more quickly than would otherwise have been possible.

The structure of political opportunity for a women's movement had expanded rapidly in the early 1960s, paving the way for the movement to burst on the scene when NOW organized in 1966. Changing circumstances emanated from the president, Congress, executive agencies, and competing elites within the government and the parties. Some of the individuals involved in this transformation were committed feminists, but most were not. It seems likely that the prospect of a bloc of women's votes, along with evidence that the New Deal voting coalition that had kept the Democrats in power since 1936 was coming apart, pushed candidates and parties to court women as a constituency in ways that had not been evident since the 1920s. Contributing to this change were government insiders who welcomed an opportunity to add women as a new source of external pressure to the interest groups such as black civil rights and big business groups that already lobbied them. In some cases, this freed them to pursue women's rights policies that they had long been interested in. In other cases, it created a countervailing source of pressure to balance the old policy coalitions that limited their freedom of decision.

The new organizational capability and the favorable structure of political opportunity would not have been enough to generate a women's movement if changes in women's consciousness had not been taking place at the same time. These changes, along with those already discussed, flowed from demographic shifts that brought women new experiences—ranging from more years spent in the labor force to having fewer children and living for more of their lives in female-headed households.

## Consciousness Raised

In 1971, Abbott Ferriss's book, *Indicators of Trends in the Status of Women*, was published by the Russell Sage Foundation.[57] With the rise of a new women's movement in the late 1960s, this data book posed the timely question of "whether changes in the objective status of women might account for the rise of protest movements."[58] His answer seemed to be no. For although significant changes could be observed in several important social and demographic variables, they did not appear to add up to either the kind of anger or the new resources that existing theories of the formation of social movements had predicted. The specific changes in long-term trends that emerged from the data were an increase in the rate of women getting degrees from American educational institutions; a decline in the percentage of married women as divorce became more common *and* single women married later; a decline in fertility starting in the 1950s; and a rise in the number of women in the labor force.

Klein analyzed these trends and concluded that the direction of these shifts set the stage for the women's movement to attract a mass following.[59] Women were freed from long decades of mothering at the same time that work and life independent of men allowed them to develop the consciousness that was necessary to work for change in their status. Susan Carroll extended this notion of autonomous women in American society into an explanation of the emergence of the gender gap in voting behavior in the 1980s.[60] As women lived through a wider range of experiences, in the work world and at home, where they might be the principal wage earner, they began to see public issues differently from men. Their problems of discrimination in the workplace, single parenting, low wages, and uncertainty about the future began to be interpreted politically, often leading them to support Democratic party candidates.

The transformation from feelings of powerlessness to a willingness to identify problems collectively and use the political process to work for change is, of necessity, a slow one that is often shaped by existing institutions. As Piven and Cloward observed, "For a protest movement to arise out of these traumas of daily life, people have to perceive the deprivation and disorganization they experience as both wrong, and subject to redress."[61]

Part of this process came about through the changing of women's objective circumstances. Backing for the status quo which was based on the assumption that men would provide for the financial needs of families while women stayed home and raised children, no longer matched with the realities of American life. Similarly, the presidential and state commissions on the status of women gathered and publicized information about the legal, social, and economic hardships faced by most women. These difficulties, which had seemed individual and inevitable, such as lower wages than men, sexual harassment on the job, and inadequate day care for the children of working mothers, came to be seen as patterns amenable to change through government actions.[62] Finally, the early legislative initiatives of Congress and the president suggested that government was a plausible vehicle for bringing about change. As the Democratic and Republican parties increasingly competed for women's votes, the electoral arena became an outlet for women to make their interests felt, through running for electoral office and through voting for candidates who seemed to recognize their values.[63]

## Conclusions

Although organizational strength, collective consciousness, and political opportunities all increased for women in the early 1960s, the most decisive change seemed to involve government's willingness to act. At the presidential, congressional, and executive agency levels, new initiatives were offered with little tangible evidence that women were yet ready to organize and press their concerns. It is more accurate to assume that government officials anticipated the rise of the women's movement than that they promoted it.

Nevertheless, discerning the balance between governmental response to outside pressures and internally generated initiatives on women's issues is more difficult than it first seems. This confusion is evident in a briefing paper on the women's movement and the U.S. government prepared to give background information to the U.S. delegation to the International Women's Year World Conference.[64] The paper begins with emphatic denials that the government initiated any changes in women's status.[65] This denial accords with standard textbook interpretations that the U.S. government responds to changes urged by the people rather than promotes change. Subsequently, in describing government's contribution to change in women's status, these disavowals ring rather hollow. The briefing paper discusses the role of the Women's Bureau of the Department of Labor in the following terms:

> The Bureau holds national and regional conferences that for many years furnished the primary means of communication among [women's] organizations. The Bureau has also been a catalyst. For example the organizing meeting of the National Association of Commissions on Women was called by the Women's Bureau and technical assistance was provided for several years. The Bureau also seeks to mobilize support of women's organizations for change within the Government.[66]

The paper further acknowledges that "individual women in key positions within the Government have also provided information and technical assistance to the [women's] voluntary organizations, helping them to maximize their impact."[67]

The stage was set for the new women's liberation movement to gain political influence quickly when it emerged in 1966. Without downplaying either the degree to which women's organizations had succeeded in transcending old rivalries and accepting a common agenda or the extent to which the changing social and economic circumstances of most women were translating into a new political consciousness, it is difficult not to regard government as a prime determinant of the timing and initial political agenda of the movement.

# 3 A New Women's Movement Emerges

After receiving substantial assistance from political institutions in the early sixties, by the mid-sixties, women's groups were ready to seize the initiative in organizing a new movement. By starting NOW in 1966 to increase and focus public pressure on government to change its policies toward women, feminists began the process of bringing together traditional women's groups and newer movement groups. The founding of NOW has been recognized as a seminal event in the development of the contemporary women's movement, but its equally important role of reconciling diverse groups with widely divergent objectives and members has not been emphasized sufficiently. NOW played a bridging role between the more radical new "liberation" groups springing up on the left and the more conservative, traditional women's groups, which were in the process of rediscovering feminism.

## New Organizational Strength

NOW's founding was both carefully planned and somewhat spontaneous. Betty Friedan, whose widely read book *The Feminine Mystique* first alerted many women to their collective discontent, was actively recruited to take steps to organize a group representing women and their interests. Richard Graham and Sonia Pressman of the EEOC, Mary Eastwood of the Justice Department, and Catherine East of the Citizens' Advisory Council on the Status of Women, wanted Friedan to form a group to bring pressure on government to listen to women's concerns about public policy.[1] In addition to these government-linked activists, Friedan's mail was filled with pleas from the general public to do something concrete.[2] Many people felt that the barriers keeping women from full participation in society needed to be challenged and that Friedan was an ideal person to organize this challenge.

The political situation in Washington in 1966, with the EEOC as a group unwilling to enforce the section of the Civil Rights Act of 1964 that barred discrimination based on sex, even by prohibiting the practice of advertising jobs under "male" and "female" categories, finally persuaded Friedan. She concluded that absent pressure "from organizations who would speak out on behalf of equality for women as the Civil Rights Movement had done for Negroes,"[3] there was little chance that the government would proceed to improve conditions for women. The major women's organizations already in existence refused to take the initiative in speaking out because they were afraid of being labeled as feminist.[4]

The decisive moment came when Catherine East invited Friedan to attend the third Conference of the Commissions on the Status of Women in Washington. At this meeting, delegate Kathryn Clarenbach, leader of the Wisconsin State Commission on the Status of Women, and other concerned delegates were told that Clarenbach could not introduce resolutions supporting the reappointment of Richard Graham as an EEOC commissioner or stronger enforcement by the EEOC of the Civil Rights Act Title VII's ban on sex discrimination since these would be interpreted as criticisms of the Johnson administration, which had organized the conference. Clarenbach, Friedan, and thirteen other women who had met the night before in Friedan's hotel room to discuss women's civil rights took over two tables at the conference luncheon and began to organize NOW. It had become clear to them that the government was unwilling to allow commissions that it created and controlled to be used to apply pressure on other parts of the government.[5]

By the end of the conference, Friedan headed a twenty-eight member organization called the National Organization for Women (NOW). Despite the founding members' disappointment with the conference, they were careful to deny even "implied criticism of any existing group or conference, but rather a realization of the limitations of various organizations."[6] NOW members also took pains, initially, not to go further in their stated goals than the recommendations of the Presidential Commission on the Status of Women.[7] In its first year, NOW neither endorsed the ERA nor supported loosening restrictions on abortion. What NOW did was apply pressure on the executive branch of government. Within hours of NOW's founding, its leaders had sent telegrams urging the reappointment of Graham to the EEOC, mailed letters asking the EEOC to rescind its directive on "help wanted" listings in the newspaper, which allowed private employers to specify "male" or "female" positions, and contacted House and Senate offices supporting legislation mandating equal federal jury service for women and men.[8]

Despite meetings throughout this first year with high government officials, including Ramsay Clark, the attorney general, and John

Macy, the chair of the Civil Service Commission,[9] concrete accomplishments were relatively modest. In 1967, President Johnson, at the urging of Esther Peterson, and despite objections from some labor-union officials, added gender as a protected category under Executive Order 11246, which is the basis for federal affirmative action policy. Johnson, however, did not reappoint Graham to the EEOC nor intervene in the controversy over "help wanted" advertising.

Dissatisfaction was apparent at the second national conference of NOW, held in November 1967. Members passed a NOW Bill of Rights, which for the first time endorsed both a woman's right to have an abortion and the passage of the ERA. They had now moved substantially beyond the more cautious recommendations of the presidential commission. The immediate impact of these actions was fragmentation within NOW, as many labor-union women left the group over its stand on the ERA, which organized labor continued to oppose. Politically conservative NOW members quit after the conference because of NOW's endorsement of abortion.[10] These desertions allowed NOW to move to the left politically, bringing it closer to the women's liberation groups that were forming across the United States in the late sixties.

Friedan's priorities for NOW are clear from a 22 September, 1969 memorandum to NOW board members and chapter presidents.[11] Friedan warned them that those under 40 years old would be more central to NOW's future development than would those over 40. Consequently, she urged that they take care to bring young people into the organization's leadership. She also cautioned that the current leaders of NOW should pay more attention to those who criticized NOW for not doing enough rather than to those who complained that it was doing too much.

Despite NOW's move to the left and its vision of attracting younger (and often more radical) movement adherents, it suffered a further schism in 1968 as Ti-Grace Atkinson, president of the New York City chapter of NOW, resigned along with several other NOW members over what they saw as the hierarchical, undemocratic character of the organization. Atkinson organized the women's liberation group, "The October 17th Movement," later called "The Feminists."[12]

After its second national conference, NOW not only adopted a more radical agenda of issues, but its tactics became less conventional. In 1967, members of NOW started picketing EEOC offices throughout the United States to pressure the commission to stop sanctioning sex-segregated want ads.[13] In 1968, NOW sponsored a number of protest actions, including a week of sit-ins, picketing, and demonstrations against male-only public accommodations, a "Fast to Free Women from Poverty Day" on May 18, and—to protest religious bias against women—a "national unveiling," burning veils that women wore to church.[14] The year 1969 was unofficially dubbed "the year of protest" for NOW. The week before Mother's Day was designated "Freedom for Women Week." A Washington march sponsored by NOW was the largest demonstration for women's rights in America since the early 1900s. NOW members met in front of the White House "to dramatize—with chains, aprons and a skit by the New Feminist Theater—that women are bound to the home and to the lowest rung jobs, as well as second class status."[15]

During the late sixties, NOW members sometimes joined with members of liberation groups like the Society to Cut Up Men (SCUM) to stage protest events. The periodical press in this period covered the women's movement more for its sensationalist value than its political significance. Consequently, magazine articles in the late sixties focused on the more extreme liberation groups rather than on the more moderate organizations such as NOW. One of the more inflammatory, but by no means isolated, examples of this early coverage is from *Time* magazine:

> Many of the new feminists are surprisingly violent in mood, and seem to be trying, in fact, to repel other women rather than attract them. Hundreds of young girls are learning karate, tossing off furious statements about "male chauvinists," distributing threatening handouts ("Watch out! You may meet a *real* castrating female!") and even citing with approval the dictum of the late revolutionary Frantz Fanon: "An oppressed individual cannot feel liberated until he kills one of his oppressors." This is all borrowed, of course, from the fiery rhetoric of today's militant black and student movements, but a deep feminine resentment is there nevertheless.[16]

A *New Republic* story starts out with members of the local chapter of Women's International Terrorist Conspiracy from Hell (WITCH) hexing First Lady Pat Nixon as she visits Portland, Oregon.[17] *Life* magazine featured a lengthy discussion of women's liberation groups that rejected marriage and had quotas for the number of married women they would accept as members.[18] In these articles, NOW is usually written off as boring, with its alleged strategy of concentrating on just one legal or legislative issue at a time. In a few cases, NOW is treated as similar to the extreme groups. "For despite differences of opinion [among WITCH, Women's Liberation, and NOW], the demands of the new activists are radical."[19]

The leadership of NOW was sufficiently alarmed at being identified with some of these more radical groups for the board of directors of

NOW, who met in December 1968, to lay down "Guidelines on Public Relations" that forbade anyone speaking for NOW to offer an opinion on any issue that was not already official NOW policy if there was "any chance that it would be controversial."[20]

NOW's more extensive organizational base, with a national membership of over four thousand by 1970, attracted women from many of the liberation groups.[21] These new and predominantly young members brought new issues, such as lesbianism, to NOW, along with enthusiasm for unconventional political activities, which expanded the repertoire of tactics within NOW.

At the same time, more conservative groups became more accepting of both the agenda and tactics of NOW. Among these groups was WEAL, formed in 1968 after its founder Elizabeth Boyer left NOW in protest over its support for abortion rights. As NOW was increasingly willing to join with younger, more radical women in protest, WEAL tried to preserve NOW's earlier tradition of applying conventional pressure for change. The frustration of WEAL's officers with continuing these tactics, however, is apparent even in the organization's first newsletter, dated 1970. The newsletter reports on a day of meetings at the Labor Department where WEAL had been invited to discuss ways to implement the theme of the fiftieth anniversary of the founding of the Women's Bureau.

> WEAL was chiefly concerned with the delay in issuing the Guidelines [on sex discrimination compliance with the Civil Rights Act of 1964], stemming from the meetings in August 1969, and asked if a committee from the group might go to the Secretary's office to request the Guidelines. . . . WEAL's request was regarded as inappropriate. . . . Later, another request that a motion be forwarded asking that the Women's Bureau be elevated to a higher policy-making status was also set aside as being inappropriate to the purposes of the meeting. . . . In general, the meetings did not meet the expectations of WEAL. Perhaps our eager enthusiasm for action on the part of the Bureau was unrealistic . . . or should I say "inappropriate"? [22]

WEAL became involved in litigation in the late 1960s and early 1970s, trying to force government agencies, including the Departments of Labor and Health, Education and Welfare, to begin monitoring laws prohibiting sex discrimination. Its most striking successes were a series of legal challenges to universities' hiring, promotion, and termination practices based on President Johnson's executive order that prohibited sex discrimination by federal contractors.

By the early 1970s, WEAL, a holdout in adopting disorderly tactics, had also changed. In 1970, Boyer had told the press, "We do not picket or chain ourselves to the White House gates. . . . And we are not a clutch of people getting together for group therapy."[23] Boyer sent a letter in March 1971 assuring members that "we are not oriented to demonstrations nor to flamboyant publicity tactics."[24] But by 1973, WEAL had reversed its stand on abortion, now supporting it, and had become more tolerant of protests. A WEAL promotional pamphlet from about 1973 explained: "While demonstrations and picketing may serve a certain purpose in attracting attention to the problem, WEAL believes primarily in another avenue of approach: *since the present situation is the result of women's inertia, it will have to be corrected by women's action.* . . . Rebellion is inevitable and WEAL stands for responsible rebellion" (italics in original).[25] By 1973, consciousness raising, borrowed from liberation groups, had become an accepted activity within WEAL. An undated leaflet from the WEAL archives gives advice about how to start "support/consciousness-raising" groups.[26] When Arvonne Fraser became president of WEAL in 1972, she recruited new leaders for the organization from a consciousness-raising group called "The Nameless Sisterhood," which met at her home in Washington, D.C.[27] WEAL had not fundamentally changed from seeing itself as "the right wing of the women's movement." But it had become more tolerant of protest and unorthodox methods of raising political consciousness because of its frustration at getting the government to alter its policies through quieter approaches.

*New York Times* coverage of the women's movement in the late sixties and early seventies gives hints of this convergence among movement groups. It covered NOW protests over access for women to public accommodations and over newspaper handling of "help wanted" ads, along with some of the actions of women's liberation groups, including the picketing and release of mice during the bridal fair at Madison Square Garden by WITCH and the storming of the New York marriage license bureau by The Feminists, the women's liberation group founded by Atkinson. The *New York Times* article that reveals the most about the joining together of disparate women's groups reports on the northeastern regional meeting of the Congress to Unite Women, attended by twenty-five chapters of fifteen organizations, ranging from WITCH to NOW to unidentified professional women's groups. In the congress's press release, the group puts forth a common agenda, emphasizing the need to work together for the liberation of all women.[28] Women's groups seem to have agreed that unity was the key to bringing about social change.

While the increased acceptance of consciousness raising and public protest moved the separate wings of the women's movement closer, the start of coordinated lobbying in Washington by women's movement groups, such as NOW, the NWPC, and WEAL, solidified cooperation with traditional women's groups. Serious efforts to establish an ongoing, well-organized lobby to pressure Congress and the executive branch on behalf of women's concerns did not begin in earnest until 1972. Members of women's groups had to see concrete legislative benefits coming out of Congress such as Title IX of the Education Amendments Act of 1972, which barred discrimination based on gender in federally funded education programs, and the ERA before they were willing to commit the resources and take the risks inherent in participating in coordinated Washington lobbying.

Lobbying creates a need for groups to accept common strategies to achieve legislative objectives. Since movement groups attracted individuals whose primary commitment was to feminism and ending the oppression of women, the compromises necessary to accomplish purely legislative ends seemed to many of their members like selling out. Further, the women's movement had, historically and in the early 1970s, experienced serious factionalism, ranging from the decades-long controversy over the ERA to recent splits precipitated by the abortion issue. As evidence that the groups' fears were not without foundation, when NOW and NWPC opened Washington legislative offices in 1973, both groups became ensnarled in internal dissent, ranging from dues protests to leadership struggles.[29]

Despite the problems these controversies created for the expansion of lobbying activity in both groups in the early 1970s, a structure of cooperative effort to foster women's interests was established that linked older organizations such as the National Federation of Business and Professional Women's Clubs and the American Association of University Women to the newer groups. In interviews conducted in 1974–75 with lobbyists and officers from many of the women's groups active in Washington, it was evident that the older organizations played a major role in helping the newer women's movement groups organize to start lobbying. The League of Women Voters held training sessions for lobbyists from NOW and the NWPC.[30] The American Association of University Women and the National Federation of Business and Professional Women's Clubs shared information with women's movement groups about people to contact on Capitol Hill. Longtime lobbyists, such as Olya Margolin of the National Council of Jewish Women, used her entree as an ally of organized labor to help get the new groups included as witnesses in committee hearings. This outpouring of assistance from traditional groups came despite real reservations on the part of some of these organizations about the wisdom of trying to represent "women's interests." One lobbyist for the League cautioned that "for women to be protected . . . , they must take a broader view [than just women]. The minorities [including women] must present a common front [to Congress]."[31]

However, the representatives of many of these traditional groups reported that working on women's rights had a very beneficial effect on their members. Ellen McCartney, lobbyist for the American Association of University Women, commented that her group had been going through its own period of feminizing and consciousness raising, spurred by its 1974 theme "Woman Searching for Self."[32] League members also seemed to be energized by working on women's issues. The League raised over $250,000 for the ERA. Judith Norrell, lobbyist for the League, observed that she had never seen so much unity and excitement within the League as on the ERA issue.[33] The League also experienced the negative aspect of this membership enthusiasm when the Massachusetts League took a strong pro-abortion stand. After losing nine hundred members in the state, it was forced to reverse its position. In general, however, established women's groups found that they were able to cooperate with the newer organizations to their mutual benefit.

The newer movement groups experienced more conflict within their organizations than did the older groups. Internal disagreement in NOW and the NWPC over the amount of national legislative work they should undertake limited NOW and the NWPC's ability to work with other women's groups that were lobbying Congress. Many of their members felt that the application of pressure in states and communities was more effective than national lobbying. Still others believed that protest would gain more attention than lobbying.

Conflict between women's groups erupted occasionally as each competed with the others for the membership of committed feminists. When one organization seemed to be less effective than another, it feared loss of members to other groups. By contrast, such traditional organizations as the League and the American Association of University Women were able to attract women from the younger generation through their successful lobbying on feminist issues—women who, otherwise, would have likely not joined either the League or the American Association of University Women or the more strident movement-oriented groups.

In summary, by the early 1970s, there was a marked convergence of women's groups from the left, right, and center of the political spectrum. Organizationally this meant that significant resources were now available to mount an effective challenge to the status quo. Most of these resources were drawn from traditional women's organizations. The League, United Methodist Women, the National Woman's Party (the original drafters of the ERA), the American Association of University Women, and the National Federation of Business and Professional Women were among the established women's groups that contributed significant resources to ERA ratification efforts.[34] The spectrum of women's movement groups, ranging from liberation groups such as WITCH and The Feminists to "conservative" movement groups like WEAL, brought new recruits and fresh ideas to the feminist cause. Although nonfeminist groups, including Common Cause, the American Civil Liberties Union, and the National Education Association, also materially aided women's efforts to achieve legal change, their assistance, although beneficial, was not crucial to the movement. Protest, consciousness raising, and ongoing Washington lobbying were all a part of the organizational repertoire of the movement in the early seventies. The structure of political opportunity within this period, while favorable on balance, was more mixed than in the early sixties, with a blend of government facilitation and tentative efforts at repression.

## Political Opportunities

After the death of President Kennedy in 1963, the impetus behind governmental efforts to assist the development of a women's movement slowly shifted from the executive to the legislative branch. President Johnson took credit for the Equal Pay Act, which guaranteed women equal wages for equal work, passed at the end of the Kennedy administration.[35]

Johnson saw women's problems as stemming from biases in employment and jobs, and he grouped their difficulties with those of racial minorities. He quietly supported the addition of a ban on sex discrimination in the Civil Rights Act of 1964;[36] cited the Democratic party platform with approval, noting its support for eliminating employment discrimination based on sex;[37] and issued his executive order (No. 11375) in 1967 that included women under federally mandated affirmative action programs.

Johnson saw these three new laws—the Equal Pay Act, the Civil Rights Act, and the affirmative action order—as providing the basis for eliminating legal barriers to the employment of women. But he went further by using the federal government as a model employer of women and the presidency as a "bully pulpit" to advocate equal job opportunities for women. Many of his public statements reflect these concerns. At a reception in 1964 for newly appointed women in government, he expounded his philosophy.

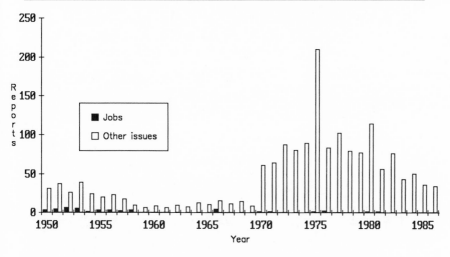

Fig. 3-1. *New York Times* reports on employment and all other women's issues.

Providence has distributed brains and skills pretty evenly over our people. To conclude that women are unfitted to the risk of our society seems to me the equivalent of closing male eyes to female facts. We need skill and intelligence and capacity for leadership. We need dedication and application and we need them wherever we find them. . . .

We can open and we are opening, the doors of public service [to women] and I think this is going to influence some other sectors as well. My whole aim in promoting women and picking out more women to serve in this administration is to underline our profound belief that we can waste no talent, we can frustrate no creative power, we can neglect no skill. . . . There is no place for discrimination of any kind in American life.[38]

Language that rejected "stag government" permeated Johnson's speeches.[39] He made frequent announcements about the number of women he had appointed or who had received promotions to high government posts under his administration. In 1965, he stated that he had appointed 114 women to major positions in government, and 3,000 other women had risen to the highest grades in the career civil service. That same year, he accused those responsible for selecting the recipients of the National Civil Service League's Career Service Awards (all of which were awarded to men) of neglecting women, expressing undisguised skepticism that merit was really divided, ten for men and nothing for women.[40]

Somewhat surprisingly, given Johnson's frequent references to

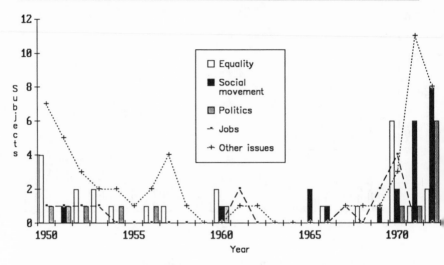

Fig. 3-2. Subjects initiated by women.

women in the work force, there are few reports about women and work in the *New York Times* in these years (Fig. 3-1). The stories that are attributed to the president and his staff deal with his political appointments of women. The president's frequently stated linkage between employing people based on merit and reducing discrimination against women in the general work force did not seem to reach the public.

Perhaps this message failed to reach the public because Johnson did not use the most visible public occasions, such as State of the Union addresses, to make his observations about job discrimination against women. He never made more than pro forma references to "men and women" in State of the Union, nomination, or inaugural speeches. His record is also marred by a "sensitivity gap." One illustration came in July 1965 when he told members of the Citizens' Advisory Council on the Status of Women and the Governors' Commission how much he appreciated the support he received from women. He then went on to read a letter sent by a mother, which said the following: "I want to tell you how proud I am of our country and our Government, and our Congress, and our President for standing up and facing the enemy and not appeasing. . . . I have 3 boys and one of them died in Vietnam, the other was wounded yesterday in the Dominican Republic, and the third one enlisted to be a paratrooper."[41] Johnson failed to recognize the aversion most women feel toward use of deadly force, compounded by the thought of risking their children's lives in controversial wars. He also did not understand women's desire to be

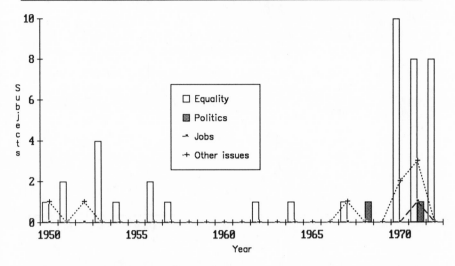

Fig. 3-3. Subjects initiated by Congress.

judged as human beings, not as sex objects. In response to a reporter's question at a presidential press conference in 1964, Johnson observed, "You are going to find more attractive, capable women working for this Government than you ever saw before."[42] In 1968, he told those attending the Federal Woman's Award Ceremony the following story:

> One of the ladies on my staff advised me that I should not speak to you women of your charm, or your grace, or your beauty. "They don't want to hear that," she said. I paused and then said, "Well, that has not been my experience." She said that I should compliment you instead on your great influence in the high councils of your Government and that is good advice.[43]

Johnson defined women's issues in terms of jobs and economic need. His record and words amply demonstrate that he felt the injustice of women being excluded from the job market and being underpaid because of their gender.[44]

Despite a good record of legislation to further women's employment opportunities and of political appointments of women to government posts, there was surprisingly little political resonance to Johnson's initiatives. The job and employment concerns of women failed to gain attention as public issues in the late 1960s. Figures 3-2 and 3-3 demonstrate that neither feminists nor Congress raised employment issues during this period.

Congress and women's groups were turning their attention instead

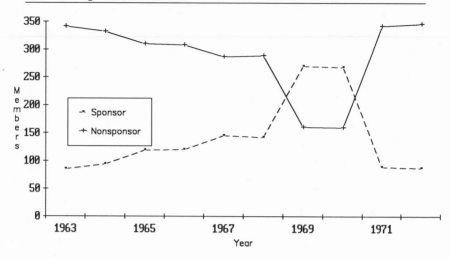

Fig. 3-4. House sponsors versus nonsponsors of the ERA.

toward the equal rights amendment to the U.S. Constitution and legislation that removed legally mandated unequal treatment of men and women. Women's groups, with help from the President's Commission on the Status of Women and the Civil Rights Act of 1964, which cut the legal underpinnings from protective legislation for women workers, had at last coalesced in support of an equal rights amendment. The Ninety-first Congress (1969–70) underwent a radical shift on the ERA. For the first time since its introduction in 1923, a majority of members of the House signed on as ERA sponsors (Fig. 3-4). This was almost double the number of sponsors in the previous Congress.

There was also a sizeable jump in the volume of bills introduced containing the ERA starting in 1969. Members of Congress moved from introducing 154 such resolutions in the Ninetieth Congress (1967–68), to 282 in the Ninety-first Congress (1969–70). Representatives Griffiths and Green then seized the initiative to push equality for women ahead in Congress. Green scheduled hearings on sex discrimination in education beginning on 17 June, 1970. These hearings became a vehicle for examining discrimination against women generally and helped to build a case for the ERA.[45] Griffiths started to circulate a petition to discharge the ERA from the House Judiciary committee chaired by Emmanuel Celler (D, N.Y.), a fervent ERA opponent. Griffiths got 218 members of the House to sign the discharge petition in just six-weeks' time, bringing the ERA directly to the floor of Congress for debate.

This was an extraordinary and audacious accomplishment. In the

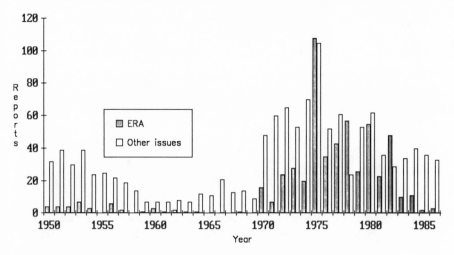

Fig. 3-5. ERA and all other women's issues, as reported in the *New York Times.*

sixty-year history of the discharge rule, members of Congress had filed 829 discharge petitions, but only 24 had actually gathered enough signatures to have bills discharged.[46] Also, in 1970, members of a Pittsburgh chapter of NOW disrupted Senator Birch Bayh's (D, Ind.) Senate judiciary subcommittee hearings on allowing nineteen-year-olds to vote. Bayh promised to schedule ERA hearings in the next session of Congress.

There is no single reason why congressional support for the ERA increased so rapidly in 1969. The *New York Times* did not have many stories on the ERA until 1970, when pressure both within and outside Congress mounted (Fig. 3-5). Both major political parties had actually dropped support for the ERA from their platforms at their 1968 conventions.[47] President Johnson displayed no interest in the ERA as a political issue. Public opinion on the ERA seems to have been static in the late sixties.[48]

Gary Orfield is one of the few scholars who has noticed and tried to explain this rapid shift.[49] He attributed Congress' willingness to act to "the emergence of a widely publicized women's movement in 1970."[50] Yet, the 214 bill introductions in the first session of the Ninety-first Congress in 1969 precede most of the coverage of the women's movement by the media. Similarly, organized lobbying on behalf of the women's movement is practically nonexistent in the late 1960s. It was not until 1971 that NOW became the first nationally organized feminist group to establish a lobbying office in Washington. Most of the early pressure on Congress to pass the ERA was coordinated

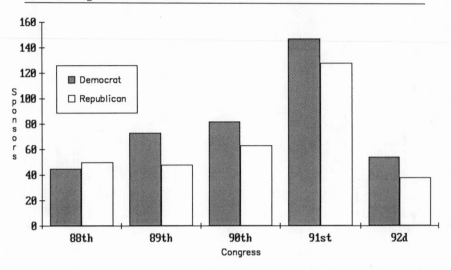

Fig. 3-6. ERA sponsors, by party affiliation.

through Griffiths' congressional office. It consisted primarily of Washington-area housewives who came to the Capitol several days a week to speak with whomever they could about the need for an ERA.

A frequent participant in these ERA forays around Congress afterwards described how several dozen suburban women would mass in the halls of Congress looking for an uncommitted member to confront.[51] A call would come from down the corridor, and they would be off to surround, press literature on, and generally hold the attention of the representative. Since many male members seemed to one participant at least to regard women as looking alike, they frequently heard mutterings from captured members that women were overrunning Congress. Their standard reply was that they were just representing the thousands marching in the streets. Mail in support of the ERA ran high. By some accounts, it surpassed the volume received by congressional offices on the war in Vietnam.[52] Yet, it was not so much the perception of pressure from women or women's groups that got Congress to pass the ERA, as it did in 1972, but the crumbling of organized opposition to the ERA.

Because the votes on the ERA were so one-sided in its favor when it passed in the Ninety-second Congress (354 to 23 in the House and 84 to 8 in the Senate), the only way to get a sense of where support and opposition to the amendment came from within Congress is by looking at sponsorship. The identity and change in congressional sponsors of ERA during this period suggests that the issue was becom-

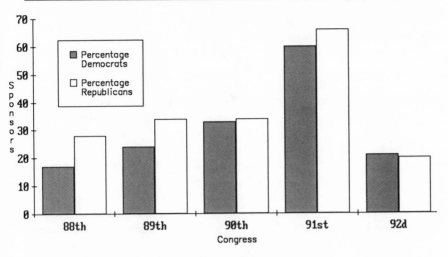

Fig. 3-7. Percentage of ERA sponsors within each party.

ing more sharply defined in the late sixties. Party support was rarely determinative. In the Eighty-seventh and Eighty-eighth Congresses, there were more Republican than Democratic cosponsors of the ERA in the House of Representatives, where the amendment had always faced the greatest opposition (Fig. 3-6). Then, the numbers shifted so that more Democrats than Republicans sponsored the ERA in the four Congresses leading up to the amendment's passage. Yet, as Figure 3-7 illustrates, because there were more Democrats than Republicans in the House in these years, there was a correspondingly greater likelihood that Democrats would sponsor the ERA. Yet, proportionately, with the exception of the Ninety-second Congress, Republican members of Congress were more likely than Democrats to be sponsors.

This stronger Republican backing for the ERA in the late sixties is not surprising. Historically, Republicans had always been more supportive of the ERA than Democrats. They were the first to include endorsement of the ERA in their party platform, and Republicans were also the first party to receive the support of the National Woman's Party, the prime proponent of the ERA. In 1928, the National Woman's Party endorsed Herbert Hoover and his running mate for the presidency. This was the first time the Woman's Party backed a presidential ticket. Their stated reason for the endorsement was that the Republican vice presidential candidate Charles Curtis had introduced the ERA in the Senate.[53]

The major reasons that the Democratic party rejected the ERA were the opposition of organized labor and a preference for legislation that

protected women workers over legislation that mandated legal equality. As these factors became less significant in the late 1960s and early
1970s, Democrats in Congress became more likely to support the ERA.
As a result of passage of the Civil Rights Act of 1964, labor-union
hostility toward the amendment waned. In 1970, the United Auto
Workers (UAW) union endorsed the ERA at its national convention.[54]
Although an official AFL-CIO endorsement of the ERA did not follow
until late 1974, it was widely recognized that the unified opposition
of organized labor to the amendment was unraveling.

It is more surprising that representatives' ties to organized labor did
not seem to account for their support or opposition to the amendment.
Given the historical hostility of the AFL-CIO to the ERA, one would
expect to find that members of Congress with high performance ratings from the AFL-CIO would be less likely to sponsor the amendment
in the early sixties, when labor's opposition was still unwavering. As
labor's dislike of the amendment weakened in the late sixties, one
would expect to find these members increasingly willing to become
sponsors.

Figures 3-8 through 3-12 show that in 1963–64, when labor's opposition was high, amendment sponsors were more likely to have low
AFL-CIO Committee on Political Education (COPE) scores than nonsponsors. But, by the mid-sixties, when labor opposition remained
firm, new sponsors of the ERA were disproportionately pro-labor and
liberal. High COPE scores (assigned by the AFL-CIO to individual
representatives based on their votes on issues of special importance to
organized labor in the previous Congress) are used to determine
members' support for organized labor. Similarly, the Americans for
Democratic Action (ADA), a liberal interest group, gives high scores
to members of Congress who voted for the liberal side on key issues
in the previous Congress and low scores to those who did not. This
is a commonly used indicator of liberalism. The analogous measure
of conservatism is the rating assigned by the Americans for Constitutional Action (ACA). Like the liberals in the ADA, the conservatives
in the ACA award scores to individual members of Congress based on
their "correct" voting on a range of conservative issues in the previous
Congress. This pattern of liberal, pro-labor support for an amendment
was temporarily reversed in the Ninetieth Congress as a group of more
conservative, anti-labor members became ERA sponsors for the first
time, but the pattern reappears in the Ninety-first and Ninety-second
Congresses. Breaking this process down by political party shows with
even greater clarity the extent to which the ERA garnered support
among members of Congress who, relative to their respective parties,
were liberal and pro-labor (Figs. 3-13 through 3-22).

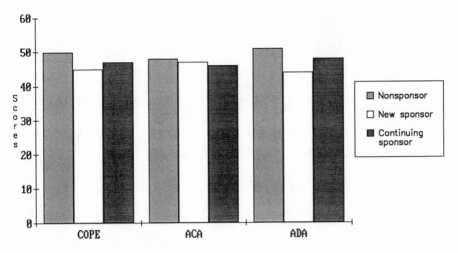

Fig. 3-8. Interest group ratings of ERA sponsors, 88th Congress.

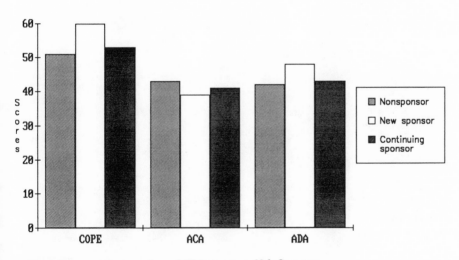

Fig. 3-9. Interest group ratings of ERA sponsors, 89th Congress.

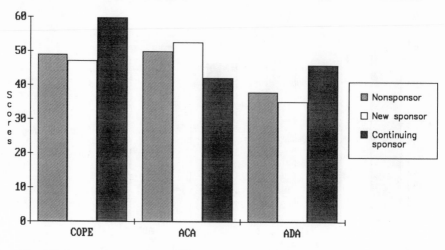

Fig. 3-10. Interest group ratings of ERA sponsors, 90th Congress.

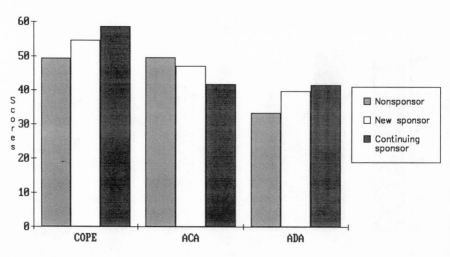

Fig. 3-11. Interest group ratings of ERA sponsors, 91st Congress.

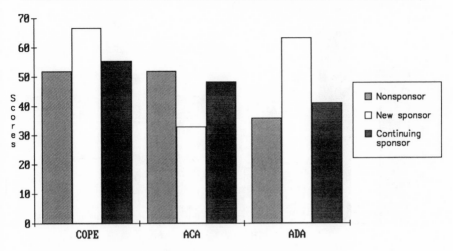

Fig. 3-12. Interest group ratings of ERA sponsors, 92d Congress.

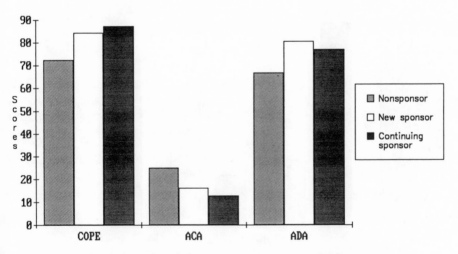

Fig. 3-13. Interest group ratings of Democratic ERA sponsors, 88th Congress.

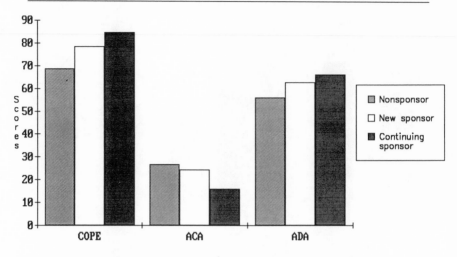

Fig. 3-14. Interest group ratings of Democratic ERA sponsors, 89th Congress.

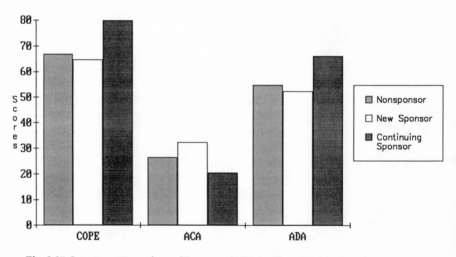

Fig. 3-15. Interest group ratings of Democratic ERA sponsors, 90th Congress.

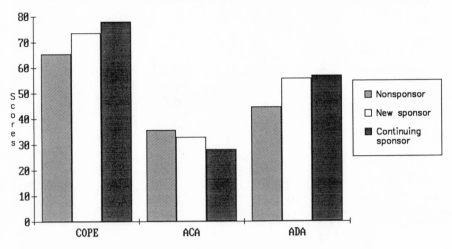

Fig. 3-16. Interest group ratings of Democratic ERA sponsors, 91st Congress.

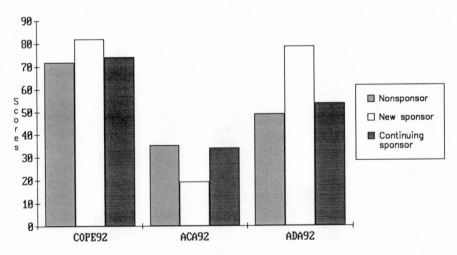

Fig. 3-17. Interest group ratings of Democratic ERA sponsors, 92d Congress.

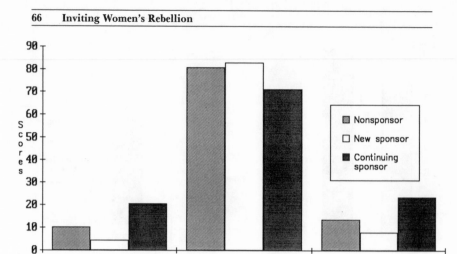

Fig. 3-18. Interest group ratings of Republican ERA sponsors, 88th Congress.

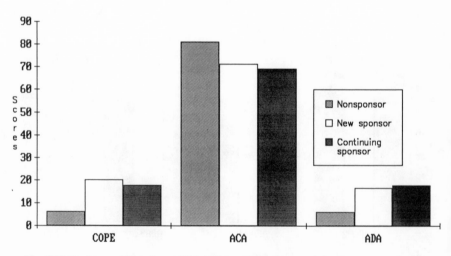

Fig. 3-19. Interest group ratings of Republican ERA sponsors, 89th Congress.

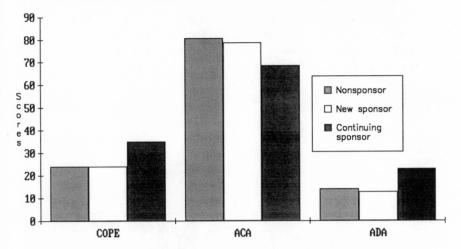

Fig. 3-20. Interest group ratings of Republican ERA sponsors, 90th Congress.

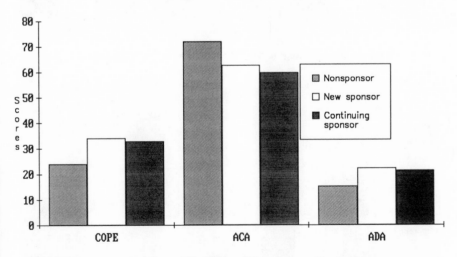

Fig. 3-21. Interest group ratings of Republican ERA sponsors, 91st Congress.

Throughout the sixties, the ERA was an issue that was more popular among members of Congress from the Northeast and less likely to attract support from Southern and Midwestern members of Congress. Only the position of Western representatives changed over time, shifting from strong support in the early years to significant lack of support in the seventies (Figs. 3-23 through 3-27).

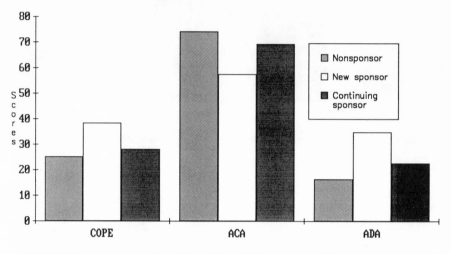

Fig. 3-22. Interest group ratings of Republican ERA sponsors, 92d Congress.

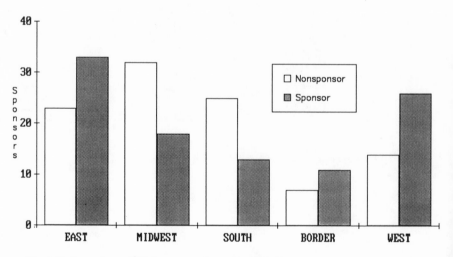

Fig. 3-23. Percentage of ERA sponsors by region, 88th Congress.

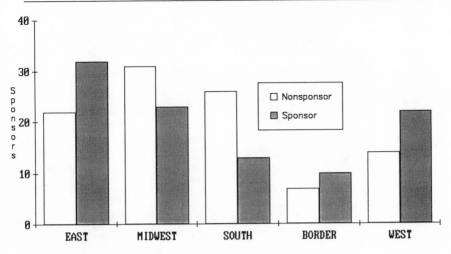

Fig. 3-24. Percentage of ERA sponsors by region, 89th Congress.

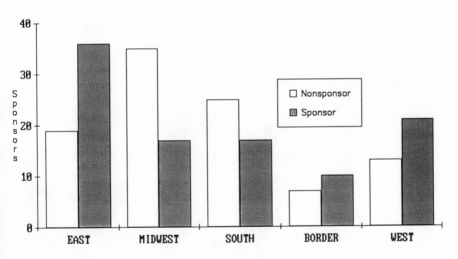

Fig. 3-25. Percentage of ERA sponsors by region, 90th Congress.

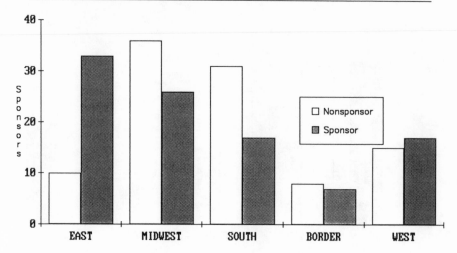

Fig. 3-26. Percentage of ERA sponsors by region, 91st Congress.

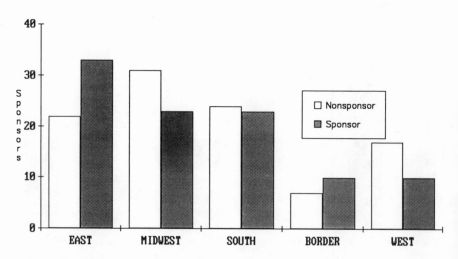

Fig. 3-27. Percentage of ERA sponsors by region, 92d Congress.

To assess how much influence these factors had on the individual decisions of members of Congress about whether to sponsor the ERA, a discriminant analysis was performed for each of the five Congresses (the Eighty-eighth through the Ninety-second). Discriminant analysis is structured to assign individuals to two or, in this case, three non-overlapping categories, based on independent predictor variables, such as party, region, or liberalism. It does this by selecting the combined score (or vector) of independent variables that is most successful in placing individuals in their correct categories.[55] Representatives were divided into three categories: (1) nonsponsors, (2) first-time or new sponsors, and (3) continuing sponsors. This represents a kind of scale of intensity of commitment to the ERA. First-time sponsors are likely to have less invested in the joint House-Senate resolution's success than repeat sponsors. The independent variables are liberalism/conservatism (measured by ACA and ADA ratings); labor support (COPE ratings); region (based on home state and divided into the East, Midwest, South, Border, and Western regions); and political party. They were used as likely predictors of individual decisions. The equations vary from a 62-percent probability of correct assignment of individuals to the three categories of nonsponsor, new sponsor, or continuing sponsor to 44-percent accuracy.[56]

Although all are significant improvements over random guessing—which would be accurate in only about one third of the cases, depending on the actual distribution of individuals among the three categories—clearly, much of the variance is not explained. This is not particularly surprising, since other research attempting to explain mass opinion on attitudes toward sex discrimination has explained less than 10 percent of the variance in roughly the same time period.[57] Cleavages that reflect gender tolerance and discrimination were not sharply defined as political issues this early and thus did not fit comfortably into the existing belief systems of Congress.

In the Eighty-eighth Congress, region, political party, and higher than average COPE scores combine to explain more than 60 percent of the sponsorship decisions. Specifically, the regional variables West and East are positively related to ERA sponsorship. Midwest is negatively related to sponsorship. Republican party affiliation and high approval ratings by the AFL-CIO make it more likely that an individual will introduce the ERA in this Congress (Table 3-1).

For the Eighty-ninth Congress, knowing the political party and COPE and ACA scores, as well as whether the legislator represented a Midwestern state, in combination permit individuals to be placed in the category they actually fell in (e.g., nonsponsor, new, or continuing sponsor) 48 percent of the time. Republican party affiliation, high

Table 3-1. Discriminant Analysis Results for the Eighty-eighth Congress

| Variables | Wilks' Lambda | Significance |
|-----------|---------------|--------------|
| West      | .963          | .001         |
| East      | .939          | .000         |
| Party     | .925          | .000         |
| COPE 88   | .907          | .000         |
| Midwest   | .874          | .000         |

Table 3-2. Discriminant Analysis Results for the Eighty-ninth Congress

| Variables | Wilks' Lambda | Significance |
|-----------|---------------|--------------|
| Party     | .983          | .05          |
| COPE 89   | .954          | .001         |
| Midwest   | .931          | .000         |
| ACA 89    | .919          | .000         |

COPE scores, and low ACA scores, as well as not being a Midwestern representative, make ERA sponsorship more likely (Table 3-2).

In the Ninetieth Congress, Midwest (negative), South (negative), ADA score (positive), party (Republican) and East (positive), combine to place representatives in their correct category 50 percent of the time (Table 3-3). In the Ninety-first Congress, the three regional variables— East, West, and Border states—along with party, permit 44 percent of the members to be identified correctly as nonsponsors, new sponsors, or continuing sponsors.

Finally, in the Ninety-second Congress, ADA and ACA scores, along with representation from the East, Border states, and South, correctly divide the members in 51 percent of the cases (Table 3-5). Although attitudes toward the ERA cut across most traditional cleavages in Congress, there is evidence that by the time the amendment passed in the House, it had been identified by many there as a liberal/conservative issue, and they responded to it as such.

While Congress struggled to come to grips with the ERA, President Richard M. Nixon's public statements showed little personal involvement with women's issues, including the ERA. When Nixon became president in 1968, he had no evident plan to appeal to women voters. During most of his first term, he neglected even the traditional presi-

Table 3-3. Discriminant Analysis Results for the Ninetieth Congress

| Variables | Wilks' Lambda | Significance |
|---|---|---|
| Midwest | .964 | .000 |
| South | .932 | .000 |
| ADA 90 | .925 | .000 |
| Party | .919 | .000 |
| East | .913 | .000 |

Table 3-4. Discriminant Analysis Results for the Ninety-first Congress

| Variables | Wilks' Lambda | Significance |
|---|---|---|
| East | .935 | .000 |
| West | .918 | .000 |
| Border | .910 | .000 |
| Party | .903 | .000 |

Table 3-5. Discriminant Analysis Results for the Ninety-second Congress

| Variables | Wilks' Lambda | Significance |
|---|---|---|
| ADA 92 | .971 | .005 |
| ACA 92 | .957 | .001 |
| East | .939 | .001 |
| Border | .939 | .001 |
| South | .930 | .001 |

dential strategy of appointing a number of women to political positions in the new administration. Shortly after taking office, he missed a traditional opportunity to spotlight female appointees in his administration. He remarked to the Seventeenth Annual Republican Women's Conference that he was particularly proud of the wives of the men he had appointed to high office.[58]

At a news conference in June 1971, Marianne Means of the Hearst newspapers criticized the president for his lack of appointments of women to government jobs. She noted that of the top 10,000 federal jobs, only 150 were held by women and that in Nixon's two and a half years in office, he had appointed only 200 women, 62 to a single arts commission. Nixon's sole response was that he appointed women when they were the best qualified.[59]

In 1971, Nixon seemed to become aware of the electoral importance of women voters. In April of that year, he directed a memorandum to the heads of executive departments and agencies, asking them to increase the number of women in the civil service at grades GS 13 to 16 and above and the number of women serving on advisory boards and committees.[60] Then, in an address to delegates to the Girls Nation Annual Convention, in August, he began to talk about women as a potential electoral majority, concluding that "any candidate for office had better get along well with women."[61]

In April 1972, as the November election drew near, the president issued a paper entitled "The Status of Women Within the Administration," asserting that his administration had appointed and promoted more women to top-level policy posts in government than any of its predecessors.[62] The Nixon administration seemed to be preparing for the November election by increasing the number of women in management-level positions in government to avoid further questions such as those from Means.

Because Congress was so actively engaged in supporting the ERA between 1969 and the spring of 1972, when the amendment was passed by an overwhelming margin, it is somewhat surprising how little the president chose to say about the ERA in this period. His support was both unequivocal and practically unvoiced. Nixon sent the following letter to Senate minority leader Hugh Scott (R, Pa.) in mid-March 1972, just *four days* before the final vote on the ERA in Congress, describing his position on the amendment.

> As you remember, as a Senator in 1951 I cosponsored a Resolution incorporating the original Amendment; in July of 1968 I reaffirmed my support for it as a candidate for the Presidency.
>
> Throughout twenty-one years I have not altered my belief that equal rights for women warrant a Constitutional guarantee—and I therefore continue to favor the enactment of the Constitutional Amendment to achieve this goal.[63]

Aside from this letter to Senator Scott, President Nixon's public papers contain no reference to the ERA until 1 March, 1973, almost a year after congressional passage. At this rather late date, in a "State of the Union Message to the Congress on Human Resources," Nixon pledged to continue support for ratification of the ERA.[64] In Nixon's final State of the Union message, in a part of the speech that was written but not delivered, he strongly endorsed the ERA, along with legislation extending equal credit to women.[65]

Although Nixon was on the record as supporting equality for women in employment, law, and politics, he seems to have devoted little attention to the issue. He appeared content throughout his presidency to allow Congress and women's groups to seize the initiative in defining the issues and drafting legislation to deal with them.

Many of the representatives of active women's groups whom I interviewed in 1974 expressed a general unease at the White House's role on women's issues during the Nixon administration. Although Anne Armstrong, counselor to the president, and her aides appeared on the membership lists of national coalitions in support of the ERA and other women's rights issues, they were not perceived as being very involved in providing assistance to those working for passage. More seriously, several of the groups, including the United Methodist Women and some of the more active feminist groups, felt that the Central Intelligence Agency (CIA) was responsible for break-ins and phone taps in their offices during the Nixon administration. They attributed this activity to administration concern about their contacts with women's groups abroad.

It is difficult to gauge the impact these fears had on these groups. Certainly, it was more difficult as a researcher to schedule interviews with group representatives. It was often first necessary to convince groups that one was not working for the CIA. Yet, despite these alleged efforts by the executive branch of government to repress the women's movement, congressional support along with both public and private assistance from feminists within government continued, on balance, to facilitate the movement's growth.

The final noteworthy governmental group assisting the activities of the women's movement during these years was the so-called woodwork feminists, the individuals in elected office and government service with a strong commitment to women's rights issues.[66] Individuals such as Mary Eastwood, Catherine East, Richard Graham, and Sonia Pressman have been publicly recognized as urging Betty Friedan to found NOW, revealing to feminists the lack of change and even hostility toward women's rights they saw within government. Feminists on congressional staffs provided vote-counting networks both for women's groups and feminist members of Congress such as Martha Griffiths, Edith Green, and Margaret Heckler (R, Mass.), who were rounding up support for women's rights legislation.

In the course of conducting interviews with congressional staff and lobbyists for women's groups in 1974–75, I was told the names of wives and mistresses of members of Congress who were active in conveying information from women's groups to the member. One enthusiastic legislative assistant in a congressional office argued strongly that girl friends of representatives were a greatly underutilized resource in lobbying campaigns. Although it is difficult to quantify the amount of help that the women's movement received from these rather unorthodox sources, it is likely that they reinforced the impression that there was widespread public support for these issues, when, in fact, support was still building across the country.

From the late 1960s through the early 1970s, Congress and feminists within government helped facilitate the growth of the women's movement. The ERA was the key issue that allowed women's groups to unite, to build public support, and to demonstrate significant political power. The structure of political opportunity, despite some ambiguity in the White House, was favorable for allowing the movement to peak in the mid-1970s.

## Psychological Change

Available evidence suggests that there was a dramatic increase in egalitarian attitudes towards women in the early 1970s, just as women's organizations began to take the initiative in pushing for change in public policy on gender. The longest across-time measure of prejudice toward women is a question that has been repeated periodically since 1937: Were individuals willing to vote for a qualified woman for president? As Ferree argued persuasively, this question probably tells less about people's likely behavior, if given the opportunity to vote for a woman president, than about their willingness openly to express prejudice toward women.[67] It is also at least a rough indicator of their degree of discomfort with the idea of women playing a serious political role.

After twenty years (between 1949 and 1969) in which there was little change in public attitudes toward voting for a woman president (roughly 55 percent of the population would), suddenly, between 1969 and 1971, women's willingness to vote for a woman for president jumped a full 18 percentage points, from 49-percent approval in 1969 to 67-percent approval in 1971 (see chap. 5). Men's approval in this period increases from 58 percent in 1969 to 65 percent in 1971.[68]

The abruptness of this change has been variously attributed to the rise of a women's movement and to increasing public awareness of the egalitarian legislation Congress passed in the mid-1960s, including the Equal Pay Act of 1963 and the Civil Rights Act of 1964. Both events are presumed to have made prejudice against women less socially acceptable. This new tolerance of a greater political role for women can itself be viewed as creating the preconditions for further growth in the women's movement. As women revised their earlier view that they were not suited to play a strong political role because of their sex, they began to develop the type of political consciousness that allowed them to work for change in their own situation.

During this same period, more women were both entering the work force and changing their attitudes about the suitability of married women working.[69] In 1960, 38 percent of adult women were in the labor force. By 1970, this figure had risen to 43 percent. By 1980, the figure was 52 percent. As Burstein noted, the available evidence indicates that public opinion on this issue changed rapidly starting in the late 1960s. Between 1946 and 1969, popular approval of married women working increased at a rate of just 0.7 percent per year. From 1969 to 1975, this rate of increase more than doubled to a 1.9-percent rise in public approval.[70]

Women's lives were in the process of changing from their previous narrow focus on home and family, as more entered the work force. Their opinions were also being transformed as they became more likely to approve of wider political and employment roles for women. These changes began to be reflected in the growing recognition among women that they faced discrimination because of their sex. In 1970, 54 percent of women felt that women of equal ability to men have less chance of becoming corporate executives, 50 percent believed that they faced discrimination in attaining executive-level jobs in business, and 40 percent expressed the view that there was discrimination against women in the professions.[71] As attitudes toward sex roles became more egalitarian and awareness of discrimination grew more pervasive, the stage was set both for the women's movement to grow in size, as new recruits were added to its ranks, and for government to respond to an increasingly public and popular issue.

## Conclusions

In the late 1960s and early 1970s, an organizational revolution occurred among women's groups. It consisted of both a "mushrooming"[72] of movement-related groups of the left, right, and center and a drawing together of existing and new women's groups. From a variety of motives, women's organizations began to cooperate with one another, pooling resources, blending tactics, and accepting a common political agenda led by a drive for equality.

As women's groups marshalled their indigenous strength, Congress took the lead in boosting the legislative fortunes of the ERA. Despite the different executive agenda of President Johnson, who felt that issues of employment discrimination were key, and the lack of involvement with women's issues during the Nixon administration, congressional support increased until the ERA passed in March 1972. As the ERA headed to the individual states in the fight for ratification, it continued to provide the prime catalyst that united and energized the women's movement. Organizationally, individually, and in the calculation of women's prospects to bring about change, the movement was about to peak.

# 4

# The High Point
# of the Women's Movement

The peak of the women's movement and of activity on the ERA occurred in the same year—1975 (Fig. 4-1). This is not particularly surprising, since the ERA was the issue that had divided women's organizations into warring camps for more than forty years.[1] The developing consensus among women's groups on the desirability of the ERA in the 1960s was an important, and perhaps even necessary, precursor to the formation of a women's social movement. After old divisions had vanished, the ERA continued to serve as a rallying point for women, comparable to suffrage in the first women's movement.[2] Both were sweeping solutions to women's concerns. Optimists believed that first the vote and, later, legal equality would usher in a more just social order.

By the mid-1970s, there was also extraordinarily broad agreement among organizations as diverse as the Republican National Committee, the International Union of Electrical, Radio and Machine Workers, and the American Civil Liberties Union that an equal rights amendment should be added to the U.S. Constitution. Each of these groups, along with many others, had representatives serving on the Equal Rights Amendment Ratification Council, the umbrella group that coordinated national activities in support of the ERA.[3]

The fortunes of the women's movement seemed to rise and fall along with the ERA in this period. Between 1970 and 1980, 419 of the 1,072 women's events reported in the *New York Times* dealt with the ERA. This represents 39 percent of *all* coverage of women's issues in the seventies. The high point, in numbers of stories as well as in the percentage featuring the ERA, was reached in 1975, when more than half of the 213 stories (108) dealt with ERA (Fig. 4-1). The ERA had become the leading issue drawing press attention to women's concerns. From 1950 to 1986, there was a correlation of more than 90 percent between the number of women's events per year covered in the *New York Times* and those dealing with the ERA.[4] It seems evident that the ERA drew attention to women's issues generally.

Despite the close relationship between the ERA and the visibility of women's concerns, the dominance of the ERA as an issue was not as

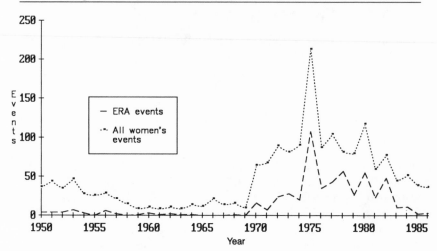

Fig. 4-1. ERA events compared with total women's events in the *New York Times*.

inevitable as many accounts of the period asserted. There was a second, competing agenda within the women's movement that centered around the special problems women face because of their gender. The ERA and its focus on legal equality did not completely overwhelm this "special needs" agenda until the mid-seventies. When this happened, the preeminence of the ERA seemed to owe more to the actions and encouragement of government officials than to choices made by women or their advocates.

## Organizational Growth

This division of issues into equality and special-needs concerns was a carryover from the earlier pro- and anti-ERA debate.[5] Groups favoring the ERA argued that nothing less than equality would make women full citizens with the same rights and responsibilities as men. Anti-ERA groups answered that, for most women, equality could never be a realistic option, burdened as women were with unique family and home responsibilities and disadvantaged by less physical strength, formal education, and training than most men. Protective laws to safeguard working women and abused or abandoned wives were a more pressing need to them than some abstract vision of equality. Although, in the second half of the twentieth century, the pro-ERA argument was predominant, this did not mean that concerns for women who combined child care with work that often paid little more than the minimum wage and single heads of households who tried to raise children in the shadow of poverty had vanished completely. There was widespread agreement that legal equality was necessary, but there was still strong interest in responding to the biological and socially determined family roles of women.

The modern version of this "equality" versus "special needs" debate divides laws so that "special needs" issues are those that address particular concerns of women rather than simply try to extend to women treatment identical to men. These issues include, among others, maternity leave for pregnant workers, child-care support, extra food stamps for pregnant and nursing mothers and their infants, and restrictions on conditions and hours for working women. Also fitting into this category are rape laws and special programs dealing with problems that may affect women differently from men, such as drug and alcohol dependency, small business ownership, and specific health problems.

The justification most often advanced for these programs is that they enable women to compete on an equal basis with men, despite their sometimes different circumstances. The Supreme Court decision *California Savings and Loan v. Guerra*[6] used this logic in upholding a California law that guaranteed leave without pay and some job security for pregnant women workers. The court argued that if women were to have the same chance as men to be promoted and earn high levels of compensation, it was reasonable for a state to guarantee them a longer period of leave when they became pregnant than was offered to men or women who otherwise became temporarily disabled. For, if women risked losing their jobs at every pregnancy, they were likely to continue to lag behind men in job advancement and salary.

By contrast, the equality agenda emphasizes the similarities between men and women. It presumes that in most endeavors women have a range of capabilities similar to men's. If so, they should be allowed to try anything that men can, succeeding or failing as individuals without any special supports or obstacles placed in their way by government because of their gender.

Although women's groups had reached agreement before the start of the women's movement that a constitutional guarantee of equality for women was a desirable goal, this did not mean that they relinquished the special-needs agenda. Of the eight explicitly political demands put forth in the NOW's 1968 Bill of Rights, four demanded equality with men and four hinged on government recognition of women's special needs. The equality demands included passage of the ERA; enforcement of legislation barring sex discrimination in employment; provision of equal educational opportunities; and passage of laws mandating equal job training and subsidies for poor women. The special-needs agenda consisted of maternity-leave rights in employment and social security benefits; tax deductions for home and child-care expenses for working parents; child-care centers; and the right for women to control their reproductive lives.[7] Those who drafted and passed this bill of rights were well aware that a woman's biological role gave rise to needs that even legal equality would not fully address.

In 1974 and 1975, I conducted lengthy interviews in Washington, D.C., with the legislative representatives of fourteen groups that were actively engaged in trying to influence government policies on women's issues.[8] The representatives reported working on six different special-needs issues, five different equality issues, and one issue, social security reform, that had elements of both. The special-needs issues mentioned were flexible hours; abortion; family planning; child care; rape; and discrimination against women in the military. The equality issues included equal access to credit; the ERA; minimum wage for domestics and tip credit for restaurant workers; and educational equality (the Women's Educational Equity Act, for curriculum issues, and enforcement of Title IX of the Educational Amendments Act of 1972, for access to education). Equality issues attracted a greater number of women's organizations to their coalitions than the special-needs issues did. The fourteen groups reported thirty-two instances of working on equality issues, twenty-three on special-needs issues. But it is clear that women's groups in the mid-1970s were pushing for both equality and special needs.[9]

In these same interviews, at the peak of the women's movement, representatives of the four groups that were most closely linked to the women's movement—Women's Lobby, NOW, the NWPC, and WEAL—voiced a set of issue priorities that was far broader than just the ERA and legal equality. Carol Burris, founder and president of Women's Lobby, stated that her group was committed to economically oriented issues. She observed, "You can do more about equality when you have some money."[10]

The head lobbyist for the NWPC, Jane McMichael, was just as emphatic about her group's priorities. The NWPC was created to "overcome the barriers to women in political office."[11] It recruited and funded women candidates for elected office and then worked to help them get good assignments within legislative bodies. The caucus also pressured government officials to appoint qualified women to nonelective positions. McMichael described her work as getting the unique perspective of women brought into political decision making. Women should be represented in government not simply because they are equal but because they are also sufficiently *different* to require representation.

WEAL and NOW were in transition in 1975. WEAL was changing from its former, rather narrow, focus on legal and economic discrimination in education and employment to a much broader range of concerns. Equal rights for women had been central to WEAL's program during its early years, but by the mid-1970s, its agenda had expanded to include abortion, day care, insurance reform, social security, and the problems of women in the military—a mixture of equality and special-needs concerns.[12]

NOW's situation, as the largest women's movement group, is harder to characterize. NOW's dominant issues were the ERA and abortion— one equality and one special-needs issue.[13] In 1974, NOW's interest in the ERA and a factional split within the active membership pushed it to emphasize state and local political activities rather than national lobbying.[14] In late 1975, NOW "consolidated" its three central offices into a new "NOW Action Center" in Washington, D.C. Its fifteen staff employees in the old centers were fired with two weeks' severance pay and the right to apply for five positions in the Action Center. Each of these staff positions, ranging from receptionist to legislative assistant, was to be paid the same as the others. This was intended as a statement that NOW "oppose(s) with equal vigor the gross disparity which exists between the wages of executives and clerical workers."[15] These actions were justified by NOW as a way to strengthen NOW by cutting back on centralization in the national staff.[16] The result was largely to pull NOW out of a leading role in the developing coalition of women's lobbying groups in Washington as its staff was preoccupied with internal organizational conflict and state-level activities. NOW was ardently committed to egalitarian policies, and it focused a great deal of attention on state ratification of ERA. Yet, NOW's other key issue, making abortion available to women, by its nature was not a pure equality issue. Abortion forced the group to recognize that sometimes guarantees of equality were not enough, and it was necessary to respond to the special needs of women.

Based on these interviews as well as a review of newsletters distributed by the four groups in the mid-seventies, none of the groups could be characterized as pursuing an agenda driven exclusively, or even predominantly, by pursuit of legal equality for women. In fact, if a direction can be established for women's groups, it was toward a greater diversity of issues, not a narrower focus. The NWPC and Women's Lobby sought to address directly some of the major problems that women shared—political powerlessness and economic need. NOW and WEAL had agendas that were split between concern for equality

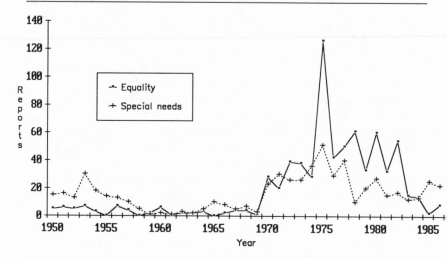

Fig. 4-2. *New York Times* reports featuring equality and special-needs issues.

(including equal access to education for women and the ERA) and an interest in women's special needs (such as continuing legalized abortion and providing government-subsidized child care).

The ERA was the issue, however, that seemed to produce the greatest degree of consensus among women's groups. The greatest number of group representatives (11) reported working on ERA coalitions. However, seven also reported working on abortion and six on child care.[17] Cooperation on the ERA existed among groups as different in membership and organizational style as NOW and the League of Women Voters, not only at the national level but at state and local levels in the unratified states.[18]

In 1975, a dramatic shift began in the balance of *New York Times* coverage of equality for women, in contrast with coverage emphasizing special needs[19] (Fig. 4-2). Before this time, there was a rough parity between equality and special-needs events. Starting in 1975, equality was clearly dominant. This dominance continued until after the final failure of the ERA to win ratification to the U.S. Constitution in 1982.

This turn of events toward equality took place despite issues of equality being more conflict laden than special-needs concerns. Figures 4-3 and 4-4 illustrate the balance of positive and negative coverage these two types of issues received in the press. Far more hostile events were targeted at equality concerns than at special needs. When just ERA events are separated from the general coverage of equality, it becomes clear that much of this controversy over equality was directed toward the ERA. It had become a lightning rod for opponents of the women's movement (Fig. 4-5).

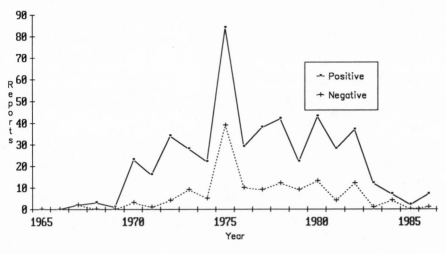

Fig. 4-3. Positive and negative reports on women's equality in the *New York Times.*

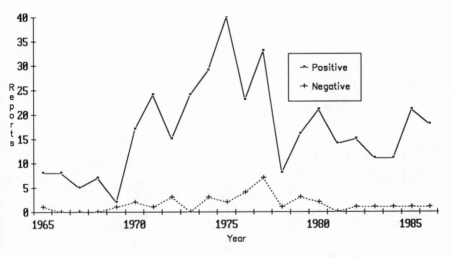

Fig. 4-4. Positive and negative coverage of special needs in the *New York Times.*

Why did this shift come about? Since there is no evidence that the shift away from special needs and toward equality originated in the women's movement, where did it come from? Government seems to be the answer. The contrast in the behavior of women's groups and government in balancing equality and special needs is striking in the seventies. Figure 4-6, based on *New York Times* press coverage, illustrates that in the early seventies, feminists and women's groups were still raising many more special-needs than equality issues. The bal-

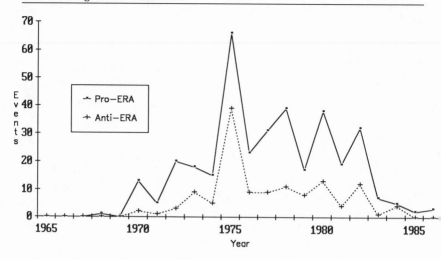

Fig. 4-5. Pro- and anti-ERA events, as covered in the *New York Times.*

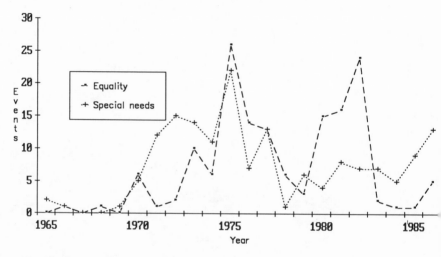

Fig. 4-6. Types of events initiated by the women's movement.

ance between these concerns, evident from interviews with group representatives and from organizational newsletters, is also reflected in the coverage in the *New York Times.*

The government, by contrast, starting in 1970, increasingly began to focus on equality (Fig. 4-7). This emphasis continued through 1984. Figure 4-8 shows the extent to which new laws on women's issues also changed decisively in the Ninety-first Congress (1970–71) from the

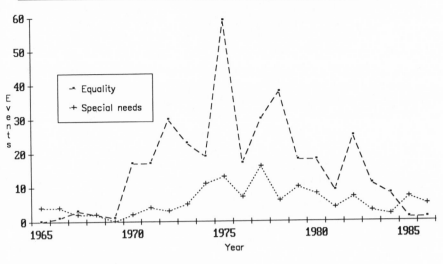

Fig. 4-7. Events initiated by government.

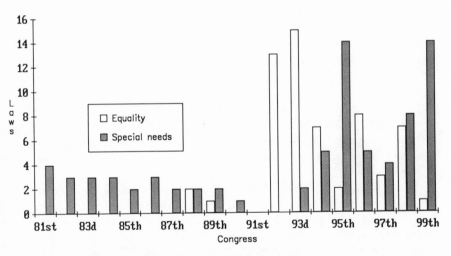

Fig. 4-8. Equality and special-needs laws passed by Congress.

traditional focus on women's special needs to legal equality. Government was first signaling and then acting on its new receptivity to claims of sexual equality. The women's movement, in turn, was gaining more by pursuing its equality than its special-needs agenda, so it is not surprising that by the mid-seventies the movement itself began to initiate more events focusing on equality than on special needs (Fig. 4-2).

As the ERA became the dominant issue in women's rights during the 1970s it seems to have been a reluctant choice of the women's movement, which wanted to balance equality with special-needs concerns. The movement was able to increase public mobilization for women's rights and to sustain pressure on government, spurred on by the ERA victory in Congress in 1972. But until the mid-seventies, the special-needs agenda also commanded the attention of many women's groups. National groups, such as NOW, the NWPC, United Methodist Women, and the American Association of University Women, worked as intensely on child care, rape, and abortion as on the ERA. It was government that by the mid-seventies seems to have tipped the balance decisively in favor of equality issues.

## The Structure of Political Opportunity

The impetus for this focus on equality came from both the executive and legislative branches. Beginning in 1970, the president and Congress first initiated and subsequently reacted far more positively to equality than to special needs. Eight of the eleven recommendations of the President's Task Force on Women's Rights and Responsibilities, issued in 1970, asked for equality not special-needs legislation.[20] Of the legislation passed by Congress that dealt with women as a group, if the annual appropriations for the Women's Bureau in the Labor Department are excluded, thirty-two of the thirty-three new laws enacted between 1963 and 1974 legislated equality, not recognition of women's special needs.[21] This indicates a structure of political opportunity that was highly favorable to equality, less so to women's special needs.

In 1974 and 1975, I interviewed twelve members of the House of Representatives who sat on either the equal opportunities subcommittee of the Committee on Education and Labor or the consumer affairs subcommittee of the Committee on Banking and Currency. Within the previous year, each subcommittee had held hearings on successful bills addressing women's rights—the Women's Educational Equity Act of 1974 and the Equal Credit Opportunity Act of 1974. My objective was not to obtain a representative cross-sample of the opinions of members of Congress on women's issues but rather to elicit the views of, by and large, sympathetic members of Congress who had recently dealt with (and been lobbied on) a women's issue. I interviewed only members of the House, not the Senate, since both these bills passed the Senate as riders to other bills without hearings or detailed legislative consideration. I also interviewed seventeen staff aides and one former aide whom members of Congress or other congressional staffers identified as actively involved with these two bills. These interviews provide a picture of consensus and a certain indifference in Congress toward women's concerns.

Those involved with both the Women's Educational Equity and the Equal Credit Opportunity Acts all agreed that the laws were needed. No one reported opposing either bill. Yet there seemed to be a wide variation in opinion about whether these bills were trivial or very popular with the public. On the Equal Credit Opportunity Act, representatives and congressional staff expressed strong feelings that discrimination against women in granting credit was an easily understood problem that struck most people as unfair and unjust. A number of the members and staff on the consumer affairs subcommittee had either participated in or were familiar with the hearings held in May 1972 by the National Commission on Consumer Finance, where there had been extensive testimony on discrimination based on gender and marital status.

One key staff member recalled the media coverage in these earlier hearings.[22] He described how a leadoff witness was an NBC newscaster in Chicago. She had tried to have her credit cards shifted to her married name, but all her charge accounts were canceled because the companies wanted her husband's name on the cards. Her husband was unemployed because he had just been defeated in the mayoral campaign against Richard Daley. He was the Republican nominee. He also recalled that several women from the Minneapolis Human Rights Commission testified about an experiment in which they sent a man and a woman with comparable jobs, comparable income, comparable marital status—everything was comparable except that one was a man and one was a woman—to various parts of the city to creditors to get loans or buy products on credit. The creditors automatically turned down the woman, but they gave the man credit.

A legislative assistant in a different office recalled a story from the hearings held in Congress two years later. She mentioned writing up this particular case about a woman denied credit to be used in some of the representative's speeches:

> She was making all the money and she was putting her husband through school. The bank wouldn't give her a car loan. She couldn't get a [credit] card with her own name on it and a doctor, a doctor she had been using all of her life, suddenly, after she got married would only address the bills to her husband, referring to her as Item: Judy Ward.[23]

By the time Congress was ready to act, in 1974, business and women's groups supported some legislation. The questions that remained concerned how comprehensive the legislation should be. Would it be limited to gender and marital status or would it also include credit discrimination based on race, color, religion, national origin, and age? Also at issue was how strict the enforcement language would be. Would suits for an entire class be allowed, or punitive damages? Various congressional offices described the legislation in one case as a "motherhood issue" and in another as an issue that attracted little notice back in the district. The dividing line seemed to be primarily economic. In affluent districts, members of Congress received letters from aggrieved constituents who reported that their Lord and Taylor and Saks Fifth Avenue credit cards were canceled when they got married. A representative of a poorer district noted that there was not much political pressure from his constituents to support this bill, but he did it because he thought that a case had been made that it was needed.[24]

Political support for equal credit legislation seemed to stem from the feeling that there was nothing to lose politically by supporting it and potentially a lot to lose by not supporting it. Since press and television coverage had been extensive, many felt that this issue was easily understood by the average voter. The philosophical justification was equally clear: It was based on support for equality between the sexes and nondiscrimination as a principle. As one male Republican member of Congress observed:

> Nobody can logically argue the case [against the legislation]. My argument is that I don't like credit discrimination because basically what you are talking about is [sic] three questions: "How much do you make?" "What do you owe?" and "What are the possibilities of your continuing to make it?" This ridiculous argumentation that a woman can get pregnant and not get her salary. So what? I could get cancer tomorrow. . . . I think that the only difference between men and women is in bed. Other than that it [gender] should be ignored.[25]

Most members of Congress and their aides reported getting their information on this issue from the hearings. They saw the bill as an issue of pure legal equality. Even those individuals who were most skeptical about the seriousness of the issue felt obliged to support it.[26]

Backing for the Women's Educational Equity Act, which provides funds to study discrimination against women in the American educational system and to develop curricular and other means of ending this bias, was also premised on the need for equal treatment of women. Support for this bill was linked both to trust in Representative Patsy Mink (D, Haw.), who was its chief sponsor and a senior member of the Committee on Education and Labor, and to a belief in equal treatment. It was evident that Mink was calling in past favors in exchange for other Congress members' support of this piece of legislation.

The other members of the subcommittee interviewed saw this as an equal rights issue. Since this subcommittee contained a number of the black representatives, including Representatives Henry Clay (D, Mo.), Shirley Chisholm (D, N.Y.), and Augustus Hawkins (D, Ca.), it is not surprising that they understood the issue in terms of equal rights. Somewhat surprisingly, Mink herself viewed the act as more of a special-needs than an equality issue. As she described it in an interview, she, along with a number of women's groups, was concerned about the amount of attention focused on the ERA. Her view was that unless society was educated to view women differently, nothing would change even if the constitutional amendment passed.[27]

Along with Mink, those closest to the process of drafting and passing the bill also saw it as a bill to meet women's special educational needs, as well as providing legal equality. Arlene Horowitz, who had worked for the Education and Labor committee earlier, reported drafting the first version of the bill with the encouragement of Jane McMichael, the lobbyist for the NWPC, as "a women's educational bill."[28] One of Mink's staff assistants, who was in charge of getting the bill out of the joint House/Senate conference committee, described her own difficulties in promoting a bill "which says women right in the title." The assistant concluded that "people [in Congress] are pretty resistant" to legislation directed at women. When she finally managed to extract the bill from committee, an employee of the staff counsel's office called her "a pushy broad."[29]

This bill, even more than the credit bill, was widely accepted as long as its backers downplayed the degree to which it was a "women's bill" and sold it as a bill to alleviate discrimination. As noted above, congressional backing for women's issues in the mid-1970s was grounded in support for legal equality, not for the special needs of women. One prominent liberal Democratic member of Congress, when asked what he believed was the greatest weakness of lobbying by women's groups, replied, "Women's organizations should be more comprehensive in their position. Those groups which testified in the Women's Educational Equity Act [hearings] should talk about equal rights generally, not just the special interest of women."[30] Only one of the people interviewed in the mid-1970s seemed to recognize how controversial even legal equality between the sexes would soon become. A liberal Democratic member of Congress explained: "Women's issues are broader [than business and labor issues]. [Women's groups] lobby on important things—sex discrimination, peace—you know, things where you really have to go out and offend people. Did you know that if the Equal Rights Amendment passes, we will all have to use the same bathroom" (laughs).[31]

The White House was just as strongly focused as the Congress on the issue of equality for women and not women's special needs. At the start of Gerald R. Ford's administration in 1974, discussion of the ERA and legal equality for women increased exponentially. First Lady Betty Ford chose sexual equality and the ERA as "her issues." But, during Ford's first year in office, he also raised these themes far more than Nixon ever had as president. At the start of his presidency, Ford repeatedly endorsed legal equality for women and the ERA. His rhetorical commitment to equality in these days seemed unambiguous. Ford exhorted: "ERA also stands for a new era for women in America, an era of equal rights and responsibilities and rewards" and "One of the most refreshing byproducts of the search to secure rights for women is the emphasis on freeing both sexes from restrictive stereotypes. Liberation of the spirit opens new possibilities for the future of individual Americans and the Nation."[32] In addition, Ford expressed support for federal affirmative action policies and strong enforcement of existing laws that barred discrimination.[33]

When Ford began to face a strong challenge for his party's 1976 presidential nomination from conservative candidate Ronald Reagan, then governor of California, he increasingly stepped away from his earlier ringing support of the ERA. By summer 1975, he responded to a reporter's question at a news conference by answering that he would not join his wife Betty in contacting Illinois state legislators and urging them to vote in the Illinois legislature to ratify the ERA.[34] At the same news conference, when asked how important the issue of sex discrimination would be in his upcoming campaign, he retreated to the traditional presidential reply, citing his appointment of "outstanding women" to serve in the executive branch.[35] When law students at Stanford University asked him in September 1975 if he could match his wife's "ardent support for the equal rights amendment," he replied, "I voted for it in the House of Representatives. I can't do any more than that."[36]

As the Republican convention and the November election neared, Ford said less about sex discrimination, and what he said was cautious concerning his personal commitment on this issue. At a question-and-answer session with the Abilene, Texas, Jaycees, when asked about his feelings concerning equal rights for women, he explained that he voted for it when he was in the House of Representatives so that the states could decide whether or not to accept it.[37] In spring 1976, Ford addressed participants at a legislative conference held by the National

Federation of Business and Professional Women's Clubs, an organization with a long history of strong support for the ERA. He told this gathering that "Betty did ask me to say to all of you that she will be out there in the frontline, as she has been, with all of you on behalf of ERA."[38] The president's only statement about his own position was a story he told about assisting fellow Michigan representative Martha Griffiths in obtaining signatures for the discharge petition, which finally brought the ERA for a vote on the House floor. The nature of Ford's discussion of his work for the ERA—all were references to past activities—was very fitting. Contemporary politics seemed to have cooled his commitment to this issue.

Despite the actions of the First Lady, the Republican party at the presidential level, under pressure from its right wing, was in retreat from the party's long-standing support for the ERA and equality under the law. This progressive Republican retreat seems to have had little impact at the polls, as Ford maintained what was then close to a normal Republican presidential "gender gap" of 6 percent over Democratic challengers.[39]

The presidency of Jimmy Carter that followed from 1976 to 1980 can be characterized by its unprecedented level of presidential commitment to equality for women. Throughout Carter's four years in office, he met frequently with leaders of women's organizations and supporters of the ERA to plan strategy for furthering equal rights for women.[40] Although most of the discussion in these meetings is not reported in Carter's public papers, the initial meeting that Carter held with representatives of women's groups on 10 March, 1977 is an exception. In this meeting in the White House, he urged them to stay in close touch with him and with members of his administration.[41] While expressing hope that the mood of the meeting would be one of "caution" on both sides, Carter sought to start a dialogue that would include "criticism about things we haven't yet done . . . a vision of what we can do, but primarily . . . a recommitment to a partnership. . . . And I've learned from you, and I've got a lot yet to know. But I haven't forgotten for a single hour the need for me and others to correct longstanding discriminatory practices."[42]

Carter was the first president to lobby extensively for the ERA. He not only made numerous speeches and statements on its behalf, expressing enthusiastic support, but phoned state legislators, buttonholed governors of unratified states, asked members of Congress to influence public opinion on behalf of the amendment, and worked to coordinate pro-ERA activity.[43] When the time limit for state legislatures to pass the ERA was about to expire in 1978, Carter worked with women's groups to successfully convince Congress to pass a bill extending the deadline for ratification.[44] Jimmy Carter was also the first U.S. president who could accurately describe the significance of the ERA. In a telephone call-in show on the CBS radio network in March 1977, Carter explained for the first of many times as president that "the equal rights amendment just simply says that the Congress . . . [or] any State are not permitted to discriminate against women."[45]

Unlike most of his predecessors, Carter's interest in women's rights was not peripheral to the broader goals of his presidency. Throughout his tenure in office, he blended support for equal rights for women with key administration themes. Carter frequently justified the need for equal legal treatment of women in terms of his overall commitment to human rights.[46]

In 1980, Carter introduced a new theme, linking passage of the ERA to progress in extending democracy in America. Responding to a question about his personal feelings about the ERA, Carter elaborated on this view at length:

I am strongly in favor of the ratification of the ERA. . . . Since the basic concepts of equality of opportunity were first put forward . . . our Nation has made steady progress in increased democratization of our system, where people, for instance, could directly elect Senators; where women were given the right to vote; where discrimination because of race was wiped from the U.S. Constitution, and guaranteed equality was given there. Women still don't have a guarantee of equal treatment under the U.S. Constitution with men.[47]

It is clear throughout the Carter presidency that legal equality for women, particularly as conferred through constitutional amendment, was what most excited him. He worked long hours and accepted a great deal of political heat in pursuing equality for women.[48] As the 1980 election campaign began in earnest, Carter extended his basic message of the need for legal equality and constitutionally guaranteed human rights for women to include his first mentions of women's special needs. In contrast to equality, this seemed to be less of a central concern to Carter. Although he did not oppose such bills as the Pregnancy Disability Act, neither he nor his administrative aides invested the time or political capital that they did on equality issues.[49]

In his 1980 and 1981 State of the Union addresses to Congress, Carter did claim credit for several of the legislative initiatives passed during his presidency that were responsive to women's special needs. Under a section headed "Special Needs" and the subheading "Women," Carter stated that "programmatic initiatives have been developed to overcome the widespread discrimination and disparities which women have faced in education, in health and in employment."[50]

In describing what had been accomplished in his administration, Carter mentioned that more money was going to the Women's Educational Equity Act to give school boards grants to establish programs to end sex discrimination in education, to family-planning programs, and to teen-pregnancy prevention. He acknowledged that women workers still earned far less than men, but he pointed with pride to improvements in funding for the Women's Bureau of the Department of Labor to train women and to research causes of this inequity. He announced plans to pass legislation to decrease domestic violence and provide shelters for battered spouses.[51] His list of accomplishments to meet women's special needs was similar, although slightly more extensive by the next State of the Union message, in January 1981, as he prepared to turn over the presidency to his successor, Ronald Reagan.[52]

Jimmy Carter as president also had an unparalleled record of appointing women to high-level government posts.[53] From the beginning to the end of his presidency, he was far ahead of his predecessors.[54]

In Carter's last election campaign, he hammered home the view that Ronald Reagan's rejection of the ERA was a drastic break from presidential and Republican party tradition. Once again, women's rights were an integral part of the larger Carter theme that Reagan was a "radical" candidate, who would initiate drastic new directions in government. A sampling of his comments convey their tone:

This [ERA] is not a partisan issue. The first party to include the equal rights amendment in its platform was the Republican Party, 40 years ago. For 40 solid years the Republican party under Eisenhower, Goldwater, Nixon, Ford have always supported the equal rights amendment until this year when Governor Reagan changed it. Six Presidents before me, Ford, Nixon, Johnson, Kennedy, Eisenhower, Truman, have all favored the equal rights amendment. Governor Reagan's opposition to the equal rights amendment is a radical departure from the mainstream of other Presidents and also his own party.[55]

Although Carter managed to reverse the gender gap in the 1980 election, becoming the first Democratic presidential candidate to succeed in winning a noticeably larger proportion (4%) of women's votes than his rival, he lost the election.[56] Consequently, his administration, rather than representing a turning point in visibility and White House support for the cause of the ERA and women's rights, becomes an isolated high point in executive-level backing for women's equality.[57]

Figure 4-9 shows the ebb and flow of activity on women's rights by the executive branch, Congress, and women's groups. Congressional action on the ERA reached its height in 1970 and 1971, the years

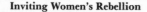

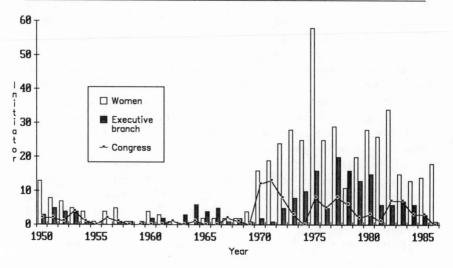

Fig. 4-9. Initiators of ERA events.

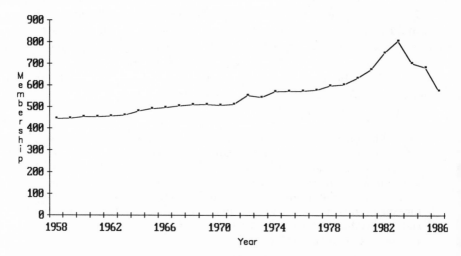

Fig. 4-10. Total membership in selected women's groups (in thousands).

preceding House and Senate passage of the amendment. Then, executive branch involvement jumps in 1974 and remains high through 1980, with just one slack year during this period, in 1976, when the conservative Republican challenge to President Ford's bid for reelection, led by ERA opponent Governor Ronald Reagan, seemed to push the incumbent to deemphasize his commitment to ERA.

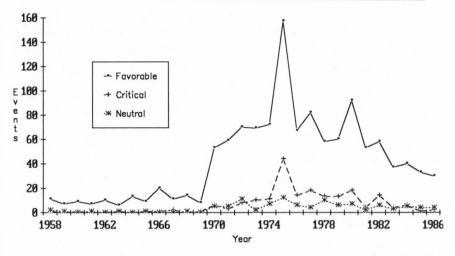

Fig. 4-11. Events dealing with women's rights, as reported in the *New York Times.*

The involvement of women and women's groups with ERA-related events, although more consistent than either the president or Congress, comes relatively late in the political process. It begins to rise in 1970 and remains high through 1986, going up once more in 1982, the last year that ERA ratification could be achieved in the state legislatures. Women and Congress, building on the recommendations of the second Presidential Task Force on Women, helped to put the ERA on the public agenda in 1970. The White House became more involved as congressional interest was flagging. The willingness of key branches of government to facilitate women's equality issues generally, and most notably the ERA, stands in contrast to their handling of special-needs concerns. It is hard to argue that in the 1970s the women's movement and its supporters were offered the same opportunity to promote their special-needs agenda as they were their equality agenda.

## Evidence of a New Group Consciousness

By the mid-1970s, a new consciousness about women's issues had permeated society. For the first time, the "gap" between those who were willing to vote for a woman for president and those who were unwilling had grown to more than 50 percent of the electorate (see Fig. 5-10 in the next chapter). Between 50 and 60 percent of those polled (depending on the wording of the question) favored adding the ERA to the U.S. Constitution.[58] The proportion of women candidates for state legislature jumped from 8 percent to 12 percent.[59] Membership in women's groups was approaching its highest point in twenty-five years (Fig. 4-10). Events data from the *New York Times* show that favorable public responses to women's issues was rising, far outnumbering hostile responses (Fig. 4-11).

Women holding state political offices by the mid-1970s had started to reach the stage that Mueller labels "group" feminism, where they felt a sense of group identification with other women and the women's movement. This led them to work for "women's issues" supported by women's groups, such as the ERA, child care, and abortion.[60]

The most dramatic evidence of new consciousness is the emergence of a gender gap in voting, starting with the 1980 election, in which women disproportionately supported Democratic candidates. Although there are a number of different explanations for the origins of the gap, which is most pronounced among young, single, college-educated, and working women, there is mounting evidence that it reflects heightened group consciousness among women voters.[61] Patricia Gurin, in analyzing three national cross-section sample surveys (1972, 1976, and 1983) carried out by the Institute for Social Research at the University of Michigan, found that gender consciousness among women became stronger in the years following the 1972 survey.[62]

The greatest changes in these years took place in women's assessment of the power men ought to have (most thought it should be less) and in their rising conviction that labor-market disparities between the sexes were illegitimate. There were also increases in the number of women who said they felt "warm" toward the women's liberation movement and in the number of women who reported feeling "close" to women as a group. Although relative to other subgroups, such as blacks, the elderly, and blue collar workers, women's group consciousness was not particularly high, it was growing in apparent response to the activity of the movement. Women were increasingly able to identify structural conditions that limited their opportunities and to see these problems as collective rather than individual.

Another significant dimension to the heightened consciousness of gender concerns among women is the parallel awareness among men that they have had too much political power and women have had too little. Gurin noted that this more "liberal" attitude toward gender issues emerged between the 1976 and 1983 surveys. In addition, virtually all studies of political trends in the 1980s have shown that despite the more conservative political climate, there has been no reversal of attitudes on gender.[63]

# Conclusions

The peak of the women's movement coincides with the high point of media attention to the ERA and a sharply concentrated focus on legal equality as a solution to women's concerns. These issues triumphed over the alternative agenda, which emphasized that women as a group have special needs that government should address, rooted in their biological, physiological, and familial differences from men. This new predominance of equality issues over special needs was less a choice of the women's movement than of the legislative and executive branches of government. Women and women's organizations seem to have split their attention between equality and special-needs issues in the early seventies. In this period, government, by contrast, consistently stressed equality, neglecting special needs. Correspondingly, newspaper coverage of equality and the ERA was far more extensive than of special needs. By the mid-seventies, equality clearly overshadowed all other women's issues. The women's movement, in turn, appears to have responded to favorable government action by shifting to a focus on equal rights, with the ERA as its centerpiece.

This narrowing of the women's rights agenda produced rewards as the movement grew in size during the 1970s. However, the increasingly single-minded focus on passage of the ERA set the stage for a dramatic decline in movement visibility in the 1980s. The movement lost its main issue when ERA failed to win ratification by the 1982 deadline. At that point, with the first president to hold office in nearly forty years who was openly antagonistic to most key women's issues and with their primary issue (the ERA) dead for the foreseeable future, the national women's movement began to fade rapidly.

# 5 Fighting Decline

The women's movement entered a period of decline after the 1980 election. With the exception of 1982, when women's groups and sympathizers initiated a final flurry of lobbying in a desperate attempt to ratify the ERA, there was far less women's rights activity in the 1980s than there had been in the 1970s (Fig. 5-1). Most of the drop-off came because government institutions, along with women and women's groups, were considerably less active in this period and initiated a smaller number of newsworthy events (Fig. 5-2). Efforts to pass the ERA, which had paced the surge in women's events from 1975 to 1982, also led the drop-off in activity once the final deadline for ERA ratification passed in March 1982 (Fig. 5-3). The timing of these trends suggests that first the election of Ronald Reagan and then the defeat of the ERA dealt serious blows to the political aspirations of the women's movement.

## Organizational Stasis

Most national women's groups adopted a defensive posture after Reagan's election. Reagan was the first U.S. president in three decades to oppose the ERA. He was also an outspoken critic of abortion rights. Interviews conducted with Washington representatives of women's movement groups in 1981 and 1984 revealed that most viewed both the political climate of the eighties and the climate with respect to women's rights as very conservative.[1] Yet, this discouragement masked the growing organizational strength of most of these groups. Women throughout the country reacted to the Reagan administration's hostility to issues they favored by swelling the membership of women's groups.[2]

Despite the influx of new people and resources, the group representatives felt that new political gains were unlikely. They cautioned that neither Congress nor the president was any longer willing to initiate bold policy change that benefitted women. Women's groups had to fight just to hang on to past victories. This is best illustrated by the

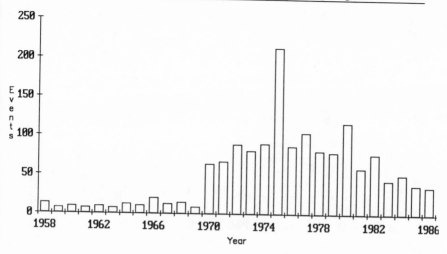

Fig. 5-1. Number of women's events reported in the *New York Times*.

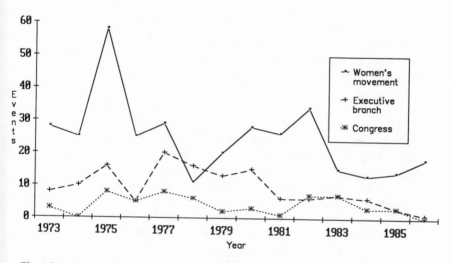

Fig. 5-2. Initiators of events reported in the *New York Times*.

highest profile "women's" issue then before Congress, a "Human Life Amendment" to make most abortions illegal. This amendment would strip women of reproductive rights that had been gained through *Roe v. Wade*, the landmark Supreme Court decision in 1973, which provided constitutional protection for a woman's right to make the choice to have a surgical abortion.[3]

Before Reagan's inauguration as president in 1981, women's groups

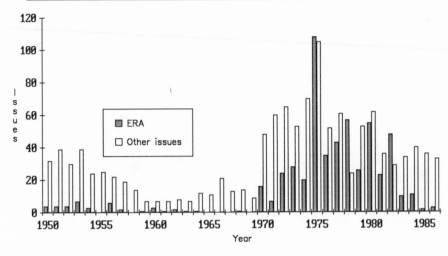

Fig. 5-3. ERA and other women's issues covered in the *New York Times*.

had already scaled back their legislative "wish lists" to fit this new perception of political reality. They agreed that legislation mandating additional domestic spending would be politically impossible to pass. Growing budget deficits and heightened defense expenditures made domestic spending a low priority for Congress and the executive in these years. As a result, it seemed that most women's movement groups working in the capital, with the exception of NOW, had modest legislative hopes for the Ninety-seventh (1981–82) Congress. Carol Bros, lobbyist for the NWPC, was typical of most group representatives in listing the ERA as her group's top priority—with most work to be done in the unratified states.[4] Similarly, she noted that if a human-life amendment, limiting access to abortion, started to gain ground in the new Congress, the NWPC would join the coalition to fight it.

The NWPC's new legislative initiatives included "efforts to clean up the Federal Code (taking out sexist provisions) . . . pension [legislation], insurance [legislation], filling in gaps in civil rights legislation and, of course, a number of straight economic issues."[5] Most of these changes were incremental, not groundbreaking. Efforts would be made to reduce discrimination based on gender in existing laws and to retain funding for programs like those set up under the Women's Educational Equity Act, to reduce sex discrimination in publicly funded educational programs, and the Women, Infants and Children program (WIC), to provide supplemental foodstamps for pregnant and nursing women and their young children. Even with this limited congressional agenda, Bros said that she would be pleased if *hearings* were held to start educating members of Congress about these issues. Patricia Reuss, lobbyist for WEAL, had a similar perspective. She described her position and that of other women's rights lobbyists as one of searching for new congressional leaders to assist them, noting that "our proposals will be more conservative and cost less money."[6] In Reuss's view, "Bills equalizing things can get through," but only because Congress views them as carrying no price tag.[7]

NOW was quite distant from this Washington-centered activity after Reagan's election. Except for anticipating a big effort to oppose a human-life bill in Congress, NOW's vice president for legislation, Jane Wells-Schooley, did not see the organization focusing its attention on national politics or on the Congress. This was not surprising, since NOW's key issues in early 1981 were "ERA, abortion, lesbian and gay rights."[8] Of these, only abortion was likely to command space on the agenda of Congress in this session and that was because *opponents* of abortion were gaining political support. Neither NOW nor any of the pro-choice advocates saw any prospect for increasing access to abortion nationally. They were merely anticipating a defensive fight to safeguard the status quo.

After three years of the Reagan administration, I again interviewed the lobbyists for the active women's movement groups. In 1984 their tone was slightly more confident. They felt that the "gender gap"— that difference in voting behavior between men and women that most often favored Democratic candidates—was making it easier for them to talk to members of Congress. Journalists and scholars first observed and labeled the gender gap in the 1980 election, but not until its continued presence in the 1982 congressional races *and* the 1984 presidential contest did most politicians begin to take it seriously. Members of Congress seemed to realize, at this rather late date, that women were a voting bloc that might aid or harm their chances for reelection. The emergence of women as a distinct political constituency in the 1980s, for virtually the first time since 1920 when women got the right to vote, made it easier for women's groups to obtain a hearing on "women's issues" in Washington. Yet, the political climate of the eighties made it difficult, nonetheless, to get these issues passed into law.

Assessments of legislative progress by lobbyists for women's groups were, on balance, still gloomy in 1984. Patricia Reuss of WEAL observed that "there have not been that many accomplishments [in the first session of the 98th Congress]."[9] She noted that there was a lot of bipartisan discussion of the issues, as members of the House and Senate competed with one another to hold hearings and claim leadership. She expressed the view that the Reagan administration's actions were even less favorable than Congress's. Reuss noted that "in 'Talking Points' [a pamphlet distributed by the White House], the administration takes credit for legislation passed [earlier] during his administration which they opposed. . . . For example, they mention job training when the administration cut almost all CETA programs helping women and flex-time [flexible working times for employees of the federal government] which Reagan opposed."[10]

Only the political presence of an electoral gender gap replaced the leverage that a more conservative Congress and White House had taken away. Catherine East, legislative director of the NWPC, expressed the view that women's groups would not have won any legislative victories in 1984 if it had not been for the "gender gap."[11] Ann Smith, director of the Congressional Caucus for Women's Issues, a group within Congress that works to coordinate legislative information on women's issues, observed that the gender gap had become "the basic mechanism that powers the whole thing."[12]

Despite disagreement among scholars[13] about whether the gender gap emerged as a result of women's reaction to Reagan's stands against the ERA and abortion, or because traditional male/female differences over issues of war and peace and "compassion" became more focused and party-centered in this period, women's group representatives expressed a holistic view of the gap. Patricia Reuss explained that "the gender gap is not card-carrying NOW and WEAL members. The gender gap is women who are concerned with jobs, fairness, inflation, employment, social security, school lunch programs . . . not just women's issues. There is a real cause and effect which we have to communicate to members of Congress. We have to teach them that there are women in their districts who care about these issues."[14] Catherine East attributed the emergence of a gender gap in voting to a variety of causes, starting with the policies of President Reagan.

> There is a widespread perception that he [Reagan] lives in the past. Many of the attitudes that he and his aides express reinforce this impression. All that discussion [by Reagan] of poverty and the poor could have been out of a different century. The peace issue is a major one, with Reagan getting us into Grenada and Lebanon. The ERA [is an important issue]. A pro-choice position on abortion with the administration opposed to reproductive freedom. There is certainly a general unease among women in this country today. It is not necessarily feminist, but it is a feeling of woman's subservient relation to many of the events that are going on around them.[15]

Ann Smith's analysis of the gender gap paralleled that of the others. She described the gender gap as representing a new collective aware-

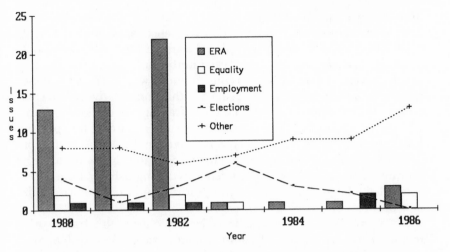

Fig. 5-4. Issues raised by women and women's groups, reported in the *New York Times*.

ness among women that certain types of problems were not being handled satisfactorily in Washington.[16]

Despite the political importance attributed to the gender gap, the representatives of most groups felt that change in the states and localities was outpacing national action in the eighties. The brightest future of feminism seemed to lie at the grass roots. The growth of women's studies programs, caucuses of women in professional associations and labor unions, along with groups of women, organized and unorganized, in schools and workplaces on guard against sexism, meant that women were becoming more knowledgeable and politically aware.[17] Scholars, including Ruth Mandel, agreed that the women's movement was diffusing. She observed that "it is spread, assimilated and incorporated throughout society at various levels and [has] become part of the social fabric."[18]

The decade of the eighties was a varied one for women organizationally. Although national women's groups were able to increase their memberships in the early eighties as a result of the new conservative political reality in national politics, most groups seemed to lack a unifying vision of what could be accomplished to further their cause. They were united in their determination to fight rollbacks in gains they had already made—most notably in abortion rights—but had few other sweeping political goals (Fig. 5-4). By contrast, the women's movement was spreading organizationally, as more and more groups continued to form on state and local levels.

By the mid-1980s, a new perspective had begun to emerge, grounded

in the gender gap. Washington feminists were starting to realize that
women throughout the country with experiences as wage earners and
heads of households were developing a sense of their own needs and
priorities that most women had lacked in the past. Most Washington-
based women's lobbyists were trying to find a way to translate these
women's concerns into a political agenda that conservative politicians
might support. Slowly and by taking advantage of the gender gap,
women's movement groups turned back to and reclaimed the special-
needs agenda that they had largely abandoned in the seventies in favor
of the massive push for equality. This recognition that women are a
unique group politically, with preferences distinguishable from other
voters, led lobbyists for women's groups to attempt to give voice to this
new political presence in Washington.

NOW, by contrast, was operating largely outside this framework,
retaining its own agenda of feminist issues (the ERA, abortion, and
gay and lesbian rights), despite the apparent political futility of this
effort. NOW similarly departed from the other groups with its pre-
nomination endorsement of Democratic presidential candidate Walter
Mondale in 1984. By this action, the group moved from the bipartisan
posture shared by most women's groups to aggressive involvement in
partisan politics. NOW's relatively extreme set of political demands
seemed to open doors for the other women's groups, as politicians (and
particularly liberal and moderate Republicans) sought to avoid NOW
but to keep contact with less radical women's organizations.

By 1989, NOW engineered another radical departure from most feminist groups, urging the abandonment of both the Democratic and
Republican parties and the formation of a third, "women's" party.
Although the NWPC immediately labeled this idea impractical, it, in
fact, moved NOW in the direction already taken by other groups,
which were looking for an ongoing voice to continue representing
women's political interests and views. Characteristically for NOW, the
organization's action came in a manner that gave increased leverage
to moderate women's groups that seemed more "reasonable" to most
politicians.

NOW's advocacy gave a strong voice to issues that others were no
longer eager to emphasize as well as to new issues that were too daring
for most to espouse. Press coverage of NOW events dwarfed that of
other women's groups during this period of the movement's decline
(Fig. 5-5). Particularly after the defeat of the ERA, NOW's sharp
rhetoric and skill in attracting the attention of the press combined to
make it the major voice of the women's movement, although it was no
longer a prominent force on Capitol Hill.

A sample of *New York Times* coverage of NOW activities in the years immediately following the ERA's defeat suggests the flavor of NOW's political involvement. In 1983, the *New York Times* reported that NOW had ended its six-year boycott of the state of Florida over its failure to ratify the ERA; formed "Women's Truth Squad on Reagan" to monitor the impact of Reagan administration policies; held a news conference on how to defeat President Reagan in the 1984 election; sent three hundred people to protest outside the White House; staged a news conference featuring Barbara Honegger, who resigned from the U.S. Department of Justice after working on the president's project to eliminate sex discrimination in federal and state laws, which she called "a sham"; and criticized Reagan's proposals to eliminate sexually discriminatory language in the law.

By contrast, 1984 was a very low-key year for NOW. The organization sponsored events that included celebrating Susan B. Anthony's birthday; giving Susan B. Anthony awards to grass-roots activists; holding a rally on Women's Equality Day; and listing the major advances and setbacks for women's rights during the year. In 1985, New York NOW held a conference on economic equity. The national office of NOW sponsored a large rally on Women's Equality Day; announced plans for a "militant" new campaign to counter the "fascist right" in America; experienced a contentious race between Eleanor Smeal and Judith Goldsmith for its presidency; and held its annual conference. In 1986, the *Times* reported that NOW was organizing support for the Civil Rights Restoration Act, then being considered by Congress; held twentieth-anniversary celebrations of NOW's founding in Washington, D.C., and in Los Angeles; asked for a recount in Vermont's defeat of a state ERA and demanded a new vote; published a state-by-state guide to women's rights; increased the number of men holding NOW leadership positions; held a national convention; and announced a renewal of the fight to pass the ERA.

NOW's quiet years in 1984 and 1985 coincide with Judith Goldsmith's leadership of the organization. When Eleanor Smeal broke with Goldsmith in 1985 and regained the presidency of NOW, the group returned to its more strident, confrontational style of political action. This style put NOW back in the papers, but the shift left the organization in debt and with a membership that had shrunk from more than 230,000 in 1983 to 150,000 in 1986.[19] Smeal and Goldsmith blamed each other for this predicament. Smeal charged that Goldsmith had failed to energize the organization. Goldsmith held that the internal conflict and bad feelings generated by Smeal led to the loss of members. Whichever version of events is more accurate, the membership did rise again by the end of the decade. NOW's increase in membership and boost in funding are largely the result of the U.S.

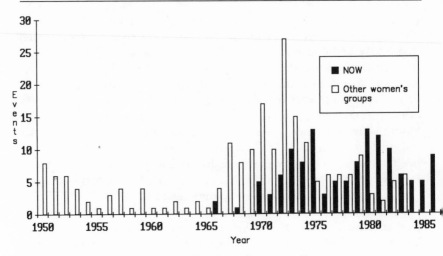

**Fig. 5-5. News events initiated by NOW and all other women's groups.**

Supreme Court handing down the *Webster v. Reproductive Health Services* decision in 1989.[20] The high court's attack on abortion rights in the *Webster* case reenergized supporters of the pro-choice position. They joined groups promoting this view, including NOW, in large numbers. As the eighties progressed, NOW remained the most outspoken as well as the most visible women's movement group in America. The other groups kept a lower profile as they continued to push for political gains in Washington.

## Shrinking Political Opportunities

As the organized women's movement groups recognized, there were no longer obvious opportunities to expand women's rights in Washington. Polls showed that President Reagan was relatively unpopular with women in the electorate, but he was very popular with men. Reagan made a number of public appeals to women, particularly during his first term. He handled women's concerns as a separate category of issues within his administration. Many felt that his focus was narrow and largely symbolic, with few concrete proposals to improve women's circumstances or respond to their problems. President Carter's programs for women, by contrast, were a part of the administration's ongoing theme of expanding human rights. Carter saw the second-class status of women in America, legally and politically, as compromising his hope that the United States could be a true model of freedom and individual rights throughout the world.

Reagan saw women's status more ambiguously. He recognized that discriminatory laws made the United States look bad abroad. But, in general, he felt that these laws could be rewritten without producing much political controversy or seriously changing the way that society operated. Reagan also resurrected the traditional White House strategy of appointing women, including some with prominent public profiles, to government posts, giving the impression that the administration was sensitive to both eliminating employment discrimination based on gender and listening to what politically active women had to say.

Although Reagan was opposed to the ERA, he did not go out of his way to debate or antagonize those who disagreed with him on this issue. His reasons for opposing the ERA were never very clearly articulated. In an interview with Ann Devroy, a reporter for the Gannett News Service, on 24 August, 1983, he explained his opposition to the ERA in the following way:

> I'm surprised that more of them [women] have not looked at how much mischief could be done, brought about by men, they could take advantage of that [ERA] and then say, "Hey, you can't make me do this because, labor regulations and so forth," that are definitely there for the benefit of women. I could see some troublemaking men, mischiefmakers just saying, "Well, look, I don't have to do that." The same would be true militarily. . . . It would put things in the hands of the courts that belong in the hands of the legislature.[21]

Reagan was clearly disturbed that certain legislation put in place to protect women or to create male-only draft registration could be overturned by the courts if the ERA were added to the Constitution. Since most "protective" labor laws for women became invalid after the Civil Rights Act of 1964 was implemented, it is difficult to believe that the president still thought that women in the eighties might lose extra sitdown breaks or heavy lifting exemptions. These were already long gone. It is more likely that Reagan was reacting to a right-wing agenda that was opposed to the ERA. As president, Reagan frequently was asked and spoke about the ERA, often, as above, in a confused fashion.

Reagan's public posture toward abortion was very different. He spoke many times about abortion and his opposition to it. His major theme, reiterated during his eight years in office, was that the key to resolving the abortion controversy is determining when human life begins. His often-repeated view was that until it could be proved scientifically that fetuses were not alive, the Declaration of Independence's guarantee of the right to "life, liberty and the pursuit of happiness" made abortion a serious violation of American values and consequently a practice that the law should prohibit.[22] The sole exception, in

Reagan's view, was when the mother's life was physically endangered. In that circumstance, abortion could be justified as self-defense by the mother.

Reagan's only other abortion "theme" was the suffering caused to the aborted fetus. Starting in January 1984, in a speech before the annual convention of the National Religious Broadcasters, the president began to cite physicians' findings that taking the life of an unborn fetus produces "pain that is long and agonizing."[23] Despite having this conclusion challenged by medical authorities, the president continued to speak of the unnecessary suffering caused by abortion.[24] He occasionally acknowledged that his views were controversial and that the decision to have an abortion was an extremely difficult one for the individual involved. Yet his conclusion remained, "With regard to this [abortion] being a personal choice, isn't that what a murderer is insisting on, his or her right to kill someone."[25]

Reagan's record on abortion was both more activist and less compromising than his stand on equality for women. He pointed with pride to his support of the Hyde amendments passed by Congresses in the late seventies and early eighties to stop federal funds from being spent on surgical abortions. He instructed the Department of Health and Human Services to explore ways to deny funds to clinics and counseling centers where abortion was presented as an option in the case of unwanted pregnancies. He also worked with abortion opponents in Congress to deny foreign aid to family-planning programs abroad that furnished abortions.[26] Finally, through the Department of Justice and public statements, he urged reversal of *Roe v. Wade*.[27]

There is a marked contrast between the president's fairly conciliatory tone on equal rights and his hard-line attitude on abortion. Reagan's official women's equality program was in place by 1981. His administration gave the highest profile to his effort to eliminate discriminatory statutes in state and federal laws. This was modeled on his California program where, as governor, he had eliminated by executive order or through legislation fourteen state statutes that discriminated against individuals on the basis of gender. As president, Reagan set up the Task Force on Legal Equality for Women, whose job was to search federal laws and find those that treated men and women differently on the basis of gender. He also organized the Fifty States Project for Women, which was supposed to identify state laws that were discriminatory. The object was to notify governors of the existence of these discriminatory statutes so that they could take steps to eliminate them.

These projects were surrounded by controversy from the beginning, as the Reagan administration promoted them as ER (equal rights) without the A (constitutional amendment) and women's groups such as NOW branded them as meaningless and cosmetic. At the same time, some conservatives complained that these "discriminatory" laws actually helped women. Anger among feminists peaked when Barbara Honegger, the Justice Department employee assigned to work on these programs, resigned in protest in 1983, saying that the projects were not really designed to eliminate legal discrimination against women.

The second part of Reagan's program focused on political appointments for women. From the start of his administration, the president returned to a traditional emphasis of chief executives, stressing the number of women he was appointing to government posts. In September 1981, Reagan asserted that "in spite of the mistaken notions [that] we are somehow lagging in women appointments [sic], the truth is just the opposite. After 8 months in office, we have selected as many women to serve in top policy-making posts as the previous administration had at the end of the first entire year."[28] In describing his administration's concern for women, Reagan regularly referred to his groundbreaking appointment in 1981 of Sandra Day O'Connor as the first woman to sit as a justice on the U.S. Supreme Court.

In 1982, the president spoke frequently about the committees he had set up and charged with eliminating unjust sex discrimination in the law.[29] He suggested that these groups were doing work that would go far to end legal discrimination against women in America. He also issued a conciliatory statement to backers of the ERA on the day the amendment went down to defeat.

I don't think that the effort [to win ratification of the ERA] was wasted because they didn't get the constitutional amendment. The only debate has been over the method of eliminating or erasing discrimination. . . . But in those 10 years, I think that their effort has brought to the attention of the people this problem. I know it did for me when I was Governor to the extent that in California we found 14 statutes that did discriminate. And we eliminated those 14 statutes or altered them.[30]

By 1983, Reagan was regularly confronted with questions about the gender gap, including why women did not like him politically. In his public statements, he continued to discuss the administration's work in eliminating sexist statutes and appointing women to high office. But at this point in his administration, with the election campaign fast approaching, he suddenly began to introduce other themes as well. He borrowed some lines from Jimmy Carter in the last election, citing the historically strong record of the Republican party in supporting women's rights. While Carter had emphasized Reagan's break with the Republican party's history of support for women's rights, Reagan began to stress the *continuity* between his administration and the Republican tradition of advocating equality for women. In his State of the Union message and throughout 1983, Reagan began to float a variety of new policies that he hoped might raise his support among women. In the State of the Union address, he asserted,

> Our commitment to fairness means that we must assure legal and economic equity for women, and eliminate, once and for all, all traces of unjust discrimination against women from the United States Code. We will not tolerate wage discrimination based on sex, and we intend to strengthen enforcement of child support laws to ensure that single parents, most of whom are women, do not suffer unfair financial hardship. We will also take action to remedy inequities in pensions. These initiatives will be joined by others to continue our efforts to promote equity for women.[31]

In four separate gatherings of women throughout the year, Reagan continued to test public response to specific policies toward women, claiming credit for eliminating estate taxes for surviving spouses; reducing the "marriage penalty" in the income tax; increasing allowable Individual Retirement Accounts (IRAs) for working wives inside and outside the home; toughening federal enforcement of child support; raising the child-care credit; creating the Task Force on Family Violence; expanding training opportunities for women recipients of Aid to Families with Dependent Children; extending flexible work hours for federal employees; and remedying inequities in workers' pensions.[32]

Reagan's efforts in 1983 illustrate some of the problems he had in appealing to women. When addressing the annual convention of the National Federation of Business and Professional Women's Clubs, he was genuinely puzzled that women in this group, as well as women nationally, took offense when he observed that "we have been doing a number of things here with regard to the thing of great interest to you, and that is the recognition of women's place. I want you to know I've always recognized it, because I happen to be one who believes if it wasn't for women, us men would still be walking around in skin suits carrying clubs."[33] Three weeks later, he was still asserting that he really believed that women were the great civilizers of humanity.[34] Women's responses that they wanted to be freed from this kind of outmoded, stereotyped thinking about their sex seemed to puzzle the president. Reagan, more than any president since Nixon, seemed to be out of touch with the aspirations of modern women. He clearly wanted to say something that would please them but was at a loss about what to say.

In 1984, leading up to the national election, Reagan held nine separate meetings with groups of Republican women elected officials—
an unprecedented number during his administration. He made a concerted effort at these meetings to present his administration as actively
engaged in advancing women's interests. He accused Democrats, the
press, and women's groups of making his strong support of equality
for women a "well-kept secret." Clearly, he was using these meetings
to enlist relatively sympathetic women candidates and officeholders to
spread a positive message about what his administration had done for
women. At these gatherings, he continued the theme that the Republican party had historically advanced women's rights more than the
Democratic party and that his administration, despite its opposition
to the ERA, was following in this long tradition. Finally, he emphasized his record of appointing large numbers of women to high-level
posts and his initiation of legislation to give women equality of
opportunity.

After Reagan's reelection in 1984, there was again a drop-off in his
involvement with women and women's issues. In 1985, the president
hosted just two lunches for Republican women elected officials. His
remarks on these occasions, like the preelection gatherings, included
summaries of the administration's actions that were particularly beneficial to women. But, in the postelection gatherings, he mentioned few
specific policies and instead put more emphasis on the overall achieve-
ments of his administration. Reagan also talked to the U.S. delegation
to the United Nations (U.N.) Conference on Women in 1985, which
was led by his daughter Maureen, before their departure for the U.N.
conference in Nairobi, Kenya. After joking about the meeting feeling
like a "family affair," Reagan endorsed the four issues that the delegation had chosen to pursue: women's literacy, women in development, domestic violence against women and children, and the plight
of refugee women and children. The president warned the delegates
that "the business of this conference is women, not propaganda" but
then went on to exhort them, "You, as Americans, will have a powerful story to share. For in our land of political and economic freedom,
women take part in virtually every aspect of the life of our nation."[35]
That year, he issued three proclamations marking Women's History
Week, Women's Equality Day, and Women Veteran's Recognition Day.

The only substantive women's issue with which the president was
involved this year was the congressional effort to overturn the Supreme Court's decision in the *Grove City College* case. In this case, the
Supreme Court held that only the college's programs that were direct
recipients of federal money had to comply with laws that prohibited
discrimination. The president had his deputy press secretary, Larry

Speakes, issue a statement announcing that the administration favored legislation introduced by the majority leader of the Senate, Robert Dole (R, Kan.), that would reverse *Grove City* by guaranteeing that any educational institution that received federal financial assistance would have to comply with existing antidiscrimination law in all its educational programs and activities.[36] This was a bill to insure equality of opportunity and reduce sex discrimination in education, but it was also a bill that was less sweeping in the protection it extended than alternatives offered by the Democratic party, which included corporations, small businesses, and other private organizations as well as educational institutions. When legislation that was closer to the Democratic than the Republican version passed in Congress, the president vetoed it. Congress subsequently overrode the president's veto of this bill.

In 1986, there was a steep fall-off in presidential involvement with women's issues. The only public actions on women's issues were delivering comments at a State Department reception honoring Maureen Reagan for leading the American delegation to the U.N. conference on women and issuing proclamations marking Women's History Week, American Business Women's Day, Women Veteran's Recognition Week, and Women's Equality Day. Reagan's remarks at the State Department's reception for Maureen Reagan have a more paternal than political tone. He observed that "as I said, it's always a little bit of a surprise for a father . . . to realize that that's your daughter up there on the TV screen, not only a grown woman—and I'm not that old yet—but a leader, a mover, someone who is making the world a whole lot better place to live."[37]

Without the possibility and pressure of running for reelection in 1988, 1987 was a year with only symbolic acts by the president on women's issues. He issued proclamations marking National Women in Sports Day and Women's History Month. In 1988, these two proclamations were again his only official acts on women's issues.

As this review of the president's public actions suggests, Reagan's interest and involvement in women's issues became especially salient before the 1984 election. This was part of the reelection strategy for the president. Richard Wirthlin conducted a poll for the White House that divided women into sixty-four subgroups based on age, marital status, and employment. Advertising and direct mailings were targeted toward those subgroups that were most supportive of Reagan. The most pro-Reagan group consisted of young working women and was code-named "Alice." The least favorable groups such as "Helen," young unemployed women, were ignored.[38] Supplementing this activity, 17,000 women were kept up to date with mailings on ad-

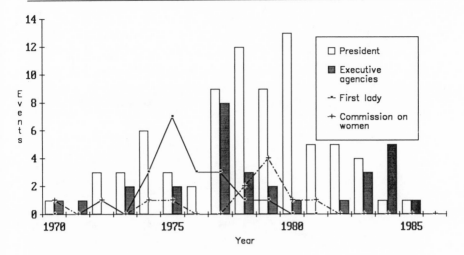

Fig. 5-6. Executive branch initiators of women's events.

ministration actions oriented toward women, a sixty-five-member speaker's bureau promoted the president's reelection, explaining how Reagan's economic program had benefitted women, and "Fact Sheets" from the Republican National Committee stressed favorable administration positions on women's issues.[39] The administration, including the president, worked hard (and successfully) to capture a majority of women's votes in the 1984 election.

With the exception of this brief period, however, Reagan limited most of his actions on women's issues (except abortion) to the ceremonial level. President Carter had met every few weeks with representatives of women's organizations in the White House. There is no evidence in public records that Reagan as president ever met with these groups. Executive branch initiatives, in general, declined steadily during this period. Not only the president but also his family and aides did little to promote women's issues (Fig. 5-6). The most dramatic drops in executive-level activity on women's issues came from the First Lady and the Presidential Commission on the Status of Women. In the six years covered in this study, Nancy Reagan initiated no news events dealing with women's issues and the presidential commission sponsored only one. The balance between positive and negative or ambiguous actions by the president that the press reported was far closer than in the past, when most presidential acts were supportive of women's issues (Fig. 5-7). The White House had moved from a publicist, ally, and sometimes cheerleader for women's rights in the Ford and Carter years to a cautious observer, offering periodic justifications for its

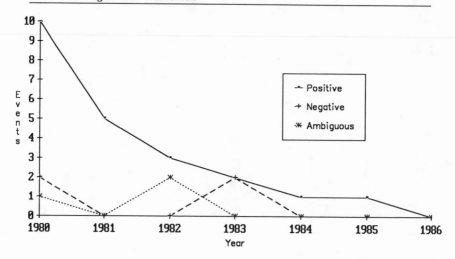

Fig. 5-7. Events initiated by the President, as reported in the *New York Times*.

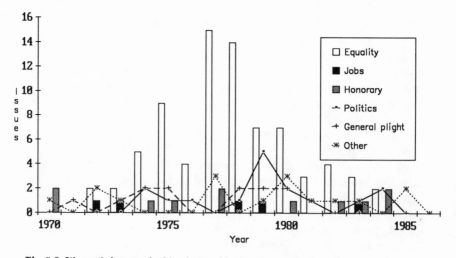

Fig. 5-8. Women's issues raised by the President and executive branch.

inaction along with preelection rhetoric to attract women's votes.

Unsurprisingly, the substance of White House involvement with women's issues also changed during the Reagan presidency. Discussion of gender equality faded from the limelight as honorary events, appointments of women to political posts, and other women's issues drew greater attention (Fig. 5-8).

Only Congress seemed relatively unchanged. Since the level of legis-

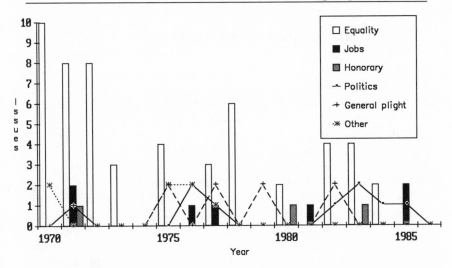

Fig. 5-9. Women's issues raised by Congress.

lative activity was so low on women's issues anyway, the fact that congressional interest did not sink further did little to reverse the momentum of decline (Fig. 5-9). Equality continued to be Congress's major focus when considering women's issues, as it had been throughout the last two decades. Women's political participation and electoral role were more often the subject of discussion in Congress in the 1980s than earlier, but there is no indication from these events that Congress was assuming a leading role on women's issues.

The structure of political opportunity faced by women in the 1980s was, in most respects, even more daunting than it had been in the sixties. The only time women's groups seemed to have been assured of a hearing from government was during the preelection period. There did not seem to be a coherent political agenda on women's issues coming out of either the White House or Congress. With the rejection of the ERA, there was no longer a flagship issue that united feminists and provided direction for the future. The most visible issues remaining were the defensive struggle to keep abortion available as an option for women who could afford to exercise it and a patchwork of efforts to improve the economic lot of single parents and other women who may be left destitute after divorce or widowhood. It is little wonder that representatives of most women's groups felt that without the presence of the gender gap in voting, they would be excluded from the political process in the 1980s.

## The Durability of Psychological Change

In the face of a women's movement that was divided and without clear direction and a government that was no longer eager to champion women's issues, public opinion remained surprisingly supportive of women's rights. This was all the more remarkable since the overall rise in conservative political attitudes that characterized the eighties failed to carry over to public opinion toward women. Egalitarian views on gender roles continued to gain strength throughout the population, but particularly among the young.[40]

Social science survey results show that the public was increasingly willing to endorse a larger political role and greater legal rights for women. This shift began in the sixties and carried into the late eighties. At the end of the sixties, just over half the public said it was willing to vote for a qualified woman presidential candidate. By the late seventies, this number had reached 80 percent, growing to 85 percent of the public by the late eighties (Fig. 5-10). Also, increasing proportions of women and men said that the country would be better off if women had more of a say in politics.[41] The Virginia Slims American Women's Opinion Poll revealed that by 1985, 73 percent of women and 69 percent of men favored "most of the efforts to strengthen and change women's status in society."[42] Several National Opinion Research Council (NORC) public opinion surveys in the late eighties revealed that young adults—women and men from 18 to 24—while somewhat more positive about Reagan and the Republican party than the population as a whole were also more favorable to gender equality than the general population. These youthful citizens were similarly more egalitarian in their attitudes than young adults had been in the seventies.[43]

The acceptance of a larger role for women in society and politics was matched by a new understanding of gender disparity. By 1983, both men and women were adopting a more structural attitude toward gender differences, concluding that the *system* discriminates against women.[44] This condition is highly conducive to the growth of a social movement. Women as a group and society as a whole had adopted the view that most women's problems are collective, rather than individual, and that women should use the political process to resolve them.

An eighteen-year panel study reinforced the view that attitudes toward women are liberalizing.[45] This study showed that there was more support in 1980 among women and men for nontraditional roles for women than there had been in 1977. Although panelists were generally more conservative than in the seventies, their political views had little effect on attitudes toward sex discrimination. Similarly, new

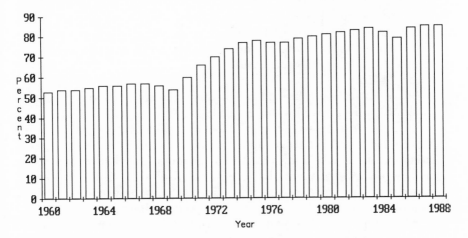

Fig. 5-10. Percentage of the public willing to vote for a woman president.

patterns of dividing work between men and women drew increasing approval from men and women in the panel.

Although both social science survey results and ongoing panel studies agree that public attitudes are becoming more supportive of nontraditional roles for women and ending sex discrimination, there is less consensus about the role played by the women's movement and broad social changes in this process. Isolated pieces of evidence suggest that the women's movement was a factor contributing to this attitudinal shift. Welch and Sigelman noted that support for a woman president in 1978 had become particularly strong among individuals who were more educated, younger, and less frequent church attenders.[46] According to this perspective, rather than diffusing throughout the population, the issues of the women's movement were taking root in clearly identifiable bases of support. This suggests a mobilization pattern more akin to movement growth, where particular subgroups in the population become heavily involved with a set of issues, rather than a more common pattern, in which opinion spreads more or less randomly through a population.

Since supporters of egalitarian attitudes toward women's political involvement are from groups that, at least in terms of their youthful age and high level of education, are becoming increasingly numerous in the population, the long-term prospect for the movement to increase its influence looks bright. As this age cohort gets older, it is likely that its members will retain these views and become even more active politically. From the other direction, Welch and Sigelman discovered that the movement's major opponents are increasingly the aged, less educated, and more religiously active non-Catholics in the population. As members of this group continue to age and lose members to infirmities and death, they will become a diminishing political force.

Susan Carroll went beyond Welch and Sigelman's cautious conclusions about the role of the movement to argue that the women's movement fostered these attitudinal shifts evident in surveys by contributing to accelerating changes in women's lives (including increasing access to higher education and employment outside the home, as well as new patterns of family life).[47] Carroll also credited the women's movement with raising women's feelings of autonomy, consequently making it easier for them to assert their political interests.

Although there is not yet definitive evidence that the women's movement is causing this significant shift in public opinion, nontraditional, egalitarian attitudes toward women are continuing to attract support among the population generally, but particularly among young people, which suggests that there may again be gains to be made by a reinvigorated women's movement. The conservative political configuration in the late 1980s and early 1990s, along with the lack of a clear direction in the women's movement, have virtually halted victories in the legislative and executive branch that characterized the 1970s. But the strength of public support for women's rights, along with the increasing sophistication of women as a voting bloc, may yet give the movement another chance to pursue its broad goal of a more egalitarian society where women's voices are heard and responded to within the political system.

## Conclusions

The downfall of the ERA and the success of the Reagan administration in moving women's rights from an active to a largely symbolic agenda item left groups within the women's movement in a state of disarray. Most groups tried to pursue women's issues that were acceptable to conservatives, while they constructed a new post-ERA agenda that would both attract and reflect the types of experiences that the women comprising the gender gap in electoral voting (working women, those who are single or divorced, and women under 30) wanted to see addressed by political leaders. These issues, including affordable, high-quality child care, access to legal abortions, and equitable pay and working conditions, drew heavily on the so-called special-needs agenda that movement groups had shifted away from in the mid-seventies in their enthusiasm for the ERA. In the eighties, NOW pursued its own direction, largely boycotting national politics while championing the ERA, abortion rights, a national women's party, and gay and lesbian issues.

In the eighties and nineties, partisans in the Democratic and Republican parties have engaged in sometimes heated debate over the desirability of new policies on child care, parental leave, women's combat exclusion in the military, government regulation of abortion, prenatal care, and legal protection against gender and race discrimination in employment. Many of these issues have and will continue to surface in election campaigns. In the 1989 off-year elections, Democratic gubernatorial candidates Douglas Wilder in Virginia and James Florio in New Jersey seemed to benefit electorally from supporting the liberal side of the abortion debate. President George Bush has increasingly positioned the Republican party on the conservative side of most of these issues, vetoing congressional efforts to strengthen laws that bar employment discrimination and to make it possible for poor women, in certain circumstances, to obtain publicly funded abortions. Bush criticizes other legislation on parenting and child care as either too costly or too great an interference with the private sector. Bush's selection of Clarence Thomas as his new nominee for the U.S. Supreme Court in summer 1991 continued the Republican party's posture of opposition to abortion rights and affirmative action policies. Approaching the 1992 presidential election, the Republican party seems positioned to concede a gender-gap advantage to Democrats, undoubtedly hoping that what the party gives up in women's votes, it will gain in votes from white males.

Examining the development of the contemporary women's movement over time, it seems evident that the movement is about to enter a new phase. Unlike the 1960s, the movement now enjoys solid popular support, which is particularly concentrated among young, well-educated voters. Although the intensity, creativity, and passion of the early movement are now largely gone, women are in the process of converting their organizations, resources, and new political sophistication into a voting bloc. This bloc, accompanied by lobbying pressure, has the potential to bring about future gains for women as a social and economic group.

Although the current condition of the women's movement is one of decline combined with the prospect for future growth, it is important to note that many options were not taken during the movement's almost twenty-five-year existence. In the next chapter, the relationship between the movement and the government during these decades is traced, with an examination particularly of the extent to which the movement allowed the government to set its political agenda.

# 6 If Government Gives, Can It Also Take Away?

Government played a key role in determining the course of the American women's movement. New governmental policies toward women began to be introduced just as the first stirrings of a new women's movement were heard. In the early 1960s, Congress and the president competed to lead public opinion on women's issues, but soon a mobilized women's movement and a public whose opinion was shifting forced government to respond to their initiatives as well. President Kennedy and many members of Congress battled each other over support of legislation that would remove legal restrictions hampering women in their working lives, education, and family lives.[1] Kennedy and the legislators seemed to believe that the influx of women into the work force, along with the imminent emergence of a new feminist movement, made it politically wise to court women as a constituency.[2] Certainly, the political environment of those years, with mounting evidence that the New Deal coalition that had kept the Democrats the majority party for thirty years was crumbling, encouraged entrepreneurial politicians to seek new blocs of support.

## Early Rumblings

Congress was the first to act. Senators and representatives signed on in growing numbers as sponsors of the ERA. This issue was an ideal one for the legislature to use to respond to women's concerns. The ERA, in one of its many versions, had been before Congress since 1923.[3] It was a proposal that was ripe for legislative action. Also, the civil rights legislation of the 1960s brought fresh light and new understanding to the issues raised by ERA. Supporters of ERA argued their case, citing efforts to eliminate racial discrimination as precedents. In addition, ERA supporters cited the Fourteenth Amendment to the U.S. Constitution, which mandates equal protection under the law. ERA advocates could argue that women's second-class treatment in America contradicted this century-old promise. Politically, the ERA built on the congressional voting bloc that had passed the Civil Rights

Act of 1964 and the Voting Rights Act of 1965 to win the two-thirds congressional vote needed to send it to the states for ratification.

At the White House, Kennedy's advisers urged him soon after he took office to move quickly to try and preempt congressional activity on ERA. His action of establishing the Presidential Commission on the Status of Women—the first in U.S. history— shifted public attention on women's issues away from Congress and toward the executive branch, providing a high-level forum to search for an alternative to the ERA (see chap. 2). Within the Democratic party, organized labor and many of the women's groups most friendly to the Democrats still adamantly opposed the ERA. Despite the commission's charge to come up with non-ERA solutions to women's legitimate demands, the ERA survived efforts to seek out alternatives. The commission uncovered and publicized the great extent of legally supported discrimination against American women. These facts, along with a progression of statutory measures equalizing treatment of women and men, combined to create a strong political consensus favoring the ERA and legal equality for women in the late 1960s (see chap. 3). The second presidential commission, the President's Task Force on Women's Rights and Responsibilities, issued its report in 1970 during the Nixon administration. It endorsed the ERA, with eight of its eleven recommendations favoring extending legal equality to women[4] (see Table 6-1). Nixon was on record as supporting the ERA and legal equality for women.

In marked contrast, neither Congress nor the president pushed legislation responding to the needs of women as a group. Government-supported child care, reproductive rights, and maternity-leave policies garnered far less support from political institutions than did simply extending rights to women that men already had. Congress cautiously passed a child-care law in 1971, providing free day care for children living in families of four or more with less than $4,300 in annual income and a sliding fee for families with higher incomes. Nixon, however, vetoed it as too costly and a threat to American families.[5] Congress failed to override the veto. In hindsight, the message to women's groups and the emerging women's movement must have seemed clear. There was political support for legal equality but not for women as a "special" interest group with needs beyond men's.

The irony of this position is that the people's representatives in Congress and the White House, by favoring equality, drew the women's movement toward a more controversial set of priorities. A comparison of positive press coverage of equality with neutral or unfavorable coverage reveals that media reactions to equality were very mixed throughout this period (see Fig. 4-3). By contrast, women's special-

Table 6-1. The Legislative Recommendations of the President's Task Force on Women's Rights and Responsibilities, 1970

Pressure for Equality versus Responding to Women's Special Needs

| EQUALITY | SPECIAL NEEDS |
| --- | --- |
| Passage of the ERA | Child care |
| Enforce law banning sex discrimination in employment | Federal support of state commissions on the status of women |
| Guarantee equal education | Tax deduction for home and child-care expenses for working parents |
| Prohibit gender discrimination in public accommodations | |
| Extend jurisdiction of the Civil Rights Commission to include gender | |
| Extend equal pay provisions to executive-level positions | |
| Amend Social Security Act to treat the dependents of female workers the same as dependents of male workers | |
| Give the dependents of female federal employees the same fringe benefits as the dependents of male workers | |

needs issues were handled in a more uniformly positive manner in the press.[6] Its more positive handling certainly should not suggest that some special-needs issues, such as abortion or lesbianism, were not controversial. They were simply not given much space in mainstream publications in the early 1970s. The major special-needs issues written about were women's general condition and their political participation as well as women's movement activities. The public seemed ready to endorse some public action to handle problems that fell into these categories.

Many elected officials were capitalizing on women's concerns to gain political support by emphasizing equality as a solution. The movement was thus confronted with a difficult tactical situation: Should the members cooperate with officials and risk charges of cooptation or should they pursue their own political agenda? The more radical "women's liberation" groups responded by eschewing cooperation with government and conventional political organizing (see chap. 2). After making little political headway and meeting harsh ridicule in the press, many of the individuals in these groups eventually joined more mainstream women's movement organizations, such as NOW. By contrast, the "mainstream" movement groups cooperated with government while sustaining a somewhat independent political agenda into the early 1970s. This mainstream agenda combined equality issues (including the ERA, equal access to education, financial credit, and job opportunities) with special-needs issues (including abortion, rape laws, and child care). During this period, elected officials responded eagerly with new laws that mandated equality but did little to meet special needs.

Tactically, the women's movement in the 1970s was directing much of its energy toward both legislative and judicial lobbying. Because most organized groups that supported women's rights were either nonpartisan or bipartisan, they were able to work comfortably with both Democrats and Republicans—as long as consensus reigned on the desirability of extending legal equality to women. A number of diverse congressional offices helped with the drafting and sponsorship of bills that ranged from ending discrimination in granting financial credit to women to prohibiting sex bias in federally funded schools.[7]

The Supreme Court, in the seventies, responded favorably to test cases brought by feminist groups, striking down, on equal protection grounds, laws that treated men and women differently.[8] A number of organizations, including the Women's Legal Defense Fund and the National Women's Law Center, were formed specifically to push for gender equality through the courts. NOW was one of several groups that spun-off legal advocacy branches, which—unlike legislative lobbies—could operate using tax-free contributions.[9] This women's "legal lobby," with the help of the American Civil Liberties Union and other sympathetic groups, persuaded a politically centrist Supreme Court to uphold most affirmative action programs, protect abortion rights against state incursions, and require legal equality in state laws.

In the mid-1970s, equality and particularly the ERA overwhelmed every other agenda item favored by the women's movement or government (see chap. 3). All major institutions and groups supported passage of the ERA, with one noteworthy exception—the political parties. After reaching a short-lived consensus in support of the ERA—reflected in their 1972 and 1976 party platforms—the parties began a historic role reversal.[10]

The Democratic party became enthusiastic in its advocacy of ERA ratification, especially with Jimmy Carter as president. The mood of bipartisan consensus on ERA in the 1970s began to show stress cracks. In contrast, the Republican party which had been the traditional advocate of women's equality and the ERA—adopting the individualistic position that women should not be barred by law from attempting to succeed or fail in any endeavor they wanted to try—began to question the wisdom of the ERA. In 1980, the Republican party platform dropped endorsement of the ERA, and its successful candidate for president, Ronald Reagan, was an unapologetic opponent of ERA.

## Who's in Charge?

The 1980 election marked a historic turning point, ending the bipartisan spirit of the 1970s. As the parties divided over women's rights issues and abortion, the women's movement underwent a corresponding shift. Movement groups changed from working inside the institutions of government, helping and encouraging them to do more on women's rights, to more electorally focused events and rising political protest. Figure 6-1 shows the overall mix of acts of institutional government (including committee hearings, legislative votes, court decisions), pressure-group acts (including electoral activity as well as events aimed at publicizing issues and putting pressure on legislators), and protest actions.

Protest and pressure rose relative to institutionalized actions beginning in the late 1970s. An increasingly conservative Congress and White House began to shun identification with women's issues as the ERA moved toward almost certain defeat. Feminists and organized women's groups used issue coalitions, political action committees (PACs), candidate endorsements, boycotts of non-ERA ratified states, and dramatic actions, such as chaining themselves to desks in the Illinois state legislature, to express their dissatisfaction with the political process.

By the early 1980s, political parties had completed their respective transformations on women's issues. Partisanship heightened as the Republican party took cues from its most conservative constituents, while Democrats followed the path laid out by President Kennedy in the 1960s, attempting to attract support from women through advocacy of women's issues (see chap. 5). Organized women's groups became more partisan, too, putting increased resources into electoral politics through candidate recruitment and PACs. They publicized high-profile issues, such as parental leave, child care, and abortion, in the hope that these might become significant electoral issues.

Meanwhile, a gender gap of from 5 to 8 percent surfaced in national, state, and local elections, with Democratic candidates the usual beneficiaries. Young working women, either single or divorced, were most likely to vote differently from men.[11] Scholars and politicians have a variety of differing explanations for this gap, ranging from a new consciousness arising from the decade-long women's movement to traditional splits between men and women voters over issues of war and peace, violence, and compassion now being reflected in Democratic and Republican differences.[12] By the 1990s it was still unclear whether women's issues, including abortion, were important in creating the

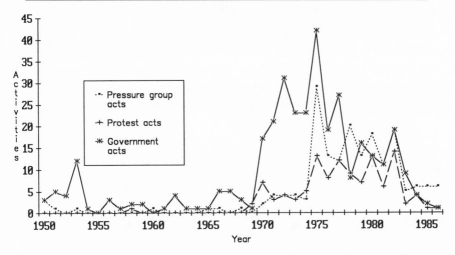

Fig. 6-1. Tactical shifts in women's rights activities.

gender gap or whether the economy (evident in such actions as Republican-led cutbacks in social welfare) and use of force (as in Republican-supported invasions of Panama and Grenada) were more significant. However, both parties and politicians self-consciously used "women's issues" to appeal to women voters.

After defeat of the ERA, the government continued to focus on legal equality for women. The women's movement, by contrast, turned to special-needs issues, including comparable worth, child care, and sexual harassment (Figs. 6-2, 6-3). While government, in general, was ready to minimize its involvement with women's issues, the women's movement was not, sustaining a moderately high level of activity into the nineties. Electoral politics rather than Congress became the principal venue for the women's movement to publicize its new initiatives.

## A Case for Shifting Initiative

The relationship between the movement, the government, and public opinion is highly complex. Both the government and the movement were competing for leadership of national policy on women. Much of this competition was over the direction of public opinion. The circumstances surrounding passage of key pieces of women's rights legislation by Congress show clearly that initiative shifted frequently during this time period. Congress sometimes played a leading

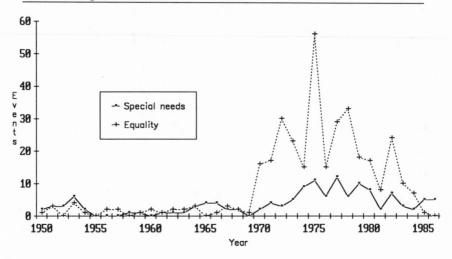

Fig. 6-2. Government events raising equality and special-needs issues.

role, "discovering" issues, publicizing them, and then passing them. At other times, Congress seemed to react either to public opinion or to the women's movement reflected through public opinion. Women's movement groups introduced still other issues, and they then pressured a reluctant Congress to act.

The Equal Credit Opportunity Act of 1974 is a strong case of legislative initiative. The importance of protecting individuals from sex discrimination in the granting of financial credit was overlooked by everyone until May 1972, when the congressionally mandated National Commission on Consumer Finance held its series of nationwide hearings on consumer-credit complaints (see chap. 4).[13] The staff of the commission noticed a pattern of grievances coming from women. Many charged that they had been denied credit in their own names or had lost their credit record after being married, widowed, or divorced. Representative Leonor Sullivan (D, Mo.), a member of the commission, asked for special hearings to determine the magnitude of this problem. Members of two women's movement groups, WEAL and the NOW Task Force on Credit, helped the commission staff schedule witnesses who could present the most effective case possible exposing sex discrimination in the credit industry.

The two days of hearings provided a graphic picture of individual cases of discrimination. They also revealed a wider pattern of systematic discrimination based on sex and marital status. Members of Congress hurried to draft legislation to seize the initiative on this issue. Senator William Brock (R, Tenn.) was the first through the gate

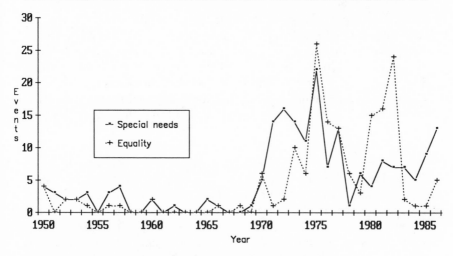

Fig. 6-3. Movement events raising equality and special-needs issues.

in this process, introducing equal credit opportunity legislation as an amendment to the Truth in Lending Act amendments in the Senate where the amendment passed the Senate 90 to 0 in July 1973. On the House side, disagreements between Sullivan, who was chair of the subcommittee on consumer affairs, and committee members Edward Koch (D, N.Y.) and Margaret Heckler drew organized women's groups, including Women's Lobby, NOW, the American Association of University Women, and the Center for Women's Policy Studies, into the process to decide what kind of bill would be acceptable: the more stringent bill favored by Sullivan or the more limited bill offered by Heckler and Koch.[14] Women's groups, although influencing the outcome by supporting Heckler and Koch over Sullivan, were clearly responding to an issue publicized by the congressional commission, discovered by the public, and subsequently seized on by Congress.

Initiative was far different for the Pregnancy Disability Act, which grew out of the court case *General Electric v. Gilbert* (1976) and quickly became a popular cause for interest groups.[15] In the *Gilbert* case, the U.S. Supreme Court rejected the argument that the anti-sex discrimination provisions of the Civil Rights Act of 1964 outlawed employment discrimination against pregnant women. By a 6 to 3 margin, the majority ruled that excluding pregnant workers from disability coverage in insurance plans was constitutional. It did not constitute sex discrimination because there were male and female "nonpregnant" workers who were advantaged by these plans. On 7 December, when the Supreme Court handed down the verdict, representatives of women's groups were waiting at the court house, ready to pick up the slip opinions handed out by the Supreme Court.[16] These opinions were photocopied and circulated among interested organizations. Meetings were scheduled in Philadelphia and Washington, D.C., for the following week to discuss possible legal and legislative responses to the Court's action. The media also reacted quickly to this case, constructing headlines such as "The Supreme Court Finds Pregnancy Unrelated to Sex."

By the time the Washington meeting was held, over a hundred interest-group and congressional representatives gathered in an event covered by all three major television networks. In this instance, despite a public outcry like that following the consumer-credit hearings, Congress was somewhat reluctant to act. Business argued that it was too expensive to extend disability coverage to pregnant workers.[17] The civil rights community was, at first, loath to agree to the first major effort to amend the Civil Rights Act of 1964. In the end, as the far-reaching implications of the *Gilbert* precedent for the economic well-being of women workers became clearer, a coalition of women's, labor, liberal, and eventually even antiabortion groups pushed Congress to enact the Pregnancy Disability Act, undoing the effects of the decision.[18]

The shift in legislative handling of the ERA provides still another case showing the way Congress and the women's movement alternated leadership on women's issues. The vast majority (214) of the 282 ERA introductions in the Ninety-first Congress were offered in 1969, preceding most of the coverage of the women's movement by the media (see Fig. 6-4). Organized lobbying on behalf of the women's movement was practically nonexistent in the late 1960s. Most of the early pressure on Congress to pass the ERA was coordinated through Representative Griffiths' congressional office. Lobbying on behalf of ERA consisted primarily of Washington-area housewives going to Capitol Hill several days a week to speak with whichever members of Congress they could find. It is unlikely that such a makeshift effort could by itself have lifted the fortunes of the ERA so dramatically.

By contrast, when Congress passed legislation in 1978 that extended the time available for states to ratify the ERA, it was not due to a congressional initiative but rather to a successful lobbying campaign by an extremely diverse coalition of groups favoring women's rights. These groups ranged from the national committees of the two major political parties to the Newspaper Guild, the United Methodist Board of Church and Society, and the American Civil Liberties Union, along with traditional women's groups, such as the League of Women Vo-

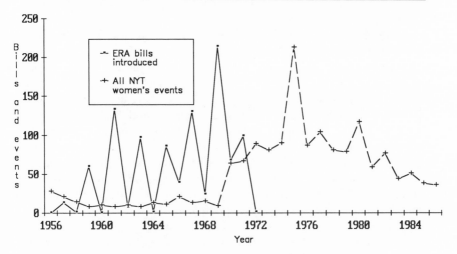

Fig. 6-4. ERA bill introductions in Congress and *New York Times* events.

ters, the American Association of University Women, and the General Federation of Women's Clubs.[19] Congress forced a compromise on this issue as the price of its acceptance, rejecting a seven-year extension of the deadline but approving a thirty-nine-month extension.[20] On the ERA, Congress moved from an initiating role to one of responding to outside pressures.

## The Balance of Power

Most women's issues before Congress can be separated according to congressional, public, or group initiation. Initiative did shift on women's issues during this period of highly visible conflict over the issues as well as extensive news coverage. But to understand how *much* influence government, public opinion, and the women's movement exerted on each other, separate measures of the activities of government, public opinion, and the women's movement have to be created. Annual measures were constructed to assess the influence of each factor.

Public opinion is represented using responses to the question, "Would you vote for a qualified woman for president [of the U.S.]?" This question was first asked by public opinion pollsters in 1937, and pollsters have regularly asked it since, making it one of the longest across-time measures of political prejudice toward women. Myra Ferree argued persuasively that this question tells us less about people's likely behavior, if given the opportunity to vote for a woman president, than about their willingness to express prejudice toward women openly.[21] This prejudice, particularly concerning women's political participation, should affect congressional willingness to legislate on women's issues. Schreiber,[22] Paul Burstein,[23] and Welch and Sigelman[24] used this question to measure changes in public attitudes toward women's rights. In an even broader sense, the responses reflect public views about women as authority figures. Willingness to vote for a woman president suggests an acceptance of women in positions of power not only in the public but also in the private sphere. Furthermore, the response is strongly correlated across time with public opinion on acceptance of women in the workplace.[25]

To measure the relative influence of activity by both the women's movement and the government on women's rights, I used a number of sources. The data are partially represented using categories from the *New York Times* events data set.[26] In addition, the number of members in five influential women's groups—the League of Women Voters, the American Association of University Women, the National Federation of Business and Professional Women, NOW, and NWPC—represents activity by organized women's groups.[27] These group membership figures, along with the coded events data, suggest how active and how organized those supporting women's rights were over the thirty-seven-year time span from 1950 to 1986.

Finally, governmental actions are analyzed through a coded measure of the percentage of bills passed by the Congress that make gender their focus. *U.S. Statutes At Large* is the source.[28] This measure represents the share of the political agenda occupied by women's laws each year.

Scholars who look at the relationship between Congress and public opinion have generally made mono-causal assumptions. They argue either that Congress reflects prevailing public opinion or that the mood of the electorate is driven by elite manipulation. The data suggest that, in the case of the women's movement, neither view is correct. The relationship between Congress and public opinion appears to have no dominant causal flow across the thirty-seven-year period investigated. The relationship is interdependent, reciprocal, and in the aggregate sense, simultaneous.

The results of the statistical analysis presented in Appendix B support the view that an interactive model is most representative of policy development on women's issues. At different times, Congress, public opinion, and the women's movement played a leading role in guiding policy affecting women. It is neither possible to divide the period and conclude, for example, that Congress was the driving force before 1975 and the movement after that date, nor to identify a single dominant actor. It is apparent that public opinion was slightly more important than either Congress or the women's movement, because statistically it mediates their influence on the women's laws that are passed. This effectively means that the movement and Congress competed to lead public opinion on women's issues. Occasionally, either the movement or Congress predominated but only for a short time. There were also times when public opinion alone seemed to impel changes in women's laws.

It is relatively easy to understand why the women's movement or energized public opinion might have wanted to initiate changes in public policy toward women. But why would Congress choose to open an area of policy as controversial as this one? Part of the answer is ideological. Representative Griffiths and a minority of members of Congress, male and female, had long supported equality for women and the ERA, reintroducing it year after year. By the late 1960s, a less ideological group of politicians, holding ambitions for higher office, began to view equal rights for women as an innovative issue with the potential to further their presidential aspirations. As Jack Walker observed, the Senate, in particular, is populated by such policy entrepreneurs, who recognize emerging issues that will attract majorities in Congress and build their national reputations.[29]

Women's rights had a more direct electoral link than most of these issues. For example, after John Kennedy's narrow electoral victory in 1960, one of his early interests was gaining greater support among women and women's groups.[30] In the 1960 election, Kennedy managed to neutralize the gender gap that had swelled Dwight Eisenhower's margins of victory in 1952 and 1956. Kennedy attracted almost the same number of women's votes as his Republican rival, Richard Nixon.

After the election, the realization that Eisenhower had received roughly 5 percent more votes from women than men in his first election to the presidency and 6 percent more women's votes in 1956 might have looked like a tempting prospect to Kennedy, who had barely eked out a slim victory.[31] Kennedy acted by urging Congress to pass new legislation and appointing the first presidential commission on women's status in the nation's history.[32] Many of the male members of Congress who were key sponsors of women's rights legislation in the 1970s were senators seeking higher office, including Walter Mondale

(D, Minn.), William Brock, and Birch Bayh. A gender gap in presidential politics, combined with the ability of women's rights issues to pass in Congress and win media attention, provided sufficient incentive to spur congressional initiative in this area of public policy.

## Conclusions

These findings suggest that intensely political concerns such as women's rights—with a mobilized social movement and changing public opinion—present circumstances in which it is possible *either* that public opinion creates legislative change *or* that constituents, the social movement, or public opinion are reacting to shifts in policy. The interactive model suggests that there is a delicate balancing act between Congress and social movement, with public opinion the lure that attracts both sides. Neither Congress nor the movement will willingly stray too far from public opinion. E. E. Schattschneider contends that when the political deck is stacked against those who have limited access to government, it is the government's role to expand the scope of conflict.[33] Only in this way can the political odds be somewhat evened and democracy served. However, in the highly charged political environment precipitated by the activity of a major social movement, Schattschneider's conclusions must be extended to include a scenario in which government is not the only actor attempting to broaden the scope of conflict. When Congress and social movements are competing for favorable public opinion, Congress is in a position of trying sometimes to broaden and at other times to narrow the scope of conflict that social movements are trying to broaden.

Then, does the political system try to coopt social movements and their leaders? Or, from a different perspective, do authorities "cave in" to movement demands prematurely, getting out in front of public opinion in their quest to appease the movement? These findings suggest that both often happen. Movements get coopted by government, at certain points in time, as legislative objectives that originate in Congress pull them in politically orthodox directions. Movements are also capable of pushing policies through Congress, largely through their impact on public opinion. Congress may quickly accede on a policy in the hope that it will thereby satisfy cries for change. By giving in to a movement's demand, government both increases the legitimacy of the movement with the public and retains the ability to direct change itself in the future.

In the case of the women's movement, the relationships among Congress as an institution, the social movement, and public opinion cannot be examined within the framework of rigid political models. Certainly, the government had great influence in its advocacy of women's equality and the ERA. The women's movement had historically based reasons to go along with this equality agenda. But, in fact, it never completely abandoned its alternative agenda, that of special needs, which is likely to become increasingly important in the 1990s. The women's movement similarly exercised initiative in introducing issues that Congress was forced to respond to as well as leading public opinion in some periods.

# 7 For a Continuing Movement

In analyzing the women's movement more than twenty-five years after its initial appearance, several conclusions are evident. First, the women's movement was guaranteed some political success from the time of its initial appearance in the 1960s. The U.S. government was willing to facilitate the emergence and early development of this movement, in part, because of structural changes in the economy, family, and workplace. Elected officials were reassessing women's political status in the United States, reacting to the rising numbers of women in the full-time work force and the new political independence of women voters. Women who married later or divorced, worked at a job outside the home, or raised fewer children became the core of a gender gap in voting that would boost the flagging fortunes of Democratic candidates in the 1980s and 1990s.

At the same time, the political system was entering a period of fragmenting electoral coalitions. The power of a mobilizing women's movement became greater relative to government because many alignments within the party system dissolved. Americans were more detached from both major political parties without lessening their interest in politics.[1] The Democrats and Republicans were looking for organized blocs of voters to help build a new majority governing coalition. As a reflection of this search, presidents and Congresses competed throughout the sixties and seventies to respond to and gain control of women's issues.

The success of the women's movement was also guaranteed because of the range of resources available to it from established and newly emerging women's groups. Once these groups resolved their historic division over the ERA, they were able to pool assets and strengths, creating a respectable lobbying presence very quickly, both nationally and in many of the states. Because of the pattern of ad hoc lobbying coalitions, which is so common in the nation's capital, women's groups could attract support from public interest and civil rights groups on issues of legal equality, from education groups, student lobbies, and teachers' unions on education issues, and from labor unions on many employment issues.[2]

Finally, in the aftermath of the civil rights movement, with influential new analyses of women's condition, most notably Betty Friedan's *The Feminist Mystique*, large numbers of women were psychologically ready to assign their discontents and their second-class status to social factors that the political system could alter.[3] The cognitive liberation of women was underway.

Most current political analyses of the women's movement overestimate the marginality and tenuousness of the movement. By assuming that the movement only just succeeded in amassing sufficient resources to attract political attention, they adopt the view that the movement gained influence by emphasizing role equity, not role change—incremental politics, not visionary politics. Those making this argument imply that the historical lesson of the movement is that tactics are highly important and that women's movements in the future must anticipate the mood of American politics and adjust to it, avoiding direct challenges to the status quo. The argument in this book is almost the opposite one. Because the contemporary women's movement came into existence as a result of nonincremental changes— including sharp rises in the number of women employed in the work force, resolution of the decades-old dispute among women's groups over the ERA, and the unraveling of the New Deal coalition—it did not need to choose issues cautiously but could have chosen boldly. Politics and society had to adjust to women's new circumstances anyway, and the question was primarily what kind of an adjustment it would be.

It is less important to ask how effective the movement's *tactics* were than it is to ask whether the contemporary movement was unduly influenced by government's agenda. Looking back over the last thirty years, when the current women's movement first arose in America in the sixties, we can see that it attracted diverse followers[4] *and* its issues were quite broad. Early political concerns of the movement had two dominant components: a search for legal equality and the transmutation of parts of the old social feminism into its modern form, that of a special-interest or special-needs agenda that emphasized policies on reproductive freedom, child care, rape and sexual harassment, maternal health, comparable worth, and family-leave policies.

By the mid-1970s, however, the movement had given up most of these social feminist priorities and instead embraced only egalitarianism. It accepted the course of action rewarded by government institutions. This analysis should not suggest that this is the *sole* reason the movement chose this course. The historic lure of equality is clear for American women in particular, as the unfinished business of the suffrage movement.[5] The American political culture assigns a lofty and possibly even preeminent place to egalitarian individualism. The ideological underpinnings of politics are imbued with the belief that in the United States, people should be equal under the law.[6]

Equality was also a comfortable solution for most government institutions, especially after their experience with the recent civil rights movement, since equality could be doled out incrementally and seemed to produce nondisruptive social and political change. However, it is far from clear that legal equality for women was the public's preference or indeed the preference of many within the movement. By contrast, issues such as child care, comparable worth, and reproductive freedom were more likely than equality to further the types of changes already taking place in society. More women were working in the paid labor force. Women were having fewer children, and those children were more likely to be cared for outside the home.

This analysis is also not meant to suggest, as movement critics have, that the movement, out of perversity or shortsightedness, undercut women's issues by allowing themselves to be either attracted unreasonably to the ERA or coopted by government.[7] It is possible that circumstances in the aftermath of the suffrage movement and the rise of the second women's movement in the shadow of the civil rights movement gave the contemporary movement no practical choice but to pursue equality and the ERA regardless of government action. However, if there were other possibilities, as I believe there might have been, the movement's own conscious decision to forego hierarchical leadership, which thereby prevented the movement from speaking in one voice, to allow women to find their own voices doomed its efforts to pursue a diverse agenda. Concerted governmental pressure relentlessly pushed the movement toward the goal of equality. Future women's movements need to weigh the risks of renouncing hierarchy in a hierarchical economic and political system against the benefits of having greater strength to guide an agenda based on women's priorities, not those that may be externally proposed or imposed.

Whatever choices the contemporary movement might have made, its neglect of the special-needs agenda in the rush to pass the ERA leaves it now in a position where the movement is virtually without government support, grappling to resurrect issues like child care, parental leave, reproductive rights, and comparable worth in the wake of the states' failure to ratify the ERA. With the rise of the gender gap and the vigor of grass-roots feminism, the cause is not dead. But how bright are its future prospects?

# The Women's Movement Confronts the Nineties

The future of the women's movement seems to hinge on two factors: first, the ability of the movement to maintain political pressure on the government through the gender gap and, second, party politics. Scholars have been criticized, and rightly so, for overselling the gender gap and linking it to feminist issues in the face of evidence suggesting that the gender gap is much more a division between women and men that is triggered by economic concerns and issues of the appropriate use of force (e.g., U.S. involvement in military conflicts or the morality of a death penalty). However, having acknowledged this basis of the gender gap, there is little doubt that the political parties are continuing to use feminist issues and appointments of women to government posts to capture women's votes; they are not using economic or war and peace issues.

Because the gender gap has been tied to divisions between the Democratic and Republican parties since the 1980 election, party-selected issues, like abortion, can be linked to the economic and coercive politics feared by women. Unwanted pregnancies have economic consequences for mothers, children, and society. Similarly, denying a woman or a minor and her family the right to make informed decisions about terminating a pregnancy reveals the coercive interference of the state. Parental leave policy and new protection against sex and race discrimination in the workplace are linked to fundamental economic and compassion issues that divide women from men in issue surveys. Polls suggest that women are more concerned than men about the plight of individuals who need to choose between having a job or having good-quality care for their children. Similarly, an issue from recent Supreme Court cases, which stated that a pattern of discrimination against women or minorities in the workplace is not sufficient proof of a violation of federal law, should underline women's feelings of vulnerability on the job.[8]

As long as the political parties are actively competing for women's votes and elections appear to be swayed as a result, the women's movement has the opportunity to resurrect a special-needs agenda. Government can no longer be regarded as facilitating the women's movement, since its main institutional branches appear to have lost interest in most women's issues following the defeat of the ERA. Political opportunities have shrunk for the women's movement. However, women's groups and their allies still appear to control sufficient resources to challenge the status quo, even though some of the smaller women's organizations such as WEAL have experienced severe budget cutbacks in the last year. In WEAL's case, the cutbacks necessitated an end to a full-time lobbying presence in Washington.[9] Public opinion polls continue to show support for a stronger assertion of women's issues. Particularly, in their enthusiasm for women's rights, people under age 25 continue to resist the overall trend toward more conservative politics.[10]

The unanswered question is whether the women's movement can reanimate its neglected special-needs agenda in the face of government indifference and the public's quiet backing of the agenda. If abortion, child care, and parental leave continue to divide the political parties and inflame election-period rhetoric, the movement will have a chance in this century to test the special-needs approach to improving women's status.

The vulnerability of gains in the area of women's rights is starkly evident. The Supreme Court seems on the verge of reversing *Roe v. Wade*, which less than two decades ago provided constitutional protection for women's right to have a surgical abortion.[11] New employment restrictions allowing companies to reassign pregnant or potentially pregnant workers away from hazardous work environments were only recently struck down by a divided (6 to 3) Supreme Court in the case *United Automobile Workers v. Johnson Controls, Inc.* (1991).[12] The courts are also becoming stricter about how individuals can prove sex discrimination on the job.[13] Congress passed a parental leave bill in 1990, but it was vetoed by President Bush—a veto that Congress failed to override.[14] Similarly, the Civil Rights bill of 1990, which eased the standard for proving job discrimination, met another presidential veto, failing to be overridden by one vote.[15] Political opportunities are closing quickly for the women's movement unless campaigns, party politics, and the largely untested special-needs agenda can extend women's influence for another decade. Caution has brought the movement to its current difficult situation. Can bold reassertion save it? If not, its failure will be the legacy upon which a third women's movement will have to build.

## Post-Social Movement American Politics

Samuel Huntington characterized the period from 1960 to 1975 as "the era of sixes and sevens."[16] He was referring not just to the decade markers but also to the extraordinary ferment and volatility of this period with its mushrooming of major social movements. Politics was transfigured by this experience, and the change has shaped subsequent events. The major social movements of this early period—the black civil rights, women's, and environmental—energized new groups of political participants, voters, and activists and redrew important partisan divisions in the United States. Curiously, all three movements trace their roots historically to the Republican party. The civil rights movement is a modern manifestation of the commitment to equality between races that first ignited the movement before the Civil War to abolish slavery. Lincoln was elected the first Republican president with the staunch support of the abolitionists. The historic conservation movement, which Republican President Theodore Roosevelt (1901-09) championed, was the predecessor of the contemporary environmental movement. Its primary emphasis was on the preservation of natural beauty and government protection of the earth's resources.[17] The women's movement likewise depended historically on the Republican party and its officeholders for its major support. The ERA was primarily a Republican issue, rejected vehemently by pre-1960s Democrats.

Yet in the 1990s, each movement was rejected by the Republican party, which instead embraced its critics. All three movements brought their ideas, issues, and, to a degree, followers to the Democratic party. Although Democrats have been criticized for their openness to such nonmainstream interests as these, the Democratic party is binding to itself bases of support in the public with long histories of appeal to the American public. Each of these movements taps issues of deep concern to most Americans, and each periodically experiences a rebirth, when millions are mobilized and its agenda becomes part of the mainstream.

The peak period has now passed for each movement: political opportunities have narrowed, consciousness has diminished, and organizations within them are preoccupied with just maintaining themselves. However, they are having much to say about who will be chosen as Democratic candidates for office and about the issues that will create electoral firestorms—abortion, racism, and environmental degradation.

Clearly, in the short term, the futures of the movements are tied to the success of the Democratic party, which is considerable in Congress but slim in the White House and increasingly slim in the Supreme Court. Even if the pattern of legislative power and executive and judicial exclusion continues for the Democrats, the issues of the women's, environmental, and civil rights movements will get a hearing and be rejected or approved based on voters' choices. The polarization of the parties over such issues retains public interest in the movements' issues and amplifies the importance of partisan victories and defeats. When recurrent social movements possess this electoral link, their issues and visions become public. They experience the shifting currents of popular approval and disapproval, but they are protected from insularity and irrelevance. When the next waves of energy sweep through these movements, as history suggests they will,[18] their supporters will be placed more strategically to bring about change than was the case in the sixties and seventies. Blacks were in chains during the first movement for black rights, the abolitionist movement. During the second civil rights movement, blacks throughout the southern United States lacked the right to vote. When the third civil rights movement comes, blacks will be voting in ever higher numbers and will hold high national office in closer proportion to their numbers, and the movement's impact will be correspondingly greater. Women were without the vote during their first social movement. The second women's movement found them excluded de facto from holding electoral offices. The third movement will build from a base in which women are voting in percentages equal to or greater than men and controlling major political offices throughout the country. Similarly, the first movement in support of the environment was largely regional (concentrated in the northeast) and class-based during America's industrial revolution.[19] Only a relatively narrow spectrum of upper-class individuals took time to notice and bemoan the despoiling of the U.S. environment. The current environmental movement is far less regional and class-based, and it has succeeded in placing its supporters in high elected and appointed offices.[20] The next environmental movement, like the women's and the civil rights movements, will have a greater political impact than its predecessors.

## Summary

American politics is markedly different now from what it was in the 1960s. The case of the women's movement suggests that past change is likely to fuel even greater changes in the future. Belief that incremental, slow politics is the way to gain influence in the United States is less persuasive than the view that bold change, tied to unfolding social and economic restructuring, with an eye to public opinion, has the greatest chance to succeed. Women's social or special-needs agenda along with equality are likely to emerge as dual cutting edges of change when the third wave of feminism appears in the United States. If both agendas can be pursued simultaneously, the movement will be carrying out its historic mandates to better the physical and legal conditions of women.

# Appendix A:
# Coding Women's Events Data

## I. General Coding Instructions

The purpose of this code is to record all events contained in the synopses of the annual index of the *New York Times* that reflect agitation over women's rights in the period from 1950 to 1986. All story synopses under the headings "Women: General" and "Women: United States" were read and coded if they fell under the study's general guidelines.

The procedures given below as instructions to the coders were adopted from Doug McAdam's work on the civil rights movement.[1] Professor McAdam, in a telephone conversation, clarified some points that were difficult to interpret in relation to the women's movement. The results should be comparable to coding schemes used to analyze other movements.[2]

A. Only events relevant to women's rights should be coded. Omit stories that are (1) opinion generated by the *New York Times* staff or printed by them (this includes all letters, comments, opinion-type stories in the Sunday sections, surveys, ads, and editorials) and (2) stories that bear little relation to women's rights (e.g., stories about actresses or women athletes), unless the story reports a significant breakthrough for women or participation by an individual in a women's-rights related activity.

B. Two separate codings on one story should be recorded when two different and discrete events are reported. For example, if one story reports state legislative action on the ERA in two different states, each event should be coded separately.

C. Stories that report on the same event should be coded only *once*. For example, two different stories on a mass demonstration—one from the perspective of local police and one from the perspective of the demonstration organizer—should have only one code.

## II. Coding Specific Responses

A. Date of Event

B. Month, day, and year (only last 2 numbers from the year, e.g., 64)

C. Initiating Unit

PARTIES
11 Candidates
12 Party organization/spokespersons
13 Other

INTEREST GROUPS
2011 NOW
2012 NWPC
2013 WEAL
2014 Federally Employed Women (FEW)
2015 Congressional Caucus on Women's Issues
2016 SCUM
2017 Redstockings
2018 Multiple feminist groups
2019 Other feminist group, specify
2020 Traditional women's group
2030 Civil rights
2040 Civil liberties
2050 Anti-feminist group
2060 Pro-abortion group
2070 Anti-abortion group
2080 Labor
2090 Business
2100 Multiple interest groups
2110 Other interest group, specify

GOVERNMENT
3010 President/White House
3020 Cabinet members/Executive department
3030 First Lady
3040 Governor/staff
3050 Member(s) of Congress
3060 Congressional committee
3070 Congress

3071 House
3072 Senate
3080 State legislator(s)
3090 State legislature
3100 Mayor/staff
3110 City council, city commission, individual member of urban legislative body
3120 Individual judge
3130 Judicial body
3140 Law-enforcement personnel
3150 EEOC
3160 Women's Bureau of the Department of Labor
3170 State human rights/civil rights commissions
3180 City/municipal human rights or civil rights commissions
3190 State Commission on the Status of Women
3200 Presidential Commission on the Status of Women/ Task Force on Women
3210 U.N. or other international agency
3220 Other, specify

RELIGION

41 Protestant spokesperson or body
42 Catholic spokesperson or body
43 Jewish spokesperson or body
44 Other religious spokesperson or body
45 Multiple religious spokespersons or bodies

PROFESSIONAL BODIES

51 Legal profession/law associations
52 Social scientists
53 Medical personnel or associations
54 Educational associations
55 Human relations councils
56 Foundations
57 Other

MEDIA

61 Newspaper
62 Television
63 Magazine
64 Artists/actors
65 Other

EDUCATION

71 Colleges and universities
72 Research centers (institutes) within colleges and universities
73 Faculty, administrators, students within colleges
74 Other

INDIVIDUALS

81 Feminist
82 Antifeminist
83 Ambiguous

90 Polling organizations

100 Foreign governments

110 Private businesses

120 Ambiguous/missing

130 Other

D. Direction of event
   1 Pro
   2 Anti
   3 Neutral

E. Level of initiating unit
   1 Local
   2 State
   3 National
   4 International

F. Target of event
   1 Governmental
   2 Nongovernmental
   3 Both

G. Level of target
   1 Local
   2 State
   3 National
   4 International

## H. Nature of event

INSTITUTIONALIZED GOVERNMENT ACTION

101 Executive orders, formation of commissions, appointments, issuing regulations

102 Signing or final passage of bill by legislative body

103 Floor action in Congress/legislature [do not include voting]

104 Legislative proposals, bill introductions

105 Committee action, hearings, testimony, and/or voting on bills or resolutions

106 House or Senate passage of a bill, resolution, or amendment

107 Court action

108 Commission reports, recommendations, rulings

109 Defeat of bill, resolution, or amendment by legislative bodies

110 Passage of laws, resolutions, or amendments through the initiative/referendum process

111 Defeat of laws, resolutions, or amendments through the initiative/referendum process

112 Rescission

113 Other

200 PRIVATE GROUP MATERIALLY AIDS THE MOVEMENT
(E.G., FOUNDATION GRANTS)

INTERNAL DYNAMICS OF WOMEN'S MOVEMENT

301 Formation of new groups

302 Disagreement over movement direction/Leadership change

303 Mergers/coalitions

304 Conventions, conferences

305 Fundraising

306 Other

400 Internal dynamics of antifeminists

ORGANIZED PRESSURE

501 Campaign to enact legislation or build public support

502 Campaign for the election of a public official

503 Survey of political candidates or public officials

504 Registration of voters

505 Petition campaign

506 Deputations, sending letters to public officials, making direct statements or phone calls

507 Filing complaints or suits

508 Applying pressure to change the practices of private business/organizations

509 Other

AGITATION

601 Threat or warning made by a group or individual who possesses the resources to carry out the threat, mentioning particular target

602 Boycott/strikes

603 Mass action (protest march, demonstration, rally, etc.) of over 100 people

604 Violent action (riot, lynching, murder)

605 Other illegal/destructive acts (attacks on persons or property)

606 Harassment or intimidation of women or their supporters by anti-movement forces

607 Job action/labor protest (short of a strike)

608 Group action (e.g., sit-in) of under 100 people

609 Other

700 STATE CONTROL (ARRESTS, JAILINGS, CONVICTIONS, INDICTMENTS, FINES, ETC.)

800 CONFERENCES, WORKSHOPS, COURSES

900 RELEASE OF REPORTS OR POLLS

1000 SPEECHES, DEBATES, STATEMENTS, NEWS CONFERENCES

1100 PARTY PLATFORMS, NOMINATING PROCEDURES, PARTY RULES

1200 AWARDS, HONORS, LUNCHEONS, RECEPTIONS

1300 OTHER (SPECIFY)

1400 MEETINGS BETWEEN LEADERS

1500 RESOLUTIONS (E.G., PASSED AT NONPARTY CONVENTIONS)

I.  Issues at stake
    1 Equality under the law and discrimination
    2 History of women/history of movement
    3 Honoring women/honorees/breakthroughs
    4 Economic and social status of women (not political)

5  Political status of women/political participation
6  Employment/jobs
7  The women's movement
8  ERA
9  Women's health/abortion
10  Organizational concerns
11  Internal dissent
12  General plight of women
13  Education
14  Military
15  Administration of justice
16  Media treatment
17  Sports
18  Religion
19  Arts
20  Elections
21  Family
22  Crime
23  Other
24  Black women
25  Lesbians/gay rights
26  International Women's Year/women internationally

VIOLENCE (NOTE: INCLUDES HARM TO INDIVIDUALS OR PROPERTY)

1  Yes
2  No
3  Uncertain

# Appendix B: Assessing the Relative Influence of Government, Public Opinion, and the Women's Movement

In working with these data on government, public opinion, and the women's movement, I quickly found that many of the social movement indicators derived from the *New York Times* were highly correlated with one another. Because of the high intercorrelation between actions initiated by government and those initiated by movement actors, it seemed desirable to put both types of events in a factor analysis (e.g., the correlation between government-initiated acts and feminist-initiated acts is $r = .84$; government events and all organized pressure are correlated at $r = .83$; and government-initiated events and acts of protest are related with $r = .83$.)

I used factor analysis to reduce the number of independent variables.[1] After factoring, the events data formed three patterns that represent (1) activity surrounding the women's movement (Factor 1: Social Movement); (2) the organized strength of women's organizations as measured by membership in women's groups (Factor 2: Women's Organization); and (3) the influence of electoral/party events on Congress (Factor 3: Party Activity). Table B-1 presents the factors and their loadings. These factor scores were saved as regression variables for utilization in subsequent analyses.

**Table B-1. Factor Pattern Matrix and Factor Loadings**

|         | Factor 1 | Factor 2 | Factor 3 |
|---------|----------|----------|----------|
| ANTIDIR | .95281   | .03527   | .03090   |
| GOVACTS | .94889   | .04271   | .00963   |
| ERASUB  | .91972   | .15731   | .00642   |
| PRODIR  | .89655   | .04018   | .17242   |
| TARGOV  | .89055   | .05319   | .10300   |
| SPEECH  | .86865   | −.20972  | .22235   |
| FEMINIT | .83504   | .24585   | .01899   |
| NONGOVT | .83332   | .00166   | .24248   |
| ANTIFEM | .82482   | −.33250  | −.25040  |
| ELSEIGS | .80373   | .38877   | −.01981  |

| | | | |
|---|---|---|---|
| AGITACT | .72109 | .40495 | .10451 |
| GROUP | .24400 | .83372 | .03678 |
| PARTIES | -.01912 | .08243 | .91083 |
| SYMBOL | .44418 | -.23721 | .67194 |
| Eigenvalue | 10.08272 | 1.16725 | 1.02862 |

Factor 1: Social Movement—actions initiated by and in reaction to the women's movement
Factor 2: Women's Organization—the organized strength of women's groups measured by membership in women's groups
Factor 3: Party Activity—electoral and party events
ANTIDIR = Events that are negative for women's rights
GOVACTS = Government actors initiate the event
ERASUB = ERA issue is raised
PRODIR = Events that are supportive of women's rights
TARGOV = Government is the target of the event
SPEECH = Conferences, speeches, statements, etc.
FEMINIT = Feminists or feminist groups initiate the event
NONGOVT = Nongovernmental group is the target of the event
ANTIFEM = Actions initiated by antifeminist groups
ELSEIGS = Actions initiated by other organized interest groups
AGITACT = Protest activities
GROUP = Membership in selected women's voluntary organizations
PARTIES = Political parties/candidates initiate actions
SYMBOL = Honorary actions (symbolic)

Putting all the variables into an ordinary least squares (OLS) analysis yields the results in Table B-2. Although almost 80 percent of the variance in Legislative Action is explained, the model is not well specified for the data. Factors 1 and 2 (Social Movement and Women's Organization) show up as having significant *negative* regression coefficients with Legislative Action when Public Opinion is included as an independent variable. Examining Table B-3, which gives correlations for the three factors derived from the *New York Times* events data (Social Movement, Women's Organization, and Party Activity) along with Legislative Action and Public Opinion, it is evident that these negative correlations are the result of flaws in the method, rather than in reality. If Public Opinion mediates the independent effects of the Social Movement and Women's Organization variables, the equation might look this way, even though it is clear that the Women's Movement and Women's Organization are positively associated with Legislative Activity, when Public Opinion is not in the equation.

Looking at the results, below, when two separate OLS equations are run, one with Public Opinion as the independent variable and Legislative Activity as the dependent variable, and the other with Women's Movement and Women's Organization as the independent variables

**Table B-2. Social Movement, Public Opinion, and Organization as Independent Variables Affecting Legislative Action**

Social Movement

Public Opinion ⟶ Legislative Action

Women's Organization

Dependent Variable = Legislative Action
Adjusted R Square = .79
N = 37

| Variable | B | SE B | Beta | T | Sig T |
|---|---|---|---|---|---|
| Public Opinion | .94 | .11 | 1.19 | 8.90 | .00 |
| Social Movement | -1.97 | .95 | -.21 | -2.08 | .05 |
| Women's Organization | -3.64 | 1.23 | -.37 | -2.97 | .01 |
| (Constant) | -48.52 | 6.80 | — | -7.14 | .00 |

**Table B-3. Correlation Matrix of Variables**

| Correlations | Legis | PubOp | WomAct | WomOrz | PartyAct |
|---|---|---|---|---|---|
| Legislative Action | 1.00 | .87** | .31 | .45* | .19 |
| Public Opinion | .87** | 1.00 | .41* | .66** | .09 |
| Social Movement | .31 | .41* | 1.00 | -.11 | -.37 |
| Women's Organization | .45* | .66** | -.11 | 1.00 | -.15 |
| Party Activity | .19 | .09 | -.37 | -.15 | 1.00 |

N = 37; 1-tailed significance:    * - .01    ** - .001

and Legislative Activity as the dependent variable, all independent variables have significant positive relationships to the dependent variable. This strengthens the hypothesis that the combined equation is misspecified.

The three-stage least squares (3SLS) method, which unlike OLS solves a set of structural equations simultaneously, reflects the interdependence of the relationship between Congress and public opinion.[2] In the model below, public opinion mediates the influence of social movements (see Fig. B-1). The following structural equations represent the model:

Legislative Action = Public Opinion + Party Activity
Public Opinion = Legislative Action + Social Movement + Women's Organization

## Table B-4.  A Comparison of OLS, 2SLS, and 3SLS Results

| Equation 1: | Legislative Action | = | Constant | + | Public Opinion | + | Party Action |
|---|---|---|---|---|---|---|---|
| **Coefficient** | | | | | | | |
| OLS | | | -31.55 | | .67 | | .97 |
| 2SLS | | | -29.09 | | .63 | | 1.02 |
| 3SLS | | | -29.05 | | .63 | | .89 |
| **Standard Error** | | | | | | | |
| OLS | | | 4.34 | | .07 | | .79 |
| 2SLS | | | 4.59 | | .07 | | .79 |
| 3SLS | | | 4.39 | | .07 | | .43 |
| **T-STAT** | | | | | | | |
| OLS | | | -7.27 | | 10.13 | | 1.24 |
| 2SLS | | | -6.34 | | 9.02 | | 1.29 |
| 3SLS | | | -6.61 | | 9.41 | | 2.07 |
| **SIG T** | | | | | | | |
| 3SLS | | | .00 | | .00 | | .05 |
| **Standard Coefficient** | | | | | | | |
| 3SLS | | | — | | .81 | | .10 |

| Equation 2: | Public Opinion = | Constant | + | Legislative Action | + | Social Movement | + | Women's Organization |
|---|---|---|---|---|---|---|---|---|
| **Coefficient** | | | | | | | | |
| OLS | | 55.48 | | .75 | | 3.19 | | 5.41 |
| 2SLS | | 51.76 | | 1.07 | | 2.09 | | 3.86 |
| 3SLS | | 49.65 | | 1.26 | | 1.57 | | 2.34 |
| **Standard Error** | | | | | | | | |
| OLS | | 1.21 | | .08 | | .72 | | .81 |
| 2SLS | | 1.90 | | .15 | | .93 | | 1.09 |
| 3SLS | | 1.29 | | .09 | | .49 | | .58 |
| **T-STAT** | | | | | | | | |
| OLS | | 45.98 | | 8.90 | | 4.45 | | 6.70 |
| 2SLS | | 27.22 | | 7.30 | | 2.24 | | 3.52 |
| 3SLS | | 38.42 | | 14.27 | | 3.19 | | 4.01 |
| **SIG T** | | | | | | | | |
| 3SLS | | .00 | | .00 | | .00 | | .00 |
| **Standard Coefficient** | | | | | | | | |
| 3SLS | | — | | .99 | | .13 | | .13 |

**Table B–5. Three–Stage Least Squares Nonrecursive (Interactive) Model**

*Legislative Action = Public Opinion + Party Activity*

|  | B | Standard error | T | Sig T | Beta |
|---|---|---|---|---|---|
| Intercept | 29.05 | 4.39 | 6.61 | .00 | |
| Public Opinion | .63 | .07 | 9.41 | .00 | .81 |
| Party Activity | .89 | .43 | 2.07 | .05 | .10 |

Adjusted r sq = .77
N = 37

*Public Opinion = Legis Action + Social Movement ± Women's Organization*

|  | B | Standard error | T | Sig T | Beta |
|---|---|---|---|---|---|
| Intercept | 49.65 | 1.29 | 38.42 | .00 | |
| Legis Action | 1.26 | .09 | 14.27 | .00 | .99 |
| Social Movement | 1.57 | .49 | 3.19 | .00 | .13 |
| Women's Organization | 2.34 | .58 | 4.01 | .00 | .18 |

Adjusted r sq = .84
N = 37

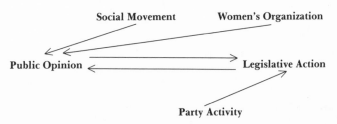

**Fig. B-1.** A nonrecursive (interactive) model of Congress, public opinion, and the women's movement.

The instrumental variables in this model are Social Movement, Women's Organization, Party Activity, and the one-year lag of Legislative Action. The correlation coefficient between Legislative Action and its lagged values is .77, and between Public Opinion and lagged Legislative Action the correlation is .86. The equations in the model have been identified by methods which satisfy both order and rank conditions. The order condition is satisfied if $K - M \geq G - 1$, where K is the number of variables in the total system. M is the number of variables in a particular equation. G is the number of dependent (endogenous) variables in the system. The rank condition is satisfied if the matrix of any equation within the multiequation system has at least one non-zero determinant.[3]

The results of the 3SLS analysis support the view that an interactive model best represents the relationship between Congress, the women's movement, and public opinion (Tables B-4 and B-5). The parameter estimates are all significant at the .05 level, and it is clear that public opinion mediates the effects of Social Movement and Women's Organization. Moreover, the variance explained is nearly the same in both equations (.77 and .84). This suggests that the relationship between Congress and public opinion is not only reciprocal over time but that the level of explained variance is almost equal. The strength of this model in comparison to the OLS model previously examined is that all the data are successfully incorporated and statistically significant. This interactive model is intuitively satisfying since it supports the case-study evidence that initiative was not unidirectional but shifted among the public, the movement, and Congress during this period.

# Notes

## Introduction

1. Jo Freeman, *The Politics of Women's Liberation* (New York: McKay, 1975), 170–229. Anne N. Costain, "Women's Claims as a Special Interest," in *The Politics of the Gender Gap, The Social Construction of Political Influence*, ed. Carol M. Mueller (Newbury Park, Calif.: Sage, 1988), 163–166.

2. For a list of the organizations whose representatives were interviewed, along with the criteria used to select these groups, see Anne N. Costain, "Representing Women: The Transition from Social Movement to Interest Group," *Western Political Quarterly* 34 (March 1981): 104n.4, 105n.5.

3. Interview, 31 October 1974, Washington, D.C.

4. See Betty Friedan, "Background Memorandum on NOW," undated, in File—President's Reports, Letters, etc. 1966–76, NOW Archive, Arthur and Elizabeth Schlesinger Library [AESL], Cambridge, Mass., 2; Judith Hole and Ellen Levine, *The Rebirth of Feminism* (New York: Quadrangle, 1971), 82.

5. Thirty-six members of Congress and congressional staff who had taken an active role in legislative consideration of either the Women's Educational Equity Act (1974) or the Equal Credit Opportunity Act (1974) were interviewed as part of this project. For a list of the members of Congress interviewed, see Costain, "Representing Women," 102n.6.

6. Interview, 25 June 1975, Washington, D.C.

7. Costain, "Representing Women," 102n.6.

8. For excellent overviews of resource mobilization theory and its application, see Doug McAdam, John McCarthy, and Mayer Zald, "Social Movements," in *Handbook of Sociology*, ed. Neil Smelser (Newbury Park, Calif.: Sage, 1988), 695–737; J. Craig Jenkins, "Resource Mobilization Theory and the Study of Social Movements," *Annual Review of Sociology* 9 (1983): 527–553; Sidney Tarrow, "National Politics and Collective Action: Recent Theory and Research in Western Europe and the United States," *Annual Review of Sociology* 14 (1988): 421–440.

9. Joyce Gelb and Marian Palley, *Women and Public Policies*, 1st ed. (Princeton: Princeton University Press, 1982), presents one of the earliest and most persuasive statements of this thesis.

10. Doug McAdam, *Political Process and the Development of Black Insurgency, 1930–1970* (Chicago: University of Chicago Press, 1982); idem, "Tactical Innovation and the Pace of Insurgency," *American Sociological Review* 48 (December 1983): 735–754; Sidney Tarrow, *Struggling for Reform*. Western Studies Paper no. 15 (Ithaca: Cornell University Paper Series, 1983).

11. See, for example, Sidney Tarrow, *Democracy and Disorder: Protest and Politics in Italy, 1965–1975* (New York: Oxford University Press, 1989); Ethel

Klein, *Gender Politics: From Consciousness to Mass Politics* (Cambridge, Mass.: Harvard University Press, 1984); Mary F. Katzenstein and Carol M. Mueller, eds., *The Women's Movements of the United States and Western Europe: Consciousness, Political Opportunity and Public Policy* (Philadelphia: Temple University Press, 1987); David Meyer, *The Winter of Discontent: The Nuclear Freeze in American Politics* (New York: Praeger, 1990).

12. For a thorough overview of the radical wing of the women's movement, see Alice Echols, *Daring to Be Bad: Radical Feminism in America, 1967-1975* (Minneapolis: University of Minnesota Press, 1989).

13. Georgia Duerst-Lahti, "The Government's Role in Building the Women's Movement," *Political Science Quarterly* 104, no. 2 (1989): 249-68. McAdam, *Political Process*, 235-250; idem, "Tactical Innovation," 735-754. Political science graduate students Evonne Okonski and Oneida Mascarenas carried out a substantial part of the coding of *New York Times* events. W. Douglas Costain joined me in coding bill introductions and laws passed.

14. Benjamin Ginsberg, "Elections and Public Policy," *American Political Science Review* 70 (March 1976): 41-49.

15. Donald R. Matthews, *U.S. Senators and Their World* (Chapel Hill: University of North Carolina Press, 1960) and David M. Olson and Cynthia T. Nonidez, "Measures of Legislative Performance in the U.S. House of Representatives," *Midwest Journal of Political Science* 16 (May 1972): 269-277, have used measures of bill introduction and bill passage to analyze the performance of individual legislators.

16. Congressional Quarterly, *Origins and Development of Congress* (Washington, D.C.: Congressional Quarterly, Inc., 1976), 123-125.

17. Paul Burstein, *Discrimination, Jobs and Politics* (Chicago: University of Chicago Press, 1985).

18. *Public Papers of the Presidents of the United States* (Washington, D.C.: U.S. Government Printing Office, 1954-1986, various volumes); Ronald Brunner and Katherine Livornese, *A Concordance of Nomination Acceptances and Inaugural Addresses*, vols. I, II (Boulder, Colo.: Center for Public Policy Research, University of Colorado, 1984); idem, *A Concordance to Presidential State of the Union Messages, 1945-1984*, vols. I, II (Boulder, Colo.: Center for Public Policy Research, University of Colorado, 1984).

# 1. Interpreting the Contemporary Women's Movement

1. Wilma Scott Heide, "The Feminist Cause *Is* the Common Cause," 27 March 1972, NOW Archive, AESL, 13; idem, "Revolution Tomorrow is NOW!" February 1973, National Organization for Women Papers, AESL, 4; "Bayh Optimistic on Voting Age of 18 after White House Backs Measure," *New York Times*, 18 February 1970, p. 20; Joyce Gelb and Marian L. Palley, *Women and Public Policies*, rev. ed. (Princeton: Princeton University Press, 1987), 50-51.

2. Sara Evans, *Personal Politics: The Roots of Women's Liberation in the Civil Rights Movement and the New Left* (New York: Alfred Knopf, 1979).

Elizabeth Boyer, the founder of WEAL, is reported to have claimed a victory for "convincing the older and better established women's organizations to become active on feminist issues. . . . I remember actually assuring someone that we were merely setting up a task force that probably would get its work done in five years." ("Tenth Anniversary Conference Draws Largest Attendance Ever," August 1978, Women's Equity Action League Archive, AESL).

3. Leslie Aldridge Westoff, "Is a Women's Revolution Really Possible? Yes," *McCall's*, October 1969, 157.

4. Freeman, *Politics of Women's Liberation*, 109.

5. Nancy Cott, *The Grounding of Modern Feminism* (New Haven, Conn.: Yale University Press, 1987), 3.

6. Anne N. Costain, "Representing Women: The Transition from Social Movement to Interest Group," in *Women, Power and Policy: Toward the Year 2000*, 2nd ed., ed. Ellen Boneparth and Emily Stoper (New York: Pergamon Press, 1988), 26–47; Gelb and Palley, *Women and Public Policies*, rev. ed.

7. Linda Charlton, "Women March Down Fifth in Equality Drive," *New York Times*, 27 August 1970, p. 1.

8. The term *gender gap* refers to observed differences in the typical voting patterns of men and women. Although such differences have been noted over the years in elections for which polling was done, before 1980, these differences were not consistently linked to support of one political party. As a result, they were often ignored or erroneously attributed to quirks in women's voting behavior. One example is the view that for a time had wide currency that women voted disproportionately for Eisenhower because he was a father figure and for John Kennedy because he was handsome. What makes gender differences distinctive in the 1980s and makes the gender gap a topic for press commentaries and political science articles is that differences are now tied to a fairly consistent preference on the part of women for Democratic candidates. For a more complete analysis of the gender gap, see Mueller, ed., *Politics of the Gender Gap*.

9. Mueller, ed., *Politics of the Gender Gap*.

10. National Information Bank on Women in Public Office, Center for the American Woman and Politics, Eagleton Institute of Politics, Rutgers University.

11. David J. Garrow, *Protest at Selma* (New Haven, Conn.: Yale University Press, 1978); August Meier and Elliot Rudwick, *From Plantation to Ghetto*, 3rd ed. (New York: Hill and Wang, 1976); John Hope Franklin, *From Slavery to Freedom: A History of Negro Americans*, 4th ed. (New York: Alfred A. Knopf, 1974).

12. Mark V. Nadel, *The Politics of Consumer Protection* (Indianapolis, Ind.: Bobbs-Merrill, 1971).

13. Norman Vig and Michael Kraft, "Environmental Policy from the Seventies to the Eighties," in *Environmental Policy in the 1980s*, ed. Norman Vig and Michael Kraft (Washington, D.C.: CQ Press, 1984), 3–26; Robert C. Mitchell, "Public Opinion and Environmental Policies in the 1970s and 1980s," in ibid., 51–74.

14. James G. Watt with Doug Wead, *The Courage of a Conservative* (New

York: Simon and Schuster, 1985); Anne M. Burford with John Greenya, *Are You Tough Enough?* (New York: McGraw-Hill, 1986).

15. *Politics of Women's Liberation.*

16. Simone de Beauvoir, *The Second Sex*, trans. H. M. Parshley (New York: Modern Library, 1961 [1949]).

17. For good summaries of this debate, see McAdam, McCarthy, and Zald, "Social Movements," 695-737; Tarrow, "National Politics and Collective Action," 421-440; Jenkins, "Resource Mobilization Theory," 527-553.

18. Steven F. Lawson, *Black Ballots: Voting Rights in the South, 1944-1969* (New York: Columbia University Press, 1976).

19. Cott, *Grounding of Modern Feminism*, 252-253.

20. William Kornhauser, *The Politics of Mass Society* (Glencoe, Ill.: The Free Press, 1959); Philip Selznick, *The Organizational Weapon* (New York: The Free Press, 1960); idem, "Institutional Vulnerability in Mass Society," in *Protest, Reform and Revolt*, ed. Joseph R. Gusfield (New York: John Wiley and Sons, 1970), 258-274; Hannah Arendt, *The Origins of Totalitarianism* (New York: Harcourt, Brace, 1951).

21. Seymour Martin Lipset and Earl Raabe, *The Politics of Unreason* (New York: Harper and Row, 1970); Seymour Martin Lipset, "Symposium-America Now: A Failure of Nerve?" *Commentary* 60 (July 1975): 58-59; Daniel Bell, ed., *The Radical Right* (New York: Doubleday, 1963); Richard Hofstadter, *The Paranoid Style in American Politics* (New York: Knopf, 1965).

22. See, for example, Paul H. Weaver, "Regulation, Social Policy and Class Conflict," *The Public Interest* 50 (Winter 1978): 45-63; Alvin W. Gouldner, *The Future of Intellectuals and the Rise of the New Class* (New York: Seabury Press, 1979); Alfred Marcus, "The Disproportionate Power of Environmentalists," *Harvard Environmental Law Review* 2 (1977): 582-595; Peter Skerry, "The Class Conflict over Abortion," *The Public Interest* 52 (Summer 1978): 69-84.

23. Lipset, "Symposium-America Now," 58-59.

24. Jeane Kirkpatrick, *The New Presidential Elite* (New York: Russell Sage Foundation, 1976), 246.

25. Ralph H. Turner and Lewis M. Killian, *Collective Behavior*, 2nd ed. (Englewood Cliffs, N.J.: Prentice-Hall, 1972); Joseph Gusfield, "The Study of Social Movements," in *International Encyclopedia of the Social Sciences*, ed. David L. Sills (New York: Crowell, Collier and Macmillan, 1968), 14:445; Selznick, "Institutional Vulnerability"; Kornhauser, *Politics of Mass Society*.

26. Ted R. Gurr, *Why Men Rebel* (Princeton: Princeton University Press, 1970).

27. Jo Freeman, "Origins of the Women's Liberation Movement," *American Journal of Sociology* 78 (1973): 792-811; idem, *Politics of Women's Liberation*.

28. *Politics of Women's Liberation*, 35-38.

29. See, for example, Jo Freeman, ed., *Social Movements of the Sixties and Seventies* (New York: Longman, 1983).

30. See Jenkins, "Resource Mobilization Theory"; Anthony Oberschall, *Social Conflict and Social Movements* (Englewood Cliffs, N.J.: Prentice-Hall,

1973); John D. McCarthy and Mayer N. Zald, *The Trend of Social Movements in America* (Morristown, N.J.: General Learning Press, 1973); idem, "Resource Mobilization and Social Movements," *American Journal of Sociology* 82 (May 1977): 1212–1241; idem, eds., *Dynamics of Social Movements* (Cambridge, Mass.: Winthrop, 1979).

31. McCarthy and Zald, "Resource Mobilization," 1217–1218.

32. This definition of social movements has been criticized for its inclusiveness. By encompassing so many groups which operate primarily through the institutionalized political system, the critics of RM assert that the unconventional, extra-systemic thrust of social movements is lost. See McAdam, *Political Process*, 23–29.

33. See Robert Salisbury's classic article that applies economic concepts to the evaluation of interest-group success: "An Exchange Theory of Interest Groups," *Midwest Journal of Political Science* 13 (February 1969): 1–32.

34. Oberschall, *Social Conflict*; McCarthy and Zald, *Trend of Social Movements*; McCarthy and Zald, eds., *Dynamics of Social Movements*.

35. J. Craig Jenkins and Charles Perrow, "Insurgency of the Powerless," *American Sociological Review* 42, 2 (1977): 249–268.

36. Gelb and Palley, *Women and Public Policies*, 1st and rev. eds.; Jane J. Mansbridge, *Why We Lost the ERA* (Chicago, Ill.: University of Chicago Press, 1986).

37. Pamela J. Conover and Virginia Gray, *Feminism and the New Right: Conflict over the American Family* (New York: Praeger, 1983).

38. Nancy McGlen and Karen O'Connor, *Women's Rights* (New York, Praeger, 1983).

39. Betty Friedan, *The Feminine Mystique* (New York: Dell, 1974 [1963]).

40. Jo Freeman, "The Tyranny of Structurelessness," *Ms Magazine*, July 1973, 76–89.

41. Tarrow, "National Politics and Collective Action."

42. McAdam, *Political Process*, 37.

43. Charles Tilly, *From Mobilization to Revolution* (Reading, Mass.: Addison-Wesley, 1978); Tarrow, *Struggling for Reform*; J. Craig Jenkins, *The Politics of Insurgency* (New York: Columbia University Press, 1985); idem, "Three Theories in Search of a Political Age," *Research in Political Sociology* 3 (1987): 269–304; McAdam, *Political Process*.

44. *Why Men Rebel*.

45. *Political Process*, 48–51.

46. Klein, *Gender Politics*, 81–93.

47. Ethel Klein, "The Diffusion of Consciousness in the United States and Western Europe," in *Women's Movements*, 23–43; Carol M. Mueller, "Collective Consciousness, Identity Transformation, and the Rise of Women in Public Office in the United States," in ibid., 89–108.

48. Patricia Gurin ("Women's Gender Consciousness," *Public Opinion Quarterly* 49 [Summer 1985]: 143–163) has made the interesting observation that men and women were changing their attitudes in tandem about women's proper role.

49. *Women's Movements.*

50. Cynthia Harrison, *On Account of Sex: The Politics of Women's Issues, 1945-1968* (Berkeley and Los Angeles: University of California Press, 1988), 211-221.

51. Duerst-Lahti, "The Government's Role," 249-268.

52. Frances Piven and Richard Cloward, *Poor People's Movements* (New York: Pantheon Books, 1977); Tarrow, "National Politics and Collective Action."

53. Using events data to trace the onset and subsequent development of social movements is an accepted method of studying social movements of the sixties and seventies. See Jenkins and Perrow, "Insurgency of the Powerless"; McAdam, *Political Process*; idem, "Tactical Innovation," 735-754; J. Craig Jenkins and Craig Eckert, "Channeling Black Insurgency," *American Sociological Review* 51 (1986): 812-829; Burstein, *Discrimination, Jobs and Politics.* Doug McAdam, whose coding rules were adopted for the current study, has concluded that this method can accurately portray "the rate of involvement of various groups over time, the different patterns of activity manifest by various parties to the conflict . . . and the interaction of various groups over time" (*Political Process*, 235). These data cannot show subtle social and psychological states, such as feelings of strain or relative deprivation among individuals. Similarly, both the onset of the movement and the end of the movement are likely to be underreported by the media, since, in the first instance, reporters may not yet recognize that these events are newsworthy and, at the other end, a waning "issue attention cycle" may lead newspapers to underreport continuing movement activities (Gurr, *Why Men Rebel*, 34).

54. These include problems of coding bias, the units of analysis selected, and measures of intercoder reliability. See Paul Burstein and Kathleen Monaghan, "Equal Employment Opportunity and the Mobilization of Law," *Law and Society Review* 20, no. 3 (1986): 355-388; Charles Johnson, "Content-Analytic Techniques and Judicial Research," *American Politics Quarterly* 15, no. 1 (1987): 169-197.

55. *Political Process*, 236-237.

56. "Insurgency of the Powerless," 253-254.

57. David Snyder and William Kelly, "Conflict Intensity, Media Sensitivity, and the Validity of Newspaper Data," *American Sociological Review* 42 (1977): 105-123.

58. Gary Marx, "External Efforts to Damage or Facilitate Social Movements: Some Patterns, Explanations, Outcomes and Complications," in McCarthy and Zald, eds., *Dynamics of Social Movements*, 94-125; Piven and Cloward, *Poor People's Movements*; McAdam, "Tactical Innovation"; Jenkins and Perrow, "Insurgency of the Powerless."

59. *From Mobilization to Revolution*, 100.

60. Anne N. Costain and W. Douglas Costain, "Strategy and Tactics of the Women's Movement in the United States: The Role of Political Parties," *Women's Movements*, 197-201.

61. Richard Cloward and Frances Piven, "Toward a Class-based Realign-

ment of American Politics: A Movement Strategy," *Social Policy* 14 (Summer 1983): 2–14; Piven and Cloward, *Poor People's Movements*.

62. *Struggling for Reform*; idem, "National Politics and Collective Action."

63. Lawson, *Black Ballots*.

64. James Q. Wilson, "The Politics of Deregulation," in *The Politics of Regulation*, James Q. Wilson, ed. (New York: Basic Books, 1980), 357–394.

65. Andrew S. McFarland, "Interest Groups and Theories of Power in America," *British Journal of Political Science* 17 (April 1987): 129–147; idem, "Sources of Countervailing Power in America: Contributions from Recent Interest Group Theory." Paper presented at the 1987 Annual Meeting of the American Political Science Association, Chicago, Illinois.

66. McFarland, "Interest Groups," 145–146.

67. Hole and Levine, *Rebirth of Feminism*, 82–85.

68. See Duerst-Lahti, "Government's Role."

## 2. The Opening of Political Opportunity for Women

1. McAdam, *Political Process*, 36–59.

2. Cott, *Grounding of Modern Feminism*, 85–114.

3. David B. Truman, *The Governmental Process: Political Interests and Public Opinion*, 2nd ed. (New York: Alfred A. Knopf, 1971); Jack Walker, "The Origins and Maintenance of Interest Groups in America," *American Political Science Review* 77 (1983): 390–406; Cynthia Harrison, "Prelude to Feminism: Women's Organizations, the Federal Government and the Rise of the Women's Movement, 1942 to 1968" (Ph.D. diss., Columbia University, 1982), 11–12.

4. Cott, *Grounding of Modern Feminism*, 89–96.

5. J. Stanley Lemons, *The Woman Citizen: Social Feminism in the 1920s* (Urbana, Ill.: University of Illinois Press, 1973), 181–196; Gilbert Y. Steiner, *Constitutional Inequality: The Political Fortunes of the Equal Rights Amendment* (Washington, D.C.: Brookings Institution, 1985), 7–12.

6. Harrison, "Prelude to Feminism," 1–20; Lemons, *Woman Citizen*.

7. Harrison, "Prelude to Feminism," 60–92.

8. Ibid., 350–354.

9. Harrison, *On Account of Sex*, 126–130.

10. U.S. President's Commission on the Status of Women, *American Women: Report of the President's Commission on the Status of Women* (Washington, D.C.: U.S. Government Printing Office, 1963), 45.

11. 404 U.S. 71 (1971).

12. J. Ralph Lindgren and Nadine Taub, *The Law of Sex Discrimination* (St. Paul, Minn.: West Publishing, 1988), 109–168.

13. Harrison, "Prelude to Feminism," 478–483.

14. Cott, *Grounding of Modern Feminism*; Jo Freeman, "Equality versus Protection" (Unpublished manuscript, 1987), 1–15.

15. Harrison, *On Account of Sex*, 160–161.

16. Evans, *Personal Politics*.

17. Hole and Levine, *Rebirth of Feminism*, 110.

18. Ibid.

19. Ibid., 111.

20. Ibid., 112.

21. Westoff, "Is a Women's Revolution Really Possible? Yes," 157.

22. Meredith Tax, "There Was a Young Woman Who Swallowed a Line" (undated manuscript, AESL, vertical file).

23. Harrison, *On Account of Sex*.

24. Jo Freeman, "Party Platforms and the ERA" (Unpublished manuscript, 1987), 1-8.

25. Piven and Cloward, *Poor People's Movements*, 198.

26. Lawson, *Black Ballots*, 150-151.

27. Henry C. Kenski, "The Gender Factor in a Changing Electorate," in *Politics of the Gender Gap*, 50.

28. Quoted in Brunner and Livornese, *Presidential State of the Union Messages*, 109.

29. Quoted in Brunner and Livornese, *Nomination Acceptances and Inaugural Addresses*, 38.

30. Dwight Eisenhower, "Radio and Television Broadcast: 'The Women Ask the President,'" 24 October 1956, *Public Papers of the Presidents of the United States: Dwight D. Eisenhower, 1956* (Washington, D.C.: U.S. Government Printing Office, 1958), 1004.

31. Ibid., 1026.

32. Dwight Eisenhower, "Remarks at Fifth Annual Republican Women's National Conference," 3 April 1957, *Public Papers of the Presidents of the United States: Dwight Eisenhower, 1957* (Washington, D.C.: U.S. Government Printing Office, 1958), 258.

33. Ibid., 57.

34. Harrison, *On Account of Sex*, 58-62.

35. *Public Papers: Eisenhower, 1957*, 258.

36. Harrison, "Prelude to Feminism," 244-293.

37. "A Chivalrous Kennedy Backs Women's Rights," *New York Times*, 9 November 1961, p. 14; Alvin Shuster, "President Names Panel on Women," *New York Times*, 15 December 1961, p. 34.

38. "President Backs Women's Drive for Fair Pay and Chance at Jobs," *New York Times*, 13 February 1962, p. 1.

39. "Civil Rights Linked to Women's Goals," *New York Times*, 25 June 1963, p. 13.

40. Marjorie Hunter, "U.S. Panel Urges Women to Sue for Equal Rights," *New York Times*, 12 October 1963, p. 1.

41. Marjorie Hunter, "U.S. Acts to Raise Status of Women," *New York Times*, 2 November 1963, p. 27.

42. "Text of President Eisenhower's Budget Message to Congress," *New York Times*, 17 January 1957, p. 16; "President Says Women Qualify for His Position," *New York Times*, 14 January 1954; and "Mrs. Luce Is Sworn in as 'Ambasciatrice' to Italy," *New York Times*, 4 March 1953, pp. 1, 17.

43. Quoted in Brunner and Livornese, *Presidential State of the Union Messages*, 157.

44. Ibid., 148.

45. John Kennedy, "Transcript of Interview with Mrs. Eleanor Roosevelt Recorded for National Educational Television," 22 April 1962, *Public Papers of the Presidents of the United States: John F. Kennedy, 1962* (Washington, D.C.: U.S. Government Printing Office, 1963), 342–343.

46. Quoted in Harrison, *On Account of Sex*, 164–165.

47. *Discrimination, Jobs and Politics*, 43–51.

48. Ibid., 50.

49. Freeman, *Politics of Women's Liberation*, 53–54, 237; *Congressional Record*, 88th Cong., 2d sess., 1964. vol. 110, pt. 2; Harrison, *On Account of Sex*, 176–184.

50. Harrison, *On Account of Sex*, 201–202.

51. *Congressional Record*, 88th Cong., 2d sess., 1964. vol. 110, pt. 2, 2578.

52. Ibid., 2580.

53. Ibid., 2580–2581.

54. Ibid., 2581.

55. Harrison, *On Account of Sex*, 187; Freeman, *Politics of Women's Liberation*, 54.

56. *Politics of Women's Liberation*, 222, 228, 234.

57. New York: Russell Sage Foundation.

58. Ibid., v.

59. Klein, *Gender Politics*.

60. Susan J. Carroll, "Women's Autonomy," in *Politics of the Gender Gap*, 236–257.

61. *Poor People's Movements*, 12.

62. Myra Ferree and Beth Hess, *Controversy and Coalition: The New Feminist Movement* (Boston, Mass.: Twayne, 1985), 53–54.

63. Carol Mueller, "The Empowerment of Women: Polling and the Women's Voting Bloc," in *Politics of the Gender Gap*, 16–36.

64. IWY Secretariat, "Women's Movement in the U.S. 1960–1975: Government Role in the Women's Movement" (3 June 1975, AESL, vertical file), 21 pages.

65. The text reads:

> The U.S. Government does *not* plan social change in the sense that some other governments do—it responds to the demands for reform made by citizens and/or voluntary associations and works with them in charting the mechanisms of social change.
>
> The great changes that have occurred in the legal and economic status of women in the past 15 years have not been initiated by Government, and it seems unlikely that future changes will be initiated by Government. (Ibid., 1.)

66. Ibid., 2.

67. Ibid., 3.

## 3. A New Women's Movement Emerges

1. Harrison, *On Account of Sex*, 193; Hole and Levine, *Rebirth of Feminism*, 82.

2. Betty Friedan, "Background Memorandum on NOW," undated, File: President's Reports, Letters, etc. 1966–76, NOW Archive, AESL, Cambridge, Mass., 1.

3. Betty Friedan, "Report of the President," January, 1968, File: Mailings to Nonmembers, NOW Archive, AESL, 2.

4. Betty Friedan, "Background Memorandum on NOW," AESL, 2; Hole and Levine, *Rebirth of Feminism*, 82.

5. Margaret Hickey, outgoing head of the Citizens' Advisory Council on the Status of Women; Mary Keyserling, director of the Women's Bureau of the Department of Labor; and Esther Peterson, then White House Special Assistant on Consumer Affairs under President Johnson, told Clarenbach that they refused to allow a government forum to be used to criticize the Johnson administration. Harrison, *On Account of Sex*, 193–195.

6. National Organization for Women, "National Organization for Women," 29 June 1966, File: National Office and Policy, NOW Archive, AESL.

7. Historian Frances Kolb ("NOW and the Search for a Feminist Ideology," Lecture, 30 April 1981, Radcliffe College, Cambridge, Mass.) characterized NOW in its first year as primarily a lobbyist for *American Women*, the report of the Presidential Commission on the Status of Women; Harrison, *On Account of Sex*, 196–205.

8. National Organization for Women, "The First Five Years, 1966–1971," undated, Vertical File, NOW Archive, AESL, 2.

9. Betty Friedan, "Memo to All Board Members," 24 January 1967, File: President's Reports, Letters, etc. 1966–76, NOW Archive, AESL.

10. Freeman, *Politics of Women's Liberation*, 80–81; Hole and Levine, *Rebirth of Feminism*, 88–89.

11. National Organization for Women, "Memorandum," 22 September 1969, quoted in Hole and Levine, *Rebirth of Feminism*, 91–92.

12. Hole and Levine, *Rebirth of Feminism*, 89–91; Freeman, *Politics of Women's Liberation*, 81–82.

13. National Organization for Women, "NOW Press Release," 14 December 1967, File: 1966–1971, NOW Archive, AESL.

14. National Organization for Women, "Preconference Board Meeting, Atlanta, Georgia, December 6, 1968," File: National Office and Policy, NOW Archive, AESL.

15. National Organization for Women, "NOW Press Releases," 6 May 1969, File: 1966–1971, NOW Archive, AESL, 2.

16. "The New Feminists: Revolt against 'Sexism'," *Time*, 21 November 1969, pp. 53–54.

17. Paula Stern, "When's It Going to Be Ladies' Day?" *New Republic*, 5 July 1969, pp. 14–16.

18. Sara Davidson, "An 'Oppressed Majority' Demands Its Rights," *Life*, 12 December 1969, pp. 66–78.

19. Stern, "When's It Going to Be Ladies' Day?" p. 14.

20. National Organization for Women, "Preconference Board Meeting."

21. This is a conservative estimate of NOW's membership in this period. By comparison, Barbara Sinclair Deckard (*The Women's Movement: Political, Socioeconomic and Psychological Issues*, 3rd ed. [New York: Harper and Row, 1983], 326) estimates that in 1971 NOW had over 150 chapters and from 5,000 to 10,000 members.

22. Women's Equity Action League, *WEAL's Word Watcher* (Winter 1970), File: WEAL National Newsletter, WEAL Archive, AESL.

23. Wilma Salisbury, "Another Lib Voice Heard From," *Cleveland Plain Dealer*, 28 June 1970, p. 2-E.

24. Elizabeth Boyer, "State Chapter Development: WEAL," 27 March 1971, Folder 203, WEAL Archive, AESL.

25. Women's Equity Action League, "WEAL Holds These Truths to Be Self-Evident," c. 1973 [Washington, D.C., address], Folder 219, WEAL Archive, AESL.

26. Women's Equity Action League, "Support/Consciousness-Raising Groups," undated, Folder 220, Leaflets, WEAL Archive, AESL.

27. Interview with Bert Hartry, Women's Equity Action League, 29 January 1981, Cambridge, Mass.

28. Linda Greenhouse, "Women's Groups Pressing Reforms," *New York Times*, 25 November 1969, p. 51.

29. Costain, "Representing Women," in *Women, Power and Policy*, 28–30.

30. Interview with Judith Norrell, League of Women Voters, 14 August 1975, Washington, D.C.

31. Interview with a representative of the League of Women Voters, 8 October 1974, Washington, D.C.

32. Interview, 19 November, 1974, Washington, D.C.

33. Interview with Judith Norrell, 14 August, 1975, Washington, D.C.

34. Equal Rights Amendment Ratification Council, Notes from their 30 October 1974 meeting, Washington, D.C.

35. Lyndon B. Johnson, "Annual Message to the Congress: The Manpower Report of the President," 9 March 1964, *Public Papers of the Presidents of the United States: Lyndon B. Johnson, 1963–64*, 2 vols. (Washington, D.C.: U.S. Government Printing Office, 1965), 354; "Remarks to Delegates to the Equal Pay Conference," 11 June 1964, ibid., 767.

36. Harrison, *On Account of Sex*, 180.

37. Johnson, "The President's News Conference of February 1, 1964," *Public Papers: Johnson, 1963–64*, 259.

38. "Remarks at a Reception for Recently Appointed Women in Government," 13 April 1964, ibid., 460.

39. See, for example, Johnson, "Remarks to the Winners of the Federal Woman's Award," 3 March 1964, and "Remarks upon Presenting the First Eleanor Roosevelt Memorial Award to Judge Anna M. Kross," 4 March 1964,

ibid., 330, 335; Lyndon B. Johnson, "Remarks at the Presentation of the National Civil Service League's Career Service Awards," 19 May 1965, *Public Papers of the Presidents of the United States: Lyndon B. Johnson, 1965*, 2 vols. (Washington, D.C.: U.S. Government Printing Office, 1966), 562.

40. *Public Papers: Johnson, 1965*, 562.

41. "Remarks on the Status of Women in America—Speaking on the South Lawn to Members of the Citizens' Advisory Council on the Status of Women and of the Governors' Commission," 29 July 1965, ibid., 808.

42. "President's Press Conference," 25 January 1964, *Public Papers: Johnson, 1963-64*, 232.

43. Lyndon B. Johnson, "Remarks at the Federal Woman's Award Ceremony," 14 March 1968, *Public Papers of the Presidents of the United States: Lyndon B. Johnson, 1968-69* (Washington, D.C.: U.S. Government Printing Office, 1970), 399.

44. Lyndon B. Johnson, "Remarks at the Sixth Annual Federal Woman's Award," 28 February 1966, *Public Papers of the Presidents of the United States: Lyndon B. Johnson, 1966*, 2 vols. (Washington, D.C.: U.S. Government Printing Office, 1967), 226.

45. Steiner, *Constitutional Inequality*, 13.

46. Gary Orfield, *Congressional Power: Congress and Social Change* (New York: Harcourt, Brace, Jovanovich, 1975), 301.

47. Freeman, "Party Platforms and the ERA," 7.

48. Mansbridge, *Why We Lost the ERA*.

49. *Congressional Power*, 301.

50. Ibid.

51. Interview with Clelia Steele, 19 August 1975, Washington, D.C.

52. Freeman, *Politics of Women's Liberation*, 217-218.

53. Cott, *Grounding of Modern Feminism*, 261.

54. Deckard, *Women's Movement*, 442.

55. John P. Van de Geer, *Introduction to Multivariate Analysis for the Social Sciences* (San Francisco, Calif.: W. H. Freeman, 1971), 243-272.

56. Because several of the independent variables in this particular case are in fact not independent of each other but are instead strongly intercorrelated (e.g., conservative [ACA] and liberal [ADA] ratings), a stepwise equation based on Wilks' Lambda is used to minimize the adverse mathematical consequence of this lack of independence. For an explanation of this technique, see Marija J. Norusis, *SPSS/PC+ Advanced Statistics V2.0* (Chicago, Ill.: SPSS Inc., 1988), B-17-B-31.

57. Myra M. Ferree, "A Woman for President? Changing Responses, 1958-1972," *Public Opinion Quarterly* 38 (Fall 1974): 394.

58. Richard M. Nixon, "Remarks at the 17th Annual Republican Women's Conference," 16 April 1969, *Public Papers of the Presidents of the United States: Richard M. Nixon, 1969* (Washington, D.C.: U.S. Government Printing Office, 1971), 291.

59. Richard M. Nixon, "President's News Conference," 1 June 1971, *Public Papers of the Presidents of the United States: Richard M. Nixon, 1971* (Washington, D.C.: U.S. Government Printing Office, 1972), 690.

60. "Memorandum About Women in Government—To the Heads of Executive Departments and Agencies," 21 April 1971, ibid., 580.

61. "Remarks to Delegates to the Girls Nation Annual Convention," 6 August 1971, ibid., 864.

62. Richard M. Nixon, "Statement About the Status of Women Within the Administration," 28 April 1972, *Public Papers of the Presidents of the United States: Richard M. Nixon, 1972* (Washington, D.C.: U.S. Government Printing Office, 1974), 556–557.

63. "Letter to the Senate Minority Leader About the Proposed Constitutional Amendment on Equal Rights for Men and Women," 18 March 1972, ibid., 444.

64. Richard M. Nixon, "State of the Union Message to the Congress on Human Resources," 1 March 1973, *Public Papers of the Presidents of the United States: Richard M. Nixon, 1973* (Washington, D.C.: U.S. Government Printing Office, 1975), 143.

65. Richard M. Nixon, "State of the Union," 30 January 1974, *Public Papers of the Presidents of the United States: Richard M. Nixon, 1974* (Washington, D.C.: U.S. Government Printing Office, 1975), 76–77.

66. Freeman, *Politics of Women's Liberation*, 216–217, 234.

67. Ferree, "A Woman for President?," 391.

68. E. M. Schreiber, "Education and Change in American Opinions on a Woman for President," *Public Opinion Quarterly* 42 (Summer 1978): 174.

69. Rebecca M. Blank, "Women's Paid Work, Household Income, and Household Well-being," in *The American Woman, 1988–89*, ed. Sara Rix (New York: W.W. Norton, 1988), 127; Klein, "Diffusion of Consciousness," 23–43.

70. Burstein, *Discrimination, Jobs, and Politics*, 50.

71. Klein, "Diffusion of Consciousness," 24.

72. Freeman, *Politics of Women's Liberation*, 147–169.

## 4. The High Point of the Women's Movement

1. See chapter 2 for a discussion of the history of this long conflict among women's groups.

2. Eleanor Flexner, *Century of Struggle* (New York: Atheneum, 1973).

3. Anne Costain, "The Struggle for a National Women's Lobby," *Western Political Quarterly* 33 (December 1980): 490.

4. The Pearson product moment correlation between the number of women's events per year and the number of ERA events per year is .93. Since a sizeable percentage of the total events themselves concerned the ERA, a correlation was also run between the ERA and non-ERA events reported in the *New York Times*. This correlation was also quite high, .73 (significant at the .001 level).

5. William Chafe, *The American Woman* (New York: Oxford University Press, 1972), 3–47; Costain, "Women's Claims," 150–172.

6. 479 U.S. 272 (1987).

7. Hole and Levine, *Rebirth of Feminism*, 439-40.

8. See Costain, "Struggle for a National Women's Lobby," 476-477, for a list of the groups and dates when interviews were held.

9. Ibid., 488.

10. Interview, 3 December 1974, Washington, D.C.

11. Interview, 22-October 1974, Washington, D.C.

12. Interview, 25 November 1974, Washington, D.C.

13. Interview, 31 October 1974, Washington, D.C.

14. Costain, "Representing Women," in *Women, Power and Policy*, 29-30.

15. File: "Press Releases, 1972," 15 December 1975, NOW Archive, AESL, 2.

16. "Majority Caucus: We're Doing It NOW," *Electric Circle*, 1975, NOW Archive, AESL, 3.

17. Costain, "Struggle for a National Women's Lobby," 488.

18. Costain, "Representing Women," *Western Political Quarterly*, 109.

19. Equality concerns were those coded discrimination, equality under the law, and the Equal Rights Amendment. Special-needs concerns included history of women, political status of women, the women's movement, women's organizational concerns, internal dissent within the women's movement, general plight of women, sports, family, crime, women's health, abortion, black women, lesbians, and international women's year.

20. Costain, "Women's Claims," 158.

21. Ibid., 163-164.

22. Staff aide to Representative Leonor Sullivan (D, Mo.), interview, 18 July 1975, Washington, D.C.

23. Staff aide to Representative Parren Mitchell (D, Md.), interview, 19 February 1975, Washington, D.C.

24. Interview, 10 July 1975, Washington, D.C.

25. Interview, 16 July 1975, Washington, D.C.

26. Interviews, 3 July and 24 July 1975, Washington, D.C.

27. Interview, 26 June 1975, Washington, D.C.

28. Interview, 10 January 1975, Washington, D.C.

29. Interview, 6 December 1974, Washington, D.C.

30. Interview, 10 December 1974, Washington, D.C.

31. Interview, 14 July 1975, Washington, D.C.

32. Gerald R. Ford, "Remarks at Graduation Ceremonies at Holton Arms School," 5 June 1975, *Public Papers of the Presidents of the United States: Gerald R. Ford, 1975* (Washington, D.C.: U.S. Government Printing Office, 1977), 775; "Remarks at a Reception for Members of the National Commission on the Observance of International Women's Year, 1975," 14 April 1975, ibid., 479.

33. "Memorandum on Equal Opportunity in Federal Employment," 6 March 1975, ibid., 319; "Remarks at a Reception for Members of the National Commission on the Observance of International Women's Year, 1975," 14 April 1975, ibid., 478.

34. "The President's News Conference of July 12, 1975," 12 July 1975, ibid., 974.

35. Ibid.

36. Gerald R. Ford, "Q and A Session with Students at the Stanford University School of Law," 21 September 1975, ibid., 1482.

37. Gerald R. Ford, "Remarks and Q and A Session at the Abilene Jaycees Bicentennial Celebration," 30 April 1976, *Public Papers of the Presidents of the United States: Gerald R. Ford, 1976–1977*, (Washington, D.C.: U.S. Government Printing Office, 1979), 1393.

38. "Remarks at a Reception for Participants in the Legislative Conference of the National Federation of Business and Professional Women's Clubs," 4 March 1976, ibid., 522.

39. Kenski, "Gender Factor," 50.

40. As President Carter told delegates at the League of Women Voters' Biennial National Convention on 5 May 1980, "In the last . . . 5 or 6 months, I have met every month with the leaders of, I would guess, 15 different organizations committed to the ratification of ERA. I meet with them personally." In Jimmy Carter, "League of Women Voters. Q and A," 5 May 1980, *Public Papers of the Presidents of the United States: Jimmy Carter, 1980–81* (Washington, D.C.: U.S. Government Printing Office, 1981), 833. See also his "Equal Rights Amendment," 15 May 1980, ibid., 921–925; "Equal Rights Amendment Dinner," 18 June 1980, ibid., 1134.

41. Jimmy Carter, "Ad Hoc Coalition for Women," 10 March 1977, *Public Papers of the Presidents of the United States: Jimmy Carter, 1977* (Washington, D.C.: U.S. Government Printing Office, 1977), 358.

42. Ibid., 357.

43. Carter, "The State of the Union," 16 January 1981, *Public Papers: Carter, 1980–81*, 2969; "Digest of Other White House Announcements," 12 February 1980, ibid., 333; "League of Women Voters, Q and A," 5 May 1980, ibid., 833.

44. Jimmy Carter, "Equal Rights Amendment: Letter to Members of the House Judiciary Committee," 12 July 1978, *Public Papers of the Presidents of the United States: Jimmy Carter, 1978* (Washington, D.C.: U.S. Government Printing Office, 1980), 1266–1267; "Interview with the President," 11 August 1978, ibid., 1412; "International Women's Year, 1975: Message to the Congress Transmitting a Report," 27 September 1978, ibid., 1643.

45. "Ask President Carter," 5 March 1977, *Public Papers: Carter, 1977*, 300–301.

46. See Carter, "National Women's Political Caucus. Remarks at a Reception for Members of the Organization," 30 March 1977, ibid., 545; "Statement on Senate Action on the ERA Extension Resolution," 6 October 1978, *Public Papers: Carter, 1978*, 1719; idem, "State of the Union," 25 January 1979, *The Public Papers of Presidents of the United States: Jimmy Carter, 1979* (Washington, D.C.: U.S. Government Printing Office, 1980), 143; "AFL-CIO. Remarks at the Organization's General Board Meeting," 4 September 1980, *Public Papers: Carter, 1980–81*, 1652–1653.

47. "Q and A, Philadelphia, Pennsylvania" 9 May 1980, *Public Papers: Carter, 1980-81*, 880. See also, Carter, "Equal Rights Amendment Dinner," 18 June 1980, ibid., 1134; "Girls Nation," 18 July 1980, ibid., 1370-1371; "Remarks at a Democratic National Committee Fundraising Reception," 2 October 1980, ibid., 2044-2045.

48. Michael Malbin, "The Democrats: A Platform that Carter May Find Awkward to Stand On," *National Journal*, 23 August 1980, 1392.

49. Interviews with representatives of the Women's Legal Defense Fund, 28 April 1977; the International Union of Electrical, Radio and Machine Workers, 13 April 1977; the Federation of Organizations for Professional Women, 8 April 1977; the American Civil Liberties Union, 29 April 1977; and NOW, 6 May 1977 were conducted by the author in Washington, D.C. Congressional staff members who were closely involved in consideration of this bill were also questioned in Washington, including Barbara Dixon, on 20 May; Maria Landolpho, on 20 May; Carol Shanzer, on 24 May; and Susan Grayson, on 24 May.

50. "The State of the Union," 21 January 1980, *Public Papers: Carter, 1980-81*, 140-141.

51. Ibid.

52. "The State of the Union," 16 January 1981, ibid., 2954-2955.

53. "More than 21 percent of my appointments within the White House and the executive branch have been women, an all-time high for any Administration." Carter, "International Women's Year, 1975," 27 September 1978, *Public Papers: Carter, 1978*, 1641.

54. Early in his presidency, Carter noted: "We've only appointed now about two-thirds of the subcabinet members in the major departments, but in those major departments headed by a Cabinet Secretary, we have tripled, more than tripled, the number of women involved. I think in the last administration we had eight women. We now have 29 and the number is growing." "President's News Conference," 8 February 1977, *Public Papers: Carter, 1977*, 99.

Toward the end of his term in office, he observed that "We've had, I think, 6 women cabinet officers in 200 years, I've appointed 3 of them . . . [that is] not enough. . . . And we've got 32 Federal judges now who are women, and I've appointed 28 of the 32. And we've had a net decrease in Federal employment since I've been President, in the bureaucracy, but we've had a 26,000 increase in the number of women employed [in the bureaucracy]." "League of Women Voters. Q and A," 5 May 1980, *Public Papers: Carter, 1980-81*, 830.

55. "Memphis, Tennessee. Q and A," 31 October 1980, *Public Papers: Carter, 1980-81*, 2592-2593. For other remarks about Ronald Reagan's abandonment of the ERA by candidate Carter, see Carter, "Remarks at a Democratic National Committee Fundraising Reception," 2 October 1980, ibid., 2044-2045; "Youngstown, Ohio. Q and A," 20 October 1980, ibid., 2350; "New York, New York. Remarks at a Meeting with Civic and Community Leaders," 13 October 1980, ibid., 2197; "Remarks at a Democratic National Committee Fundraising Dinner," 20 October 1980, ibid., 2374-2375; "Remarks at the 1980 Presidential Campaign Debate," 28 October 1980, ibid., 2498-2499.

56. Kenski, "The Gender Factor," 50.

57. Despite President Carter's unprecedented degree of support for equal rights for women, he became embroiled in a controversy that for the short term, at least, detracted from his reputation as an advocate for women. His decision to fire former Representative Bella Abzug from her position as cochair of the 40-member National Advisory Committee for Women (to which he had appointed her less than six months before) following her criticism of his administration's budget proposals, angered feminists. The cochair and more than half of the committee resigned in protest over the president's action. NOW, the largest feminist group, subsequently decided not to endorse Carter for reelection in 1980. See Dom Bonafede, "Billy and Bella," *National Journal*, 20 January 1979, 105; idem, "People: Carter Treats his Bella-ache," *National Journal*, 20 January 1979, 114; Malbin, "Democrats," 1392.

58. Mansbridge, *Why We Lost the ERA*, 96.

59. Mueller, "Collective Consciousness," 102.

60. Ibid., 103.

61. Ibid.; Susan Carroll, "Gender Politics and the Socializing Impact of the Women's Movement," in *Political Learning in Adulthood*, ed. Roberta Sigel (Chicago, Ill.: University of Chicago Press, 1989), 306–339.

62. "Women's Gender Consciousness," 143–163.

63. Ibid.; Mueller, "Collective Consciousness," 102; Carol M. Mueller, "In Search of a Constituency for the New Religious Right," *Public Opinion Quarterly* 47 (Summer 1983): 213–229.

## 5. Fighting Decline

1. All the interviews were held in Washington, D.C. The following interviews were conducted in 1981: Patricia Reuss, Women's Equity Action League, on 6 January; Carol Bros, National Women's Political Caucus, on 6 January; Jane Wells-Schooley, National Organization for Women, on 7 January; and Ann Smith, Congresswomen's Caucus, on 7 January. Ann Smith of the Congressional Caucus for Women's Issues (formerly the Congresswomen's Caucus), Catherine East and Linda Anderson of the National Women's Political Caucus, and Patricia Reuss of Women's Equity Action League were interviewed in 1984. The dates of the interviews were Smith, East, and Anderson on 20 January, and Reuss on 18 January.

2. The combined membership in the American Association of University Women, the National Federation of Business and Professional Women's Clubs, the National Women's Political Caucus, the National Organization for Women and the League of Women Voters fluctuated during the late 1970s and early 1980s: 1978—598,000; 1979—603,000; 1980—634,000; 1981—674,000; 1982—750,000; and 1983—685,000.

3. 410 U.S. 113 (1973).

4. Interview, 6 January 1981, Washington, D.C.

5. Ibid.

6. Interview, 6 January 1981, Washington, D.C.

7. Ibid.

8. Interview, 7 January 1981, Washington, D.C.

9. Interview, 18 January 1984, Washington, D.C.

10. Ibid. CETA refers to the Comprehensive Employment and Training Act of 1973. It is the largest federally sponsored program that provides job training and employment opportunities for economically disadvantaged and unemployed people.

11. Interview, 20 January 1984, Washington, D.C.

12. Interview, 20 January 1984, Washington, D.C.

13. See Jane Mansbridge, "Myth and Reality: The ERA and the Gender Gap in the 1980 Election," *Public Opinion Quarterly* 49 (Summer 1985): 164–178; Klein, *Gender Politics*.

14. Interview, 18 January 1984, Washington, D.C.

15. Interview, 20 January 1984, Washington, D.C.

16. Ann Smith explained, "Most of this movement [the change in women's voting patterns] is an extension of what has gone on before. Particularly with women in the workplace, people are in a position to realize that 'What is being done to me is not fair.' There is a new political base out there. . . . When women are working, they know what is coming or not coming in their paycheck. They recognize problems in pension systems. With so many single heads of household, they know what is involved in trying to take care of a family. The peace vote is important and not just on war and peace issues. Women are concerned about crime and domestic violence. There is a whole type of compassion present on many of these issues. Women hear that a child is malnourished and want to figure out how to feed him. Men are more likely to look abstractly at the whole problem." Interview, 20 January 1984, Washington, D.C.

17. Interview, 18 January 1984, Washington, D.C.

18. Quoted in Dom Bonafede, "Still a Long Way to Go," *National Journal*, 13 September 1986, 2175.

19. Ibid., 2178–2179.

20. The case of *Webster v. Reproductive Health Services*, 106 L.Ed.2d 410 (1989), was noteworthy in two respects. First, four of the nine Supreme Court justices wrote that they wanted to terminate all constitutional rights to have an abortion by reversing *Roe v. Wade* (1973), the case that had first established women's right to have an abortion. Second, a majority of the justices on the court made it clear that state governments were welcome to begin enforcing state laws making it difficult for women to get abortions in their states.

21. Ronald Reagan, "Excerpt from an Interview with Ann Devroy of the Gannett News Service on Women's Issues," 24 August 1983, *Public Papers of the Presidents of the United States: Ronald Reagan, 1983* vol. 2 (Washington, D.C.: U.S. Government Printing Office, 1985), 1196.

22. Reagan, "Remarks and a Q and A with Women Leaders of Christian Religious Organizations," 13 October 1983, ibid., 1452.

23. Ronald Reagan, "Remarks at the Annual Convention of the National Religious Broadcasters," 30 January 1984, *Public Papers of the Presidents of*

*the United States: Ronald Reagan, 1984*, vol. 1 (Washington, D.C.: U.S. Government Printing Office, 1986), 119.

24. Ronald Reagan, "Remarks to Participants in the 1985 March for Life Rally," 22 January 1985, *Public Papers of the Presidents of the United States: Ronald Reagan, 1985* (Washington, D.C.: U.S. Government Printing Office, 1988), 62; idem, "Remarks to Participants in the March for Life Rally," 22 January 1986, *Public Papers of the Presidents of the United States: Ronald Reagan, 1986* (Washington, D.C.: U.S. Government Printing Office, 1988), 74; idem, "Remarks at a White House Briefing for Right to Life Activists," 30 July 1987, *Public Papers of the Presidents of the United States: Ronald Reagan, 1987* (Washington, D.C.: U.S. Government Printing Office, 1989), 896.

25. "Debate Between the President and Former Vice President Walter F. Mondale," 7 October 1984, *Public Papers: Reagan, 1984*, 1453.

26. Reagan, "Remarks to Participants in the March for Life Rally," 22 January 1987, *Public Papers: Reagan, 1987*, 43; "Message to the Congress on 'A Quest for Excellence'," 27 January 1987, ibid., 71; "Remarks at the Conservative Political Action Conference Luncheon," 20 February 1987, ibid., 167; "Remarks at a White House Briefing for Right to Life Activists," 30 July 1987, ibid., 896-898; idem, "Remarks to Participants in the March for Life Rally, 22 January 1988, *Public Papers of the Presidents: Ronald Reagan, 1988* (Washington, D.C.: U.S. Government Printing Office, 1990), 75-76; "Address Before a Joint Session of Congress on the State of the Union," 25 January 1988, ibid., 120.

27. 410 U.S. 113 (1973).

28. Ronald Reagan, "Remarks in Denver, Colorado, at the Biennial Convention of the National Federation of Republican Women," 18 September 1981, *Public Papers of the Presidents of the United States: Ronald Reagan, 1981* (Washington, D.C.: U.S. Government Printing Office, 1982), 811.

29. Reagan, "Address Before a Joint Session of the Congress Reporting on the State of the Union," 26 January 1982, *Public Papers of the Presidents of the United States: Ronald Reagan, 1982* (Washington, D.C.: U.S. Government Printing Office, 1983), 77 and 165-166; Reagan, "Annual Report to the Congress on the State of Small Business," 1 March 1982, ibid., 247; Reagan, "The President's News Conference," 30 June 1982, ibid., 830-831.

30. Ibid., 830.

31. "Address Before a Joint Session of the Congress on the State of the Union," 25 January 1983, *Public Papers: Reagan, 1983*, 107.

32. Reagan, "Remarks to Participants in the Republican Women's Leadership Forum," 3 June 1983, ibid., 820; "Remarks at the Republican Women's Leadership Forum in San Diego, California," 26 August 1983, ibid., 1204; "Remarks at a White House Luncheon Marking the Observance of American Business Women's Day," 22 September 1983, ibid., 1333; "Remarks at a White House Ceremony Marking the 10th Anniversary of Executive Women in Government," 19 September 1983, ibid., 1298.

33. "Remarks at the Annual Convention of the National Federation of Business and Professional Women's Clubs," ibid., 1121.

34. "Excerpt from an Interview with Ann Devroy," ibid., 1197. See also

"Interview with Robert L. Bartley and Albert R. Hunt of the *Wall Street Journal* on Foreign and Domestic Issues," 2 February 1984, *Public Papers: Reagan, 1984*, 163.

35. Reagan, "Remarks to the United States Delegation to the United Nations Conference on Women," 10 July 1985, *Public Papers: Reagan, 1985*, 907.

36. "Statement by Principal Deputy Press Secretary Speakes on a Bill Prohibiting Discrimination by Educational Institutions Receiving Federal Financial Assistance," ibid., 69-70.

37. Reagan, "Remarks at a State Department Reception Honoring Maureen Reagan," 10 February 1986, *Public Papers: Reagan, 1986*, 192.

38. Mueller, "Empowerment of Women," 32.

39. Ibid.

40. Mueller, "In Search of a Constituency," 213-229.

41. Gurin, "Women's Gender Consciousness."

42. Carroll, "Gender Politics," 317.

43. "Reagan Era Young Hold Liberal Views," *Wall Street Journal*, 30 October 1989, p. B1.

44. Gurin, "Women's Gender Consciousness."

45. The data analyzed are from a probability sample of mothers and children taken from the birth records of first, second, and fourth-born white children in Detroit, Michigan, collected in July 1961. The mothers were interviewed six times during the period from 1962 through 1980. The children born in 1961 were interviewed in 1980. The sample stayed intact quite well over the years. In 1980, full interviews were obtained with both mother and child in 916 families or roughly 85 percent of the families interviewed in 1962 in which both mother and child were still alive in 1980. For more information on the panel and its findings, see Arland Thornton, Duane Alwin, and Donald Camburn, "Causes and Consequences of Sex-Role Attitudes and Attitude Change," *American Sociological Review* 48 (April 1983), 211-227; Arland Thornton and Deborah Freedman, "Changes in the Sex-Role Attitudes of Women, 1962-1977," *American Sociological Review* 44 (October 1979), 831-842.

46. Susan Welch and Lee Sigelman, "Changes in Public Attitudes Toward Women in Politics," *Social Science Quarterly* 63 (June 1982), 320.

47. "Gender Politics," 321-322.

## 6. If Government Gives, Can It Also Take Away?

1. Harrison, *On Account of Sex*, 69-115; Freeman, *Politics of Women's Liberation*, 170-229; Anne Costain and W. Douglas Costain, "Movements and Gatekeepers: Congressional Response to Women's Movement Issues, 1900-1982," *Congress and the Presidency* 12 (Spring 1985): 21-42.

2. Harrison, *On Account of Sex*, 259-260n.10.

3. Susan D. Becker, *The Origins of the Equal Rights Amendment* (Westport, Conn.: Greenwood Press, 1981); Mansbridge, *Why We Lost the ERA*, 8-19; Steiner, *Constitutional Inequality*, 1-25; Cott, *Grounding of Modern Feminism*, 117-142.

4. President's Task Force on Women's Rights and Responsibilities, *A Matter of Simple Justice* (Washington, D.C.: U.S. Government Printing Office, 1970); Costain, "Women's Claims," 158.

5. Child Development Act of 1971 (H.R. 6748 and S. 1512). See Freeman, *Politics of Women's Liberation*, 202.

6. These issues include the history of women and the women's movement; political status of women; the general plight of women; sports; family; crime; women's health; abortion; black women; lesbians; International Women's Year; and women's organizational concerns.

7. Gelb and Palley, *Women and Public Policies*, 1st ed.

8. Herma Kay, *Sex-Based Discrimination*, 3rd ed. (St. Paul, Minn.: West Publishing, 1988), 13-138.

9. Gelb and Palley, *Women and Public Policies*, 1st ed., 32-35.

10. Anne N. Costain, "After Reagan: New Party Attitudes Toward Gender," in *American Feminism: New Issues for a Mature Movement*, ed. Janet Boles, *The Annals* 515 (May 1991): 114-125.

11. Carroll, "Women's Autonomy," 236-257; idem, "Gender Politics," 306-339.

12. Mueller, ed., *Politics of the Gender Gap*; Robert Y. Shapiro and Harprett Mahajan, "Gender Differences in Policy Preferences: A Summary of Trends from the 1960's to the 1980's," *Public Opinion Quarterly* 50 (1986): 42-61; Mansbridge, "Myth and Reality," 164-178.

13. Charles Holstein, administrative assistant to Representative Leonor Sullivan, Interview, 18 July 1975, Washington, D.C.

14. Anne Costain, "Lobbying for Equal Credit," in *Women Organizing*, ed. Bernice Cummings and Victoria Schuck (Metuchen, N.J.: Scarecrow Press, 1979), 90-93.

15. 429 U.S. 125 (1976).

16. Kathy Miller, American Civil Liberties Union, Interview, 29 April 1977, Washington, D.C.; Judith Lichtman, Women's Legal Defense Fund, Interview, 28 April 1977, Washington, D.C.

17. See, for example, "Pregnancy Coverage Held Too Costly for Many Firms," *Washington Post*, 30 April 1977, p. A17; Wendy Susco, "Pregnant with Sexism," *New York Times*, 6 February 1977, "Connecticut Weekly," p. 24.

18. Ruth Weyand, International Union of Electrical, Radio and Machine Workers, Interview, 13 April 1977, Washington, D.C.; Nina Hegsted, National Organization for Women, Interview, 6 May 1977, Washington, D.C.

19. Costain, "Struggle for a National Women's Lobby," 490.

20. Steiner, *Constitutional Inequality*.

21. "A Woman for President?," 391.

22. "Education and Change," 174.

23. *Discrimination, Jobs and Politics*.

24. "Changes in Public Attitudes," 312-321.

25. See Burstein, *Discrimination, Jobs and Politics*, 50: "Attitudes toward women both as members of the labor force and as presidential candidates became more favorable fairly rapidly before the late 1940s, as far as we can tell, at a rate of about 2.2 percent per year on labor force participation (data

available for 1938–46) and 3.8 percent on the presidency (1945–49). The rate then slowed dramatically for both attitudes until the late 1960s, to 0.7 percent per year on labor force participation (1946–69) and 0.3 percent on the presidency (1949–69). At the beginning of the 1970s attitudes on both questions, again moving in tandem, started rapidly becoming more favorable again, at an annual rate of approximately 1.9 percent on labor force participation (1969–78) and 2.8 percent on the presidency (1969–75)."

26. The following categories are included: actions that are negative for women's rights; events initiated by government actors; ERA issue raised; events that are supportive of women's rights; actions where government is the target; conferences, speeches, and statements; feminists or feminist groups that initiate the event; a nongovernmental group that is the target of the event; actions initiated by antifeminist groups; all organized pressure; protest activities; political parties/candidates who initiate actions; and honorary or symbolic actions.

27. Early figures were taken from Ferriss's *Indicators of Trends*. Later figures draw on a number of sources. Theses sources include Gelb and Palley, *Women and Public Policies*, 2d ed.; Deckard, *Women's Movement*, 3rd ed.; and Maren Carden, *The New Feminist Movement* (New York: Russell Sage, 1974). In addition, some figures were collected through personal interviews with group representatives. For a list of the organizations whose representatives were interviewed before 1980, see Costain, "Representing Women," *Western Political Quarterly*, 101–102. In 1981, the following group representatives were interviewed in Washington, D.C.: Patricia Reuss, Women's Equity Action League, January 6; Carol Bros, National Women's Political Caucus, January 6; and Jane Wells-Schooley, National Organization for Women, January 7. In 1984, interviews were conducted in Washington with Catherine East and Linda Anderson, National Women's Political Caucus, January 20; and Patricia Reuss, Women's Equity Action League, January 18. Finally, when no other source was available for a particular year, annual membership figures were taken from the *Encyclopedia of Associations 1951–87* (Detroit: Gale Research, 1952–1988).

28. *U.S. Statutes at Large* (Washington, D.C.: U.S. Government Printing Office, 1950–90).

29. "Setting the Agenda in the U.S. Senate," *British Journal of Political Science* 7 (October 1977): 423–446.

30. Harrison, "Prelude to Feminism," 244–248.

31. Kenski, "Gender Factor," 50.

32. Harrison, *On Account of Sex*, 74–81.

33. *Semisovereign People* (Hinsdale, Ill.: Dryden Press 1972 [1960]), 16–18.

# 7. For a Continuing Movement

1. J. Craig Jenkins, "Interpreting the Stormy 1960s," *Research in Political Sociology* 3 (1987): 269–303.

2. Costain, "Struggle for a National Women's Lobby," 486–490.

3. Freeman, *Politics of Women's Liberation*, 25-28; Klein, *Gender Politics*, 45-46.

4. See Freeman, *Politics of Women's Liberation*, 49-62; Beth Schneider, "Political Generations and the Contemporary Women's Movement," *Sociological Inquiry* 58 (Winter 1988): 4-21.

5. Historian Ellen DuBois (*Feminism and Suffrage* [Ithaca: Cornell University Press, 1978]) makes the further argument that egalitarianism was both deeply rooted and radically-based in the suffrage movement.

6. Louis Hartz, *The Liberal Tradition in America* (New York: Harcourt, Brace, 1955); Samuel Huntington, *American Politics: The Promise of Disharmony* (Cambridge, Mass.: Harvard University Press, 1981), 13-30.

7. The most powerful statement of this point of view is Sylvia Hewlett, *A Lesser Life: The Myth of Women's Liberation in America* (New York: William Morrow, 1986).

8. Two of the key U.S. Supreme Court cases that make it more difficult for women and minorities to win job-discrimination suits are *Watson v. Fort Worth Bank and Trust*, 101 L.Ed.2d 827 (1988), and *Wards Cove Packing Co., Inc. v. Atonio*, 104 L.Ed.2d 733 (1989). "House Joins in the Standoff Over Civil Rights Measure," *Congressional Quarterly*, 4 August 1990, 2517.

9. Interview with Patricia Reuss, former national lobbyist for WEAL, June 15, 1990, Denver, Colorado.

10. "Reagan Era Young Hold Liberal Views," *Wall Street Journal*, 30 October 1989, p. B1.

11. For Supreme Court cases that cut back on rights granted in the decision *Roe v. Wade*, see *Webster v. Reproductive Health Services*, 106 L.Ed.2d 410 (1989); *Ohio v. Akron Center for Reproductive Health*, 111 L.Ed.2d 405 (1990); and *Hodgson v. Minnesota*, 111 L.Ed.2d 344 (1990).

12. *UAW v. Johnson Controls, Inc.*, 111 S.Ct. 1196 (1991). Ruth Marcus, "Supreme Court Hears 'Fetal-Protection' Case," *Washington Post*, 11 October 1990, p. A6; Steven Wermiel, "Justices Bar 'Fetal Protection' Policies," *Wall Street Journal*, 21 March 1991, pp. B1, B8; Joan Biskupic, "Supreme Court: Members Gratified by Decision on 'Fetal Protection' Law," *Congressional Quarterly*, 23 March 1991, 749.

13. "House Panel Adds Its Stamp to Civil Rights Measure," *Congressional Quarterly*, 28 July 1990, 2418.

14. "Inside Congress," *Congressional Quarterly*, 18 August 1990, 2658.

15. "House Joins in the Standoff over Civil Rights Measure," *Congressional Quarterly*, 4 August 1990, 2517; "Inside Congress," *Congressional Quarterly*, 18 August 1990, 2661.

16. *American Politics: The Promise of Disharmony* (Cambridge, Mass.: Harvard University Press, 1981), 167.

17. Samuel P. Hays, *Conservation and the Gospel of Efficiency: The Progressive Conservation Movement, 1890-1920* (New York: Atheneum, 1974 [1959]).

18. Verta Taylor, "Social Movement Continuity," *American Sociological Review* 54 (October 1989): 761.

19. Hays, *Conservation and the Gospel of Efficiency*.

20. Robert Cameron Mitchell, "Public Opinion and Environmental Politics in the 1970s and 1980s," in *Environmental Policy in the 1980s*, 51-74.

## Appendix A: Coding Women's Events Data

1. McAdam, *Political Process*, 237-250.
2. Jenkins, *Politics of Insurgency*; Jenkins and Eckert, "Channeling Black Insurgency."

## Appendix B: Assessing the Relative Influence of Government, Public Opinion, and the Women's Movement

1. In rotating the correlation matrix to derive the factors, oblique rotation was selected over orthogonal (varimax) rotation. Orthogonal rotation defines only uncorrelated patterns while oblique rotation has greater applicability to social science because patterns of relationships are sought out regardless of their level of correlation. The resulting patterns are more conceptually useful than if the correlation matrix is rotated to an orthogonal solution. On purely epistemological grounds, Rummel defends the use of oblique rotation when he writes that "the real world should not be treated as though phenomena coagulate in unrelated clusters. As phenomena can be interrelated in clusters, so the clusters themselves can be related. Oblique rotation allows this reality to be reflected in the loadings of the factors and their correlations." R. J. Rummel, "Understanding Factor Analysis," *Journal of Conflict Resolution* 11, no. 4 (1967): 477.

2. 3SLS estimates are also consistent and generally more efficient than 2SLS estimates. See Peter Kennedy, *A Guide to Econometrics* (Cambridge, Mass.: MIT Press, 1985), 126-141; Robert Pindyck and Daniel Rubinfeld, *Econometric Models and Economic Forecasts* (New York: McGraw Hill, 1981), 317-353; William Berry, *Nonrecursive Causal Models* (Beverly Hills, Calif.: Sage, 1984).

3. See Herbert Asher, *Causal Modeling* (Beverly Hills, Calif.: Sage, 1983), 53-72; Berry, *Nonrecursive Causal Models*, 39-60; and Pindyck and Rubinfeld, *Econometric Models and Economic Forecasts*, 339-344. There need not be temporal *simultaneity* between public opinion and congressional action. However, this equation assumes that across time and in the aggregate, this relationship cannot be adequately separated and a simultaneous equation model using 3SLS is indeed most appropriate. 3SLS is much more sensitive to specification error than OLS or 2SLS. Data problems generally limit the building of simultaneous equation models. However, if T statistics become more significant and standard errors decline or stay constant as the analysis moves from 2SLS to 3SLS, then a 3SLS model can be considered well specified. See Table B-5 for a comparison of the change from OLS to 2SLS to 3SLS. In particular, notice the change in Factor 3 (Party Activity) and the change within the structural equation system from 2SLS to 3SLS. The change from 2SLS to 3SLS suggests that there is cross-equation error term correlation in the model and thus the 2SLS estimates are biased and inefficient.

# Index

Abortion, xvi, 1, 7, 45, 46, 48–51, 82–84,
88, 98, 103–6, 117, 121, 124, 125, 126,
139, 141, 144, 149, 160 n, 170 n, 174 n,
176 n; legislative involvement with,
101, 102; President's stand on, 100, 104,
109, 110, 115; Supreme Court and, 108,
140
Abzug, Bella, 173 n
ACA. *See* Americans for Constitutional
Action
ADA. *See* Americans for Democratic
Action
Affirmative action, 38, 46, 52, 92, 121,
125
AFL-CIO, 60, 71, 171 n
Alwin, Duane, 176 n
American Association of University
Women, xii, 11, 28, 50, 51, 88, 129, 131,
132, 173 n
American Business Women's Day, 114,
175 n
American Civil Liberties Union, xii, 52,
79, 125, 130, 172 n, 177 n
Americans for Constitutional Action, 60,
71, 72
Americans for Democratic Action, 60, 71,
72
Anthony, Susan B., 27, 107, 160 n
Arendt, Hannah, 4, 160 n
Armstrong, Anne, 75
Arthur and Elizabeth Schlesinger
Library, xiv, xvii, 157 n
Asher, Herbert, 180 n
Atkinson, Ti-Grace, 46, 49

Bayh, Birch, 57, 134, 158 n
Becker, Susan, 176 n
Bell, Daniel, 5, 160 n
Berry, Jeffrey, 180 n
Bill introductions in Congress, ix, xviii,
xix, 57, 131, 147, 158 n
Biskupic, Joan, 179 n
Blank, Rebecca, 169 n
Bonafede, Dom, 173 n, 174 n

Boneparth, Ellen, 159 n
Brock, William, 128, 134
Bros, Carol, 102, 173 n, 178 n
Brownell, Herbert, 33
Brunner, Ronald, 158 n, 164 n, 165 n
Burford, Anne, 160 n
Burris, Carol, 82
Burstein, Paul, x, xix, 36, 77, 132, 158 n,
162 n, 169 n, 177 n
Bush, George (President), 4, 121, 140

Camburn, Donald, 176 n
Carden, Maren, 178 n
Carroll, Susan, 41, 120, 165 n, 173 n,
176 n, 177 n
Carter, Jimmy (President), 93–95, 108,
111, 115, 125, 171 nn–73 nn
Celler, Emmanuel, 56
Center for the American Woman and
Politics, ix, xi, 159 n
Center for Women's Policy Studies, 129
Chafe, William, 169 n
Charlton, Linda, 159 n
Chazan, Naomi, ix, xiv
Children, 40, 41, 54, 81, 102, 112, 113, 123,
136, 138, 139, 176 n
Chisholm, Shirley, 91
CIA, 75
Civil Rights, 4, 10, 33, 136, 145, 164 n;
groups, 16, 25, 40, 144; legislation, xiv–
xvi, 102, 107, 122, 130; movement, xvii,
1–3, 9, 15, 22, 30, 45, 138, 141–43, 158 n,
179 n
Civil Rights Act of 1957, 33
Civil Rights Act of 1964, 25, 29, 33, 37–39,
44, 45, 48, 52, 56, 60, 76, 109, 129, 130
Civil War, 4, 141
Clarenbach, Kathryn, 45, 166 n
Clark, Ramsey, 32, 45
Clay, William, 91
Clifford, Clark, 32
Cloward, Richard, 24, 32, 41, 162 nn–
64 nn
Cognitive liberation, 12, 136

Committee on Political Education of the AFL-CIO (COPE), 60, 71, 72
Common Cause, 6, 52, 158 n
Congress, xvii, xviii, 10, 58, 123, 141, 147, 150, 157 n, 158 n, 164 n, 167 nn–69 nn, 171 n, 175 n, 179 n; hearings, xii, 1, 50, 56, 57, 88–90, 102, 103, 126, 128, 130, 147; lobbying, 51, 58, 86, 93, 107, 135; members of, xiii–xv, 60, 68, 71, 72, 144, 157 n; staff of, ix, xi–xiii, xix, 39, 54, 55, 75, 83, 88, 89, 91, 128, 143–45, 157 n, 172 n; and public opinion, 132–34, 152–55; and women's issues, xviii, 10, 14, 23, 27, 29, 32–34, 37, 38, 40, 41, 59–77, 86, 87, 92, 93, 95, 97, 100–101, 104, 110, 114, 116, 117, 122, 123, 127, 129, 131, 134, 140
Congressional Caucus for Women's Issues, 104, 173 n
Congressional Record, xviii, 165 n
Conover, Pamela, 8
Consciousness about women's political circumstances, xv, 13, 25, 32, 40–43, 49, 51, 77, 97, 98, 126, 141
Consciousness raising, 25, 49, 51, 52
Consumer movement, 2
COPE. See Committee on Political Education
Costain, Anne, x, 157 n, 159 n, 162 n, 167 n, 169 n, 170 n, 176 nn–78 nn
Cott, Nancy, 159 n, 160 n, 163 n, 168 n, 176 n
Credit discrimination, xv, xvii, 10, 52, 75, 82, 88–91, 94, 104, 112, 125, 128–30, 157 n, 177 n
Cummings, Bernice, 177 n
Cummings, Milton, x
Curtis, Charles, 59

Daley, Richard M., 89
Davidson, Sara, 167 n
de Beauvoir, Simone, 3, 160 n
Deckard, Barbara, 167 n, 168 n, 178 n
Department of Health and Human Services, 110
Department of Justice, 107, 110
Department of Labor, 14, 28, 35, 42, 95, 145, 166 n
Devroy, Ann, 109, 174 n, 175 n
Discriminant analysis, 71–73
Discrimination, 53, 92, 113, 148, 170 n; in education, 56, 83, 90, 95, 102, 114,

176 n; in employment, 29, 33, 37–39, 41, 44, 52, 54, 78, 81, 83, 109, 112, 121, 129, 139, 140, 158 n, 162 n, 165 n, 169 n, 179 n; racial, 9, 94, 121, 122, 139; sex, 14, 25, 33, 38, 39, 41, 44, 45, 48, 50, 52, 54, 56, 71, 77, 81, 82, 89, 92, 94, 95, 102, 107, 109, 111, 118, 119, 123, 128, 129, 140, 163 n, 177 n
Dixon, Barbara, 172 n
Dole, Robert, 114
DuBois, Ellen, 179 n
Duerst-Lahti, Georgia, 158 n, 162 n, 163 n

East, Catherine, 44, 45
Eastwood, Mary, 44, 75
Echols, Alice, 158 n
Eckert, Craig, 162 n, 180 n
EEOC. See Equal Employment Opportunity Commission
Eisenhower, Dwight (President), 26, 33–35, 95, 133, 159 n, 164 n
Elections, xi, xviii, 2, 4, 10, 24, 33, 34, 74, 92, 94, 95, 98, 100, 103, 107, 111, 113–15, 121, 126, 133, 139, 140, 147, 149, 158 n, 159 n, 174 n
Environmental movement, 3, 141, 142
Equal Employment Opportunity Commission, 25, 39, 44–46, 145
Equality issues, xiv, xv, xvi, 2, 9, 17, 28, 29, 35, 45, 56, 60, 75, 77, 79–88, 90–95, 97, 99, 106, 107, 110, 112–14, 116–18, 123–25, 127–29, 133, 135–38, 141, 142, 148, 159 n, 163 n, 170 n
Equal protection clause, 28, 122, 125
Equal Rights Amendment, 117, 120, 125, 127, 135, 138, 139, 149, 151, 161 n; anti-ERA groups, 28, 29, 32, 80, 86; Congress and, 14, 37, 38, 56–72, 74, 75, 78, 88, 91, 122, 126, 130, 131, 133; history of, 27–30, 32, 45, 46, 50, 51, 59, 60, 79, 137, 138, 176 n; lobbying on, xiii, xv, 1, 8, 10, 11, 17, 32, 51, 52, 58, 76, 79, 81–84, 88, 98–100, 102, 103, 105–7, 121, 122, 130, 136, 167 n, and political parties, 4, 32, 59, 60, 123, 125, 141, 164 n; presidents and, 33–35, 72, 73, 75, 91–97, 104, 109, 111, 113, 173 n; in state legislatures, 21, 143
Equal Rights Amendment Ratification Council, 79, 167 n
ERA. See Equal Rights Amendment
Europe, 3, 4, 5, 13, 157 n, 158 n, 161 n

Evans, Sara, 158 n, 164 n
Events data, ix, 16, 22, 98, 132, 143, 150, 151, 162 n, 180 n

Factor analysis, 150, 180 n
Family, 36, 77, 80-82, 95, 110, 112, 113, 115, 120, 122, 136, 137, 139, 149, 161 n, 170 n, 174 n, 176 n
Federal government, 19, 20, 28, 36, 52, 163 n
Federation of Organizations for Professional Women, 172 n
Feinstein, Diane, 1
Feminism, 3, 44, 50, 98, 105, 137, 138, 142, 157 nn-61 nn, 163 n, 164 n, 166 n, 168 n, 170 n, 176 nn-79 nn
Feminists, The (organization), 46, 49, 52
Ferree, Myra, 76, 132, 165 n, 168 n
Ferriss, Abbott, 40, 178 n
Fifth Amendment, 28, 29
Fifty States Project for Women, 110
Flexner, Eleanor, 169 n
Florio, James, 121
Ford, Betty, 92, 93
Ford, Gerald (President), 92, 93, 95, 96, 115, 170 n, 171 n
Fourteenth Amendment, 28, 29, 122
Franklin, John Hope, 159 n
Fraser, Arvonne, 49
Freedman, Deborah, 176 n
Freeman, Jo, x, xii, 3, 6, 32, 39, 157 n, 159 nn-61 nn, 163 nn-66 nn, 168 n, 169 n, 176 n, 179 n
Friedan, Betty, 8, 44-46, 75, 136, 157 n, 161 n, 166 n

Garrow, David, 159 n
Gelb, Joyce, 7, 8, 159 n, 161 n, 177 n, 178 n
Gender Gap, 2, 24, 33, 35, 41, 93, 95, 98, 103-6, 111, 117, 120, 126, 127, 133, 134, 136, 138, 139, 157 n, 159 n, 164 n, 177 n
General Electric v. Gilbert, 129
General Federation of Women's Clubs, 27, 131
Ginsberg, Benjamin, xviii, 158 n
Goldsmith, Judith, 107
Gouldner, Alvin, 160 n
Government facilitation, xv, 18, 22, 23, 25, 52
Government repression, 15, 22, 52
Graham, Richard, 25, 39, 44-46, 75

Grayson, Susan, 172 n
Green, Edith, 39, 56, 75
Greenhouse, Linda, 167 n
Greenya, John, 160 n
Grenada, 104, 127
Griffiths, Martha, 38, 56, 58, 75, 93, 133
Gurin, Patricia, 98, 161 n, 176 n
Gurr, Ted, 5, 6, 12, 160 n, 162 n
Gusfield, Joseph, 160 n

Harrison, Cynthia, 162 nn-67 nn, 178 n
Hartry, Bert, 167 n
Hartz, Louis, 179 n
Hawkins, Augustus, 91
Hayes, Helen, 27
Hays, Samuel, 179 n
Heckler, Margaret, 75, 129
Heide, Wilma Scott, 158 n
Hepburn, Katharine, 27
Hernandez, Aileen, 39
Hess, Beth, 165 n
Hewlett, Sylvia, 179 n
Hickey, Margaret, 166 n
Hodgson v. Minnesota, 179 n
Hofstadter, Richard, 5, 160 n
Holstein, Charles, 177 n
Honegger, Barbara, 107, 111
Hoover, Herbert, 59
Horowitz, Arlene, 91
House of Representatives, 37, 38, 59, 88, 92, 158 n; Committee on Banking and Currency, 88; Committee on Education and Labor, 88, 90; House Judiciary Committee, 56, 171 n
Human rights, 89, 94, 108, 145
Hunter, Marjorie, 164 n
Huntington, Samuel, 140, 179 n

Indigenous resources, 22, 25
Interest groups, xi, 6, 8, 16, 24, 40, 60-68, 123, 129, 144; business, xi, xii, 16, 27, 30, 40, 50, 52, 77, 81, 89, 91, 93, 112-14, 130, 132, 137, 144, 148, 171 n, 173 n, 175 n; labor, 11, 13, 14, 16, 27-29, 33-38, 40-42, 46, 48, 50, 59, 60, 71, 77, 88, 90, 91, 95, 98, 105, 109, 123, 130, 136, 138, 144, 145, 148, 166 n, 177 n, 178 n; liberal, xii, 5, 11, 38, 60, 72, 91, 98, 106, 121, 130, 168 n, 176 n, 179 n; tactics of, xi, xiv, xx, 1-3, 8, 15, 46, 48, 49, 77, 137; traditional women's, xii, 16, 44, 50, 51, 130, 144

International Union of Electrical, Radio and Machine Workers, 79, 172 n, 177 n
International Women's Year, 42, 149, 170 nn–72 nn, 176 n
Interviews, reports of, ix, xii, xvi, xvii, xix, 39, 50, 75, 82, 83, 86, 89, 100, 170 n, 172 n, 173 n, 176 n, 178 n

Jenkins, Craig, x, 15, 157 n, 160 nn–62 nn, 180 n
Johnson, Charles, 162 n
Johnson, Lyndon (President), 38, 39, 45, 46, 48, 52–55, 57, 78, 95, 140, 166 nn–68 nn, 179 n
Johnson, Marilyn, ix

Katzenstein, Mary, 13, 158 n
Kay, Herma, 177 n
Kelly, William, 162 n
Kennedy, John (President), 3, 14, 26, 28–30, 34–38, 52, 95, 122, 123, 126, 133, 159 n, 164 n, 165 n
Kennedy, Peter, 180 n
Kenski, Henry, 164 n, 171 n, 173 n, 178 n
Keyserling, Mary, 166 n
Killian, Lewis, 160 n
Kirkpatrick, Jeane, 160 n
Klein, Ethel, 12, 13, 41, 158 n, 161 n, 165 n, 169 n, 174 n, 179 n
Koch, Edward, 129
Kolb, Frances, 166 n
Kornhauser, William, 4, 160 n
Kraft, Michael, 159 n

Landolpho, Maria, 172 n
Laws, ix, x, xi, xiii, xvi, xviii, xix, 9–11, 27–29, 37, 48, 52, 80–82, 86–89, 92, 102, 107, 109–13, 121, 125, 132, 133, 147, 158 n, 174 n; Equal Credit Opportunity Act, 10, 88, 89, 128, 157 n; Pregnancy Disability Act, 94, 129, 130; Women, Infants and Children, 102
Lawson, Steven, 33, 160 n, 163 n, 164 n
Leaders and leadership, 7, 134, 148, 172 n, 174 n; in the civil rights movement, 2: political, 103, 120; in the women's movement, 8, 10, 14, 27, 45, 49, 93, 171 n
League of Women Voters, xiii, 11, 26, 28, 50, 84, 130, 132, 167 n, 171 nn–73 nn
Legislation: Civil Rights Restoration Act, 107, 140; Equal Credit Opportu-

nity Act, 10, 88, 89, 128, 157 n; health, 10, 27, 37, 48, 81, 94, 108, 110, 137, 149, 174 n, 176 n, 179 n; protective, for women, 27–29, 39, 56, 80, 109; rape, 81, 82, 88, 125, 137; women's rights, xi, xix, 75, 127, 133
Lemons, Stanley, 163 n
Lesbianism. See Women's issues, lesbianism
Lichtman, Judith, 177 n
Lincoln, Abraham (President), 141
Lindgren, Ralph, 163 n
Lipset, Seymour Martin, 5, 160 n
Livornese, Katherine, 158 n, 164 n, 165 n
Lobbying, xi, xii, 49–52, 57, 76, 83, 91, 100, 121, 125, 130, 136, 140, 177 n. See also Congress, lobbying; Equal Rights Amendment, lobbying on
Luce, Clare Booth, 35, 164 n

McAdam, Doug, x, xv, xvii, 12, 15, 143, 157 n, 158 n, 160 nn–63 nn, 180 n
McCarthy, John, 157 n, 160 nn–62 nn
McCartney, Ellen, 51
McFarland, Andrew, x, 24, 163 n
McMichael, Jane, 82, 91
Macy, John, 46
Mahajan, Harprett, 177 n
Malbin, Michael, 172 n, 173 n
Mandel, Ruth, ix, 105
Mansbridge, Jane, 7, 8, 17, 161 n, 168 n, 173 n, 174 n, 176 n, 177 n
Marcus, Alfred, 160 n, 179 n
Margolin, Olya, 50
Margolis, Diane, ix, xiv
Martin, Jane, ix, xiv, 5, 160 n
Marx, Gary, 162 n
Mascarenas, Oneida, x, 158 n
Mass marches, 2
Mass media, 8
Mass society, 4–6, 160 n
Maternity leave, 81, 123
Matthews, Donald, 158 n
Mead, Margaret, 27
Meier, August, 159 n
Meyer, David, 158 n
Miller, Kathy, 177 n
Mink, Patsy, 90, 91
Miss America Pageant, 31
Mitchell, Robert, 159 n, 170 n, 180 n
Mobilization, xiv, xvi, 4, 6–9, 11–18, 22, 23, 25, 88, 119, 157 n, 160 nn–62 nn

Monaghan, Kathleen, 162 n
Mondale, Walter, 106, 133, 175 n
Mueller, Carol, x, xiv, 13, 98, 157 nn–
    59 nn, 161 n, 165 n, 173 n, 176 n, 177 n
Murray, Pauli, 28

NAACP. See National Association for the
    Advancement of Colored People
Nadel, Mark, 159 n
Nader, Ralph, 2
National American Woman Suffrage
    Association, 26
National Association for the Advance-
    ment of Colored People, 39
National Association of Colored Women,
    27
National Association of Women Lawyers,
    27
National Commission on Consumer
    Finance, 89, 128
National Committee to Defeat the Un-
    Equal Rights Amendment, 32
National Consumers League, 28
National Council of Jewish Women, xii,
    50
National Education Association, xii, 27, 52
National Federation of Business and Pro-
    fessional Women, xii, 27, 30, 50, 52,
    112, 132, 171 n, 173 n
National Organization for Women, xi,
    xii, xiii, xiv, xvii, xviii, xix, 1, 5, 14, 25,
    30, 31, 33, 37, 39, 40, 44, 45, 46–51, 57,
    75, 81–84, 88, 102–4, 106–8, 111, 120,
    121, 124–26, 128, 129, 132, 138, 141, 142,
    144, 157 nn–60 nn, 166 n, 167 n, 170 n,
    172 n, 173 n, 178 n
National Religious Broadcasters, 110, 174 n
National Women's Political Caucus, xi,
    xvii, 31, 50, 51, 82, 83, 88, 91, 102, 104,
    106, 132, 144, 171 n, 173 n, 178 n
National Women's Trade Union League,
    28
New class movement, 5, 160 n
New Deal, xv, 32, 40, 122, 137
New Republic, 47, 166 n
New York Times, ix, xvii, xviii, 9, 15–18,
    20, 35, 49, 53, 54, 57, 79, 80, 84–86, 97,
    98, 101, 102, 105–7, 116, 131, 132, 143,
    150, 151, 158 n, 159 n, 164 n, 169 n, 177 n
New York Times Annual Index, xvii,
    xviii, 9
Nineteenth Amendment, 26

Nixon, Pat, 47
Nixon, Richard (President), 72, 74, 75, 78,
    92, 95, 112, 123, 133, 168 n, 169 n
Nonidez, Cynthia, 158 n
Norrell, Judith, 51, 167 n
Norusis, Marisa, 168 n
NOW. See National Organization for
    Women
NWPC. See National Women's Political
    Caucus

Oberschall, Anthony, 160 n, 161 n
O'Connor, Sandra Day, 111, 161 n
Okonski, Evonne, ix, 158 n
OLS. See Ordinary least squares
Olson, Mancar, 158 n
Ordinary least squares, 151, 152, 154–56,
    180 n
Orfield, Gary, 57, 168 n

Palley, Marian, 7, 8, 159 n, 161 n, 177 n,
    178 n
Peace Corps, 35, 36
Perrow, Charles, 15, 161 n, 162 n
Peterson, Esther, 14, 28, 29, 34, 35, 38, 46,
    166 n
Pindyck, Robert, 180 n
Piven, Frances, 24, 32, 41, 162 nn–64 nn
Political action committees, 1, 126
Political opportunity theory, xv, xvi, 12,
    24–26, 32, 40, 52, 76, 88, 117, 158 n,
    163 n. See also Political process theory
Political parties, 13, 24, 32, 34, 57, 125,
    126, 136, 139, 140, 151, 162 n, 178 n;
    Democratic, 2, 4, 14, 40, 41, 52, 59, 60,
    113, 114, 121–23, 125, 126, 136, 141,
    172 n, 173 n; Republican, 4, 32, 33, 59,
    71, 93, 95, 106, 111, 113, 118, 121, 125,
    126, 136, 141; Republican National
    Committee, 79, 115
Political process theory, xv, xvi, 11–14,
    18, 21, 22, 25. See also Political oppor-
    tunity theory
President, 14, 30, 32–35, 37–41, 46, 48, 49,
    52, 54, 56, 57, 72–76, 78, 82, 88, 92–97,
    99, 100, 101, 103, 104, 107–16, 119, 121–
    26, 131, 132, 140, 141, 144, 157 n, 163 n,
    164 n, 166 nn–69 nn, 171 nn–73 nn,
    175 n, 176 n. See also specific presidents
Presidential appointments of women, 14,
    34, 35, 39, 52, 55, 73, 74, 111, 116, 139,
    167 n, 172 n

Presidential Commission on the Status of Women, 3, 14, 23, 28, 34, 38, 45, 115, 123, 145, 166 n
President's Task Force on Women's Rights and Responsibilities, 88, 124, 176 n
Pressman, Sonia, 44, 75
Protest, 1, 2, 4, 9, 18, 19, 30, 39–41, 46–49, 51, 52, 107, 111, 126, 148, 150, 151, 157 n, 159 n, 160 n, 173 n, 178 n; boycott, 107, 148; civil disobedience, 2, 3; demonstrations, 15, 31, 46, 49; sit-ins, 2, 46
Public Citizen, 6
Public interest, 5, 6, 24, 136, 141, 160 n
Public opinion, ix, 36, 37, 57, 77, 93, 118, 120, 122, 127, 128, 131–35, 140, 142, 150, 151, 152–55, 159 n, 161 n, 163 n, 168 n, 169 n, 173 n, 174 n, 177 n, 180 n
Public Papers of the Presidents of the United States, xix, 158 n, 164 n, 165 n, 167 nn–71 nn, 174 n, 175 n

Raabe, Earl, 160 n
Radcliffe College, ix, xiv, 36, 166 n
Reagan, Maureen, 113, 114
Reagan, Nancy, 115
Reagan, Ronald (President), 3, 92, 95, 96, 100, 101, 103, 104, 107–16, 118, 120, 125, 172 n, 174 nn–77 nn, 179 n
Reagan administration, 3, 100, 103, 107, 110, 120
Regions, 68–71; border, 71, 72; East, 71, 72, 75, 104, 173 n, 178 n; Midwest, 71, 72, 158 n, 161 n; South, 33, 71, 72, 160 n, 168 n; West, vi, 71, 72, 163 n, 177 n
Relative deprivation, 5, 6, 12, 162 n
Resource mobilization theory, xiv, xvi, 4, 6–9, 11–17, 157 n, 160 n, 161 n
Reuss, Patricia, 103, 104, 173 n, 178 n, 179 n
Roe v Wade, 101, 110, 140, 174 n, 179 n
Role change, 7, 136
Role equity, 7, 10, 136
Roosevelt, Eleanor, 36, 165 n, 167 n
Rubinfeld, Daniel, 180 n
Rudwick, Elliot, 159 n
Rummel, R. J., 180 n

St. George, Katharine, 39
Salisbury, Robert, 7, 161 n, 167 n
Schattschneider, E. E., 134

Schreiber, E. M., 132, 169 n
Schuck, Victoria, 177 n
SCUM. See Society to Cut Up Men
Selznick, Philip, 4, 160 n
Senate, 34, 37, 45, 57–59, 71, 74, 88, 91, 96, 103, 114, 129, 133, 145, 147, 169 n, 171 n, 178 n
Shanzer, Carol, 172 n
Shapiro, Robert, 177 n
Shuster, Alvin, 164 n
Sigelman, Lee, 119, 120, 176 n
Sills, David, 160 n
Smeal, Eleanor, 107
Smelser, Neil, 157 n
Smith, Ann, 104, 173 n, 174 n
Smith, Howard, 38
Smith, Margaret Chase, 27, 38, 104, 173 n, 174 n
Snyder, David, 162 n
Social feminism, 137, 163 n
Social movement, x, xiv, xv, xvi, xvii, xix, 1, 2, 4–6, 8, 10, 12, 15, 24, 26, 30, 31, 40, 79, 118, 134, 140–42, 150, 151, 153–55, 157 n, 159 nn–62 nn, 179 n
Social security, 27, 82, 83, 104
Society to Cut Up Men, 47, 144
Speakes, Larry, 114, 176 n
Special needs issues, 27, 80–85, 87, 88, 91, 92, 94, 95, 97, 99, 106, 120, 124–25, 127–29, 135, 137–40, 142, 170 n
State of the Union Message, xix, 33, 35, 54, 74, 94, 95, 112, 158 n, 164 n, 169 n, 171 n, 172 n, 175 n
Steele, Clelia, 168 n
Steiner, Gilbert, ix, 163 n, 168 n, 177 n
Stern, Paula, 166 n, 167 n
Stoper, Emily, 159 n
Suffrage, 2, 10, 12, 26, 27, 30, 38, 79, 137, 138, 179 n
Sullivan, Leonor, 128, 129, 170 n, 177 n
Supreme Court, 28, 29, 81, 101, 108, 111, 113, 121, 125, 129, 130, 139–41, 174 n, 179 n
Susco, Wendy, 177 n

Tarrow, Sidney, x, xv, 24, 157 n, 160 nn–62 nn
Taub, Nadine, 163 n
Taylor, Verta, 179 n
Thomas, Clarence, 121
Thornton, Arland, 176 n

Three-stage least squares (3SLS), 152-55, 180 n
Tilly, Charles, 22, 23, 161 n
Title IX, xviii, 50, 82
Truman, David, 163 n
Truman, Harry (President), 32, 34, 95
Turner, Ralph, 160 n
Twentieth Amendment, xviii
Two-stage least squares (2SLS), 153-55, 180 n

United Automobile Workers v. Johnson Controls, Inc., 140
United Auto Workers (UAW), 60, 179 n
United Methodist Women, 51, 75, 88
United Nations (U.N.) Conference on Women, 113
U.S. Constitution, amendments, xviii, 8, 17, 27, 56, 79, 84, 94, 98, 122
U.S. Statutes at Large, xviii, 132

Van de Geer, John, 168 n
Vig, Norman, 159 n
Voluntary Parenthood League, 27
Voting Rights Act of 1965, 123

Walker, Jack, 133, 163 n
Watson v. Fort Worth Bank and Trust, 179 n
Watt, James, 159 n
Wead, Doug, 159 n
WEAL. See Women's Equality Action League
Weaver, Paul, 160 n
Webster v. Reproductive Health Services, 108, 174 n, 179 n
Welch, Susan, 119, 120, 132, 176 n
Wells-Schooley, Jane, 103, 173 n, 178 n
Wermiel, Steven, 179 n
Westoff, Leslie, 159 n, 164 n
Weyand, Ruth, 177 n
Wilder, Douglas, 121
Wilson, James Q., 24, 163 n
Wirthlin, Richard, 114
Wirtz, Willard, 38
Women candidates, xiii, 82, 98, 113
Women's Bureau of the Department of Labor, 14, 28, 35, 42, 95, 145, 166 n
Women's Educational Equity Act, 82, 88, 90, 91, 95, 102, 157 n
Women's Equality Day, 107, 113, 114

Women's Equity Action League, xi, xii, xiv, 48-50, 52, 82, 83, 103, 104, 128, 140, 144, 159 n, 167 n, 173 n, 178 n, 179 n
Women's groups, xi, xii, xiii, 2, 11, 16, 21, 22, 26-31, 33, 34, 40, 44, 49-52, 55, 56, 58, 75, 76, 77, 79, 81-85, 88, 89, 91, 93, 95-98, 100, 101, 103-6, 108, 111, 113, 117, 123, 126, 129, 130, 132, 133, 136, 137, 139, 150, 151, 167 n, 169 n. See also specific groups
Women's International League of Peace and Freedom, 27
Women's International Terrorist Conspiracy from Hell (WITCH), 47, 49, 52
Women's issues, xi, xii, xiii, xiv, xix, 7, 10, 13, 18, 29, 31-33, 35, 42, 51, 53, 55, 57, 72, 75, 78, 79, 82, 86, 88, 91, 97-99, 102-4, 113-18, 120, 122, 123, 126, 127, 130, 131, 132, 136, 138-40, 144, 162 n, 173 n, 174 n; child care, xvi, 80, 82, 84, 88, 98, 120, 121, 123, 125-27, 137, 138, 140; child support, xvii, 112; comparable worth, 127, 137, 138; domestic violence, 95, 113, 174 n; draft, 27, 109, 128; education, xii, xvi, xviii, 27, 48, 50, 52, 56, 60, 80, 82-84, 88, 90, 91, 94, 95, 114, 119, 120, 122, 125, 136, 146, 149, 169 n, 177 n; employment, xvii, 25, 29, 32, 37-39, 52, 53, 55, 75, 77, 78, 81-83, 94, 104, 109, 114, 120, 121, 129, 136, 140, 149, 162 n, 172 n, 174 n; equal pay, 29, 33, 35, 37, 38, 52, 76, 167 n; jobs, 6, 27, 45, 47, 52, 55, 73, 74, 77, 81, 89, 104, 149, 158 n, 162 n, 164 n, 165 n, 169 n, 177 n; lesbianism, 48, 103, 124; in the military, xvi, 7, 27, 82, 83, 121, 139, 149; peace, xvi, 34; sexual harassment, 41, 127, 137
Women's Legal Defense Fund, 125, 172 n, 177 n
Women's liberation, 2, 31, 42, 46, 47, 49, 98, 124, 157 nn-60 nn, 165 n, 166 n, 168 n, 169 n, 176 n, 179 n
Women's Lobby, xi, xii, 82, 83, 129, 169 n, 170 n, 177 n, 178 n
Women's movement, ix, x, xi, xii, xiii, xiv, xv, xvi, xvii, xviii, xix, xx, 1-4, 6-18, 21, 22-26, 29, 31, 32, 34, 39-42, 44, 47, 49, 50, 52, 57, 75-88, 97-100, 102, 103, 105, 106, 108, 118-28, 130-43, 149-54, 158 n, 162 n, 163 n, 165 n, 166 n,

Women's movement (*cont.*)
168 n, 169 n, 170 n, 173 n; allies, xiv,
xvi, 7, 14-17, 27, 139; emergence, xiii,
xvii, 1, 3, 8, 14, 18, 37, 39, 41, 57, 98,
103, 104, 122, 136; groups, xii, xv, 40,
50, 52, 100, 102, 103, 106, 108, 128; internal conflict, 50, 107; radicals, xvii, 9,
32, 44, 46-48, 56, 95, 106, 124, 158 n, 160 n

Women's votes, xiii, 24, 32, 40, 41, 95,
115, 116, 121, 133, 139

Young Women's Christian Association
(YWCA), 28

Zald, Mayer, 157 n, 160 nn-62 nn

Designed by Laury A. Egan

Composed by Blue Heron, Inc.
in Baskerville text and display

Printed on 50-lb., Sebago Antique Cream
and bound in Holliston Roxite
by The Maple Press Company